Ex Libris

Lowell R. Kantzer

JUSTICE

and the

SOCIAL ORDER

Emil Brunner

JUSTICE
and the
SOCIAL ORDER

Translated by Mary Hottinger

HARPER & BROTHERS
New York and London

... Contents ...

TRANSLATOR'S NOTE

The translation of a work such as the present presents peculiar embarrassments to the translator owing to certain radical differences between the manner of thought of the original and English thought on the same subject. This comes out most clearly in the fact that the very words on which the whole work turns have in German a wider angle of reference than in English. Thus *Gerechtigkeit* is not only justice, but also righteousness, and is used in both senses in this book. *Gleich* is equal, like, same; *ungleich* is unequal, unlike, different. As for *Recht*, Holland in his *Jurisprudence* has pointed out that it denotes "not only the sum total of Laws, but also the sum total of Rights and the sum total of all that is just." Further: " . . . the German *Recht* . . . expresses not only "a right" but also "law" in the abstract. In view of these differences, certain very forcible formulations have had to be split up in English to avoid confusion, and the possible gain in concreteness has involved a sacrifice of their original pregnancy. Professor Brunner's always illuminating criticism has helped to overcome some of these difficulties, but the basic incommensurability of the two manners of thought is insuperable, and a certain inadequacy in the translation is the inevitable result.

M.H.

JUSTICE
and the
SOCIAL ORDER

... Foreword ...

FEW WORDS ARE MORE CURRENT THAN "JUSTICE" and "injustice," yet who knows what justice is? Who can say what is just and what unjust? Nobody can say what justice is, we are told, because justice is a relative thing. But the judge and the legislator should know what a just penalty or a just law is; the employer should know what just wages are; mankind today should know whether Communism or capitalism is the just economic order, whether the totalitarian state or the liberal state is the just political order. Every would-be Christian has to face the question whether interest, so-called unearned income, is just. Where are we to find a standard by which these questions may be answered if we are ignorant of the very principle of justice? Mankind today does not know what that principle is, but Christians might know it. While the Catholic church, drawing on centuries of tradition, possesses an impressive systematic theory of justice, Protestant Christianity has had none for some three hundred years past. That may sound a bold statement; it can, unfortunately, be proved. It is doubtless one of the main reasons why the Protestant church is so unsure of itself in questions of the social order, economics, law, politics and international law, and why its statements on these subjects are so haphazard and improvised that they fail to carry conviction.

If this is indeed the case, there is no need to justify the attempt to establish a doctrine of justice on Protestant principles. There is urgent need of such a doctrine at a time which has not only seen its whole social order shaken to the foundations, but has also lost any sense of what justice is. The fact that we have so long lacked a doctrine of justice may serve to extenuate the imperfections of this first attempt. In particular, the second part presents many a point of attack to criticism, and cannot fail to lay the author open to the charge of dilettantism. But who could hope to have secure and expert knowledge in all these fields? After all, every one of the questions raised involves whole branches of science, in which the individual can hardly hope to gain a general view, and yet these are questions in which practical experience, and not science, would appear to have the last word. Who shall venture to speak on all these questions at once?

There are, however, in the world of mind and spirit, things that simply have to be ventured. The world cannot wait until its men of science have concluded their researches and are in a position to assert unanimously what is just. Protestant Christians, moreover, have a right to be instructed by their Christian leaders, whether theologians, philosophers or statesmen, as to what is required in the name of social and political justice on the basis of the Christian faith. We are, after all, convinced that the foremost requirement of our day is justice. Must we not first know what we mean, and why we mean it, when we say that the just, justice, is our foremost need? The attempt, therefore, had to be made.

This attempt, however, lays no claim to exhaustive treatment of the individual problems. It only sets forth what is required as just by Christian faith in each field. Hence a thousand questions are raised in the course of the consideration of these problems, only to be left unanswered. Many justified points of view are not taken into account, many pronouncements of weight unquoted. Indeed, what is quoted and what omitted, what views illustrate an argument and what not, is to a certain extent a matter of chance. In the main, however, the course laid down is strictly followed. In Part I we are concerned with the discovery of principles, in Part II the principles discovered are applied to some of the most vital domains of life in which the question of justice is particularly important. But this book can be regarded only as a first step. I trust that the day is not far distant when Protestant jurists, sociologists and economists will continue and improve on these inadequate beginnings. I shall be perfectly satisfied with their assurance that this book offers at least a useful basis for further work.

I owe, however, a special word of apology to the historians.

The problem of justice, as we see it today, must always be grasped, as a whole and in detail, on the great background of European history. That necessitates certain schematic generalizations which must be almost intolerable to the scientific historian, with his predilection for the multitudinousness of history, for the fine shades of historical personality. I can only plead in extenuation that even historians are, on occasion, driven to similar violent foreshortenings.

Finally, the purpose of this book is not primarily theoretical, but practical, as all theological work should be. Its aim is not contemplation but action. But the basis of its belief is that all action must proceed from knowledge. A knowledge of the just on a clear and firm foundation is a first, and even indispensable step towards putting justice into action. My present office as rector of the university should, perhaps, have withheld me from writing this book at the present time, but who can refrain from writing when he feels he must write? And who can deny that it is high time for anyone with anything to say on the subject of justice to do so?

Zurich, September, 1943

... Chapter 1 ...

THE DISINTEGRATION OF THE
WESTERN IDEA OF JUSTICE

THE WHOLE WORLD IS CRYING OUT FOR JUSTICE
All suffering is bitter, but unjust suffering is doubly bitter. The
suffering which is fate unites men; unjust suffering breeds strife.
There is a kind of suffering which belongs to the life of the
creature as it were by nature, but unjust suffering is unnatural.
Unjust suffering does not merely thwart man's desire for happi-
ness; it also destroys an established order; it deprives me of my
due. Unjust suffering arouses indignation; it affects the life of
the spirit; it eats into the personality. It is the injustice which
constitutes the real suffering, not the wrong which has been
unjustly done. Only man knows this kind of suffering, because
only man knows an order of things in virtue of which something
is, or is not, his by right.

Injustice there has always been, but no age has yet witnessed
such a measure of injustice as ours. Mankind has passed through
epochs of cruelty, but not yet an epoch like this, when wrong is
done in the name of right, indeed when wrong has become
systematic, when the reversal of the very principle of justice has
become the order of the day and the system of the state. To
violate the order of justice by dis-orderly passion is one thing;
to set up dis-order as a principle of order is a very different
thing. Wrong as a setting aside of order is evil; wrong as a
system, as an approved and permanent perversion of a just order,
is intolerable. There have at all times been men of power who
have called right wrong and wrong right, but it was reserved to
our time to turn that perversion into a political principle, a
standard of public order. A perversion of such a kind cannot be

explained merely by a peculiar degree of evil in individuals. It only becomes possible when the perversion has long been preparing in the depths of the spirit. The ulcer is not the disease; it is only the symptom and manifestation of the poison in the blood. The ideologies and principles of the totalitarian state—for that is the name given to systematic wrong in our time—are deeply rooted in the spiritual history of the Western world. The systematic perversion of wrong into right and right into wrong was prepared long beforehand by the breakdown of the idea of justice in Christendom.

Every human being has a sense of right and wrong. Every schoolboy feels the wrong done to him by an unjust and partial teacher. Every coolie protests if he is cheated of just wages for his work. "There is no doubt that certain notions of right and justice are innate in the human mind, and that a light of justice shines in them."[1] We speak of justice as an instinct. The term is not apt. Instincts belong to the sphere of nature, but the sense of right and wrong belongs to the domain of the spirit, for it is a realization, however obscure, of an order of things, of something that is "right," that ought to be, that *must* not be violated. This instinctive insight into right and wrong exists wherever men have awakened to human, personal existence. However various its forms, however restricted its domain, no human being is quite ignorant of justice, whatever race, whatever stage of civilization, whatever religious creed he may belong to. It is a constant factor in all human history.

What is not constant is the theory of justice, the way in which that blind sense of justice has emerged into the clear light of consciousness and has been interpreted in terms of philosophy or religion. A good deal of spiritual history consists of such interpretation—true or false. Human life, especially when it is concerned with the framing of social institutions, requires such interpretation. The vague sense of just and unjust must be transformed into clear thought, into the principle of justice, and comprehended as the idea of justice, if the institutions of human society are to express justice. This interpretation of right and

[1] Calvin, Works, pp. 49, 37.

wrong, this exegesis of justice, is a matter in which religion and philosophy must take a predominant part.

The Western theory of justice is derived from two main sources—classical philosophy, in which the Roman element should not be underrated, and Christianity. No writer has taught more clearly the nature of justice and more deeply influenced jurisprudence by his teaching than Aristotle; nowhere is the demand for justice so clearly and so powerfully expressed as in the Hebrew prophets. The primal, mythical notion of an order of law established by the gods found its philosophical expression in Aristotle's dictum that all human law is based on a primal divine law, the φύσει δίκαιον, the just by nature, which is the criterion and creative foundation of all human legislation and jurisdiction (1).

In the Christian era, this idea was blended with the Scriptural doctrine of the order of creation and the commandment of justice laid upon men by the one holy and just God. The two coalesced in the conception of the Christian law of nature. This conception of justice as eternal, supernatural and absolutely valid, which was, in its Latin form, incorporated in Justinian's *Corpus juris civilis* as the *jus naturale*, dominated the jurisprudence of the end of the classical world, the Middle Ages, Renaissance, Reformation and post-Reformation down to the Age of Reason. It was the Western conception of justice for two thousand years.

Its disintegration set in with the Age of Reason. Firstly, the *divine* law of nature, the objective, superhuman standard of justice, became the subjective law of human reason, its substance soon being narrowed down into the individualistic notion of subjective rights of man. Later, following the trend of the time, the element of "nature" in law was reinterpreted in a naturalistic sense. The historicism of the Romantic period then declared war on a timelessly valid justice, replacing it by the conception of justice as a historical growth. It was, however, the positivism of the nineteenth century, with its denial of the metaphysical and superhuman, which dissolved the idea of justice by proclaiming the relativity of all views of justice. Thereby the idea of justice was stripped of all divine dignity and law abandoned to the vagaries of human will. The view that justice is of its nature relative became the dogma of the jurists, and the proof seemed to lie at hand in the concrete facts of history. Men ceased to believe in an eternal standard of justice transcending all human legislation; the difference between right and wrong became a convention, law was conceived as the mere product of the reigning power. Finally the idea of justice was reduced to a mere husk by the complete codification of law at the beginning of the nineteenth century, after which it meant nothing more than the demand for a system of law without contradiction in form, but without any value as a criterion in substance (2).

Hence it was only to be expected that one day a political power devoid of all religious scruples should discard the last vestiges of the traditional idea of justice and proclaim the will of the ruling power as the sole canon of appeal in matters of law. The totalitarian state is simply and solely legal positivism in political practice, the abrogation in actual fact of the classical and Christian idea of a divine "law of nature." If there is no divine standard of justice, there is no criterion for the legal system set up by a state. If there is no justice transcending the state, then the state can declare anything it likes to be law; there is no limit set to its arbitrariness save its actual power to give force to its will. If it does so in the form of a logically coherent system, it thereby fulfils the one condition to which the legality of law is bound in the formalistic view of law. The totalitarian state is the inevitable result of the slow disintegration of the idea of justice in the Western world.

Thus the history of the interpretation of the idea of justice in the Western world has culminated in its total dissolution; it has been annulled, both in theory and practice. The long road has led into the void. The totalitarian state, and the positivistic theory which prepared the way for it, have room neither for the rights of man nor for any eternal standard of justice whatever. They consist solely in the system of power actually existing and enforcing its own absolutism by its own will and its own means. No wonder that the era of the totalitarian state should be the era of an unprecedented lawlessness and of systematic injustice.

It is only now, when Western humanity is faced with the appalling result of its work of destruction, that it is beginning to realize what has happened and to look back on the road it has travelled. It is overwhelmed with the horror of a terrible reality, which it sees taking shape in the totalitarian state. Yet it has not reached the point of admitting that this totalitarian state is not the invention of a handful of criminals in the grand style, but its own product, the ineluctable consequence of its own positivism, a positivism void of faith and inimical to metaphysics and religion. It will not yet believe that this is the inevitable result of man's loss of faith in a *divine* law, in an eternal justice. Yet the alternative stands clearly revealed. Either there is a valid criterion, a justice which stands above us all, a challenge presented *to* us, not *by* us, a standard rule of justice binding on every state and every system of law, or there is no justice, but only power organized in one fashion or another and setting itself up as law. Either there exist eternal, indefeasible rights of man, or there are merely the opportunities of the lucky and the lack of opportunity of the unlucky. Either there is a sacred law, which can be appealed to against every inhuman, unjust social order, against any caprice or cruelty on the part of the state, or that sacred law is a mere dream and law is nothing but another name for the chance products of the actual elements of power in a political field of force.

But if there is no sacred, eternal, divine, absolute law, there is no possibility of denouncing any form of law or polity or national act as unjust. If the positivistic theory of law is right, there is no possibility of waging war against the totalitarian state as a monster of injustice. Nor can we even say—it is unjust —but only—it does not suit me, I do not like such things.

The crisis in law and order which bears the name of the totalitarian state is the outward manifestation of the crisis in the conception of law. Humanity today is faced with the necessity of finding an issue from that crisis both in its inward and its outward aspects. One way, popular up to the present, is barred; we can no longer appeal to history. The totalitarian state has squandered the heritage of history. Now that its bankruptcy is declared, the question of the foundations on which a new world can be built can no longer be evaded. On what basis can reconstruction begin? Where is the idea of justice which alone renders such reconstruction possible? This question is not only *one* of those confronting us today. It is *the* question of the day. One thing is obvious. No reconstruction can be based on the maxim that justice is a relative thing. Nothing can be measured with an elastic yardstick. It is true that all social systems which we human beings create are only relatively just. But even such a relatively just system is only possible if we are guided by an idea of absolute justice, if we align what we build by the plummet of divine justice.

For nearly two thousand years the classical and Christian idea of justice, the "Christian law of nature," sustained and directed occidental jurisprudence, and was conceived to provide an adequate expression in philosophic terms for man's innate, underived sense of right. What would be simpler, therefore, than to return to it? Yet that is no easy matter for us, if only because the "Christian law of nature" is not an unequivocal standard. From the outset, a certain ambiguity has clung to the idea, whether in its classical or its Christian form. What is meant by the "nature" in which the principle of "divine" justice is contained? The polemic against the law of nature has by no means only been carried on by men who were prepared to surrender the idea of justice to relativism or formalism, but also by men who were well aware of the imperishable values of the classical and Christian idea of justice.[2] They felt the inadequacy of the term "law of nature." They suspected some confusion in the blend of the Christian and classical elements which came about at the end of the ancient world. It will be one of the paramount tasks of future jurisprudence to clarify this connection.

It should be no matter for surprise if Christian theology also feels bound to grapple with the problem. The Scriptural and Christian idea of justice plays a preponderating part in the

---

[2] In particular the great jurist Gierke in his work *Johannes Althusius*. (English translation: *Natural Law in the Middle Ages*.)

formation of the occidental standard of justice; for instance, it can be shown that the conception of the rights of man arose and found expression in connection with Christian ideas(3). Hence it can hardly be contested that it is the right and the duty of the Christian theologian to take his share in the work of reconstruction. On the other hand, the Christian theologian can hardly fail to realize that this theme of secular justice—for our subject is the divine standard for the systems of this world—is merely incidental in the Gospel. It is obvious that the central teaching of the divine Gospel as "the righteousness of God,"[3] the message of atonement for the sinner by Jesus Christ, is only indirectly connected with the question of just reward for labour, just punishment, a just polity, and so on. And vice versa, it cannot escape anyone living entirely in the world of Christian thought that, when questions of justice in the political or economic world arise, it is not from the theological expert in Scriptural matters that advice and authoritative information will be sought. These are questions in which even the most orthodox and exclusive Scripturalists among the Christian teachers have felt it incumbent upon them to sit at the feet of philosophers and jurists. Hence the question of justice in the systems of this world is clearly one which lies on the borderline between the faculties, and it is not mere chance that Christianity and classical antiquity should have co-operated in mastering the problem. But borders are not only the places where the most momentous decisions are arrived at in politics and war, but also in the history of the spirit. Only the man who can look beyond frontiers can be their guardian. It is high time that theologians, philosophers and jurists should unite in order to comprehend and clarify the meaning of this great idea, the idea of justice, of what is just, so that devastation may be checked and a reconstruction of just institutions begun on the ruins.

[3] See translator's note, p. vii.

...PART I...

PRINCIPLES

... Chapter 2 ...

WHAT IS MEANT?

IF WE ARE TO ELUCIDATE THE ESSENTIAL NATURE of justice, we must first be clear what we mean when we speak of justice. Justice may mean many things. If we take as our starting-point the saying of the ancient sage Theognis: "All virtue is subsumed in justice,"[1] or if, as would appeal to a Christian theologian, we set out from the Scriptural use of the word justice,[2] we should be speaking of something which has nothing to do with our theme. When we moderns speak of justice, of just and unjust, we do not mean the sum total of all goodness or all virtue: nor do we mean, as the Bible does, real devoutness, confidence based on faith in the grace of God. Both in ancient Greece and in the Bible the word just has a depth and scope which it has long since lost.[3] When we speak of just and unjust, we have something far more restricted in mind than when we simply distinguish good from evil.

Even Aristotle was faced with the necessity of drawing this distinction(4). He realized that in his day the word "just" was used in a double sense, firstly in that comprehensive sense in which it means righteousness, and secondly in a narrower, more specific sense in which it means a just rendering to every man his due. Since Aristotle's time that broader, more comprehensive sense has almost vanished from our minds. No man of today but would find it strange if, because he was kindly, devout, charitable, grateful and God-fearing, he should be called just, as in the language of the Bible and, in another fashion, in the

---

[1] Diehl: *Fragmente der Vorsokratiker.*
[2] See translator's note, p. vii.
[3] Cf. *Theologisches Wörterbuch des Neuen Testaments*, Vol. II, pp. 176-229.

older Greek which survives in the saying of Theognis. This narrowing down of the term has been fateful to us. We can no longer use the word "just" as the ancient world used it without causing the gravest confusion. The use of the word in its narrow sense has, since Aristotle, become universal.

When we moderns speak of justice, we mean a mode of conduct which certainly belongs to the moral sphere, but neither embraces it entirely nor exhausts its depths. We say, for instance, of a man—he isn't what you would call kind, but we must admit that he's just. We use the word here exclusively in Aristotle's second sense, which means the just rendering to each man of his due. Thus we speak of a "just" teacher or critic when he is impartial, of a "just" tax when its burden is properly distributed, of a "just" polity when it properly determines the rights and duties of its citizens towards each other and the relation of rulers to subjects. It is in this sense that we speak of a just reward for labour and just punishment, of just and unjust distribution of property, of just laws, of just or unjust social systems.

That is the justice which is the theme of the present work. Our object is to enquire into its origin and nature, to discover the principle by which just dealing is distinguished from unjust, just criticism from unjust, just wages from unjust, a just from an unjust polity. We are not dealing with that Biblical justice, of which we read: "The just shall live by his faith,"[4] still less of that righteousness of God "which is not of the law"[5] but was revealed in the atonement by Jesus Christ. What we have to deal with is, in the language of Christian theology, "worldly justice," not "the justice of faith," but the justice of the institutions of this world. A just teacher who treats his pupils impartially, even though he is just in this narrower earthly sense, may be anything but just in the Scriptural sense of the word, while a just wage is not only not identical with what the New Testament calls the justice of faith, but stands in a notable contrast to it. The justice which metes out just punishment to

4 Hab. 2: 4; Rom. 1: 17.
5 Rom. 3: 21 ff.; Phil. 3: 9.

the lawbreaker is quite different from that "better justice" which, in the teaching of Christ, resists not evil, which, having been smitten on the one cheek, turns the other, and thus, in our manner of speaking, should rather be called forgiveness by love than justice.

Between this even-handed justice, which renders to each man his due, and that other, heavenly justice, which returns good for evil and forgives the transgressor seventy times seven, there is an ultimate, secret affinity, which we shall not ignore, but, in due course, elucidate as far as possible.[6] But what we have to deal with is earthly and not heavenly justice, the thing that satisfies the plain man's sense of justice, yet whose nature cannot be directly inferred from that elementary, unreflective sense of justice. What is, what origin and what authority has, that justice which distinguishes just from unjust payment, just from unjust punishment, a just from an unjust polity? That matter, that theme is our matter, our theme. We have spoken in the preceding chapter of the breakdown of this idea of justice, of its restoration as the prime condition for the reconstruction of just institutions in the Western world, whose life has been so terribly devastated by that breakdown. What is, in this sense, just and unjust? How can we acquire a standard for the distinction, as a whole and in detail? Can we say what makes an action, a law, a relationship just or unjust? Can we discover the principle of this justice?

[6] Cf. Chap. 14, "Justice and the Revelation of Scripture."

... Chapter 3 ...

THE PLACE OF JUSTICE IN THE SPHERE OF ETHICS

WHEN WE CALL SOMETHING JUST, WE MEAN to denote by the word something which is morally good—morally good insofar as the word justice can only be used where the human will is involved. Things or animals can of themselves be neither just nor unjust. On the other hand, it is characteristic of the term "just" that it describes not only human will, character, "virtue," but man-made relationships, conditions and institutions. This first reflection shows that by the notion of justice morality has been extended beyond the immediate sphere of the will, hence that it brings about a certain materialization of morality.

This will at once become clear if we compare justice with love—brotherly love. There is unquestionably a close kinship between the two which we shall have to enquire into later.[1] At this point, however, they mean totally different things. Love is always related to persons, never to things. We can speak of a just law or system, but we cannot speak of a loving law or system. Everybody feels at once that the union between love and personality is incomparably closer than that between justice and personality. We also realize at once that in the personal sphere, in the mutual relation of persons, love, not justice is the highest good. Everyone knows what is meant, and knows that it is right, when we say that love is more personal than justice, that is, that the relationship between human beings which is based on love is more personal than the relationship which is based on justice. While love is the acme of all moral goodness, we cannot by any means

[1] See Chap. 15, "Justice and Love."

16

say the same of justice. It is therefore our bounden duty to enquire what warrant the standard of justice can have, seeing that
it does not embrace the highest, ultimate good. Looked at from
the standpoint of love, it presents the appearance of a kind of
inferior morality, of a mere preliminary stage of the good(5).

The riddle is solved as soon as we turn our attention to the
object of justice, to the sphere it regulates and governs. Unlike
love, whose writ runs supreme in the moral sphere of personality, justice has to do not with the person *qua* person, but with
the person in view of "something," a material domain which is
not personal. From time immemorial the principle of justice has
been defined as the *suum cuique*—the rendering to each man of
his due(6). The definition of justice: *justitia est perpetua et
constans voluntas suum cuique tribuendi*, entered mediaeval
jurisprudence by way of Ulpian and the *corpus juris*,[2] side by
side with Cicero's terser definition of justice as *animi affectio
suum cuique tribuens*.[3] Who or whatever renders to every man
his due, that person or thing is just; an attitude, an institution, a
law, a relationship, in which every man is given his due is just.
Thereby justice is clearly distinguished from love. Love does
not ask what is mine and what thine: it does not render to the
other what is his due, what belongs to him "by right," but gives
of its own, gives precisely that to which the other has no right.

When Locke says that there can only be justice where there
is property, and even private property,[4] the fallacy is comprehensible, but it is none the less a fallacy. It is true that justice
is always concerned with mine and thine, and for that very reason, never with the person *qua* person, but with the person in
view of "something." That mine and thine, however, need not
necessarily be a material object, a thing owned or possessed.

That *suum*, mine or thine, comprises everything which is not
myself, but which "belongs" to me. Kant, referring to Ulpian's
familiar formula,[5] says: "That which is mine by law (*meum
juris*) is that with which I am so bound up that any use made of

[2] Dig. 1, 1. 10.
[3] *De Finibus*, pp. 5, 23.
[4] *On Government*, § 26.
[5] *Metaphysik der Sitten*, I, 1. §1. Ulpian, *neminem laedere*, Dig. 1.

it by another without my consent would injure me." It may be a man's good name, it may be due recognition, it may be freedom, or a political right—but it is always something which belongs to me or you. The sphere of justice embraces all that "belongs," all that is a man's due, all that he has a "right to."

That "right," however, does not by any means refer to the positive law of the state, firstly because it is precisely the idea of justice which enables us to distinguish between a just and an unjust law, secondly because we also speak of justice in cases where there could be no recourse to a legal settlement by the state. The schoolboy who has done his work well has a "right" to good marks, it is "unjust" if he is given lower marks than another whose work is inferior; the good marks are his "due." Hence the primitive idea underlying the idea of justice is that of "belonging." The simple statement *suum cuique*, which actually comprehends the whole essence of justice—of that justice which is dealt with in this book and which satisfies men's "sense of justice"—goes back to an underived, primal order of things established by no human lawgiver. The man who protests because something that belongs to him is taken away or withheld from him believes that that which has been taken away or withheld belongs to him in virtue of an order which no human being can administer. The possessive pronouns mine and thine cannot be eliminated from our conception of justice, nor can the idea, even though it remain only half conscious, of an order in virtue of which this something "belongs" to us. It *must* be given to us, it *must* not be removed or withheld from us because it "belongs" to us. In that "belongs" lies the whole appeal of the idea of justice to feeling. Our first question is not *what* belongs to each man, or *what* is his by right—that is the subject of this whole book. Nor do we first ask how we *know* what is each man's due, or even whether we can know it with any certainty. All those questions are justified and must be faced in their proper place, but the first unquestionable assertion we have to make is this: when we speak of justice, when we believe in justice, when we demand justice or protest against injustice, we always mean one thing—that primal order of mine and thine which stands above all human apportioning and must be the standard for all human apportioning if it is to be "just." An action or an attitude of mind, a law or an institution, can only claim to be called "just" if it corresponds to that primal order. The man who does not believe in that primal order, which renders to each man his due, cannot believe that anything "belongs to him by right"—unless in the sense that it is assigned to him by some law of the state. But he could not then distinguish between an unjust and a just law of the state, and he could not speak of justice in cases where the standard of law of the state is not and cannot be applied. The sense of "the just" cannot be given effect without reference to that primal order.

Thus in virtue of the idea of justice mankind is placed in an order. He is part of a structure, fits a certain place in that structure, and it is a structure which orders the whole of life, the relationship of every man to his fellow men and at the same time the relationship of every man to the natural constants of life. By justice, every man is "fitted in," and hence in a way is disposed of. The idea of "fitting in" is inseparable from the idea of justice. Justice always gives a feeling of stability, however far the substance of what belongs to a man by right may change with the changes of circumstance and personality. Whenever a just claim is put forward, an appeal is made to "what is fitting." It is in virtue of "what is fitting" that this is due to me, that to you, in virtue of "what is fitting" that that falls to your share, belongs to you, and this to me. That is the deepest reason why a certain impersonality clings to the idea of justice. In every case, what "belongs" to me, what is my due, is something definite, fixed. Hence if I treat a man justly, and only justly, I regard him as fitting his place in the structure, as one whose place has been decided upon, and so decided that this or that is his due or property(7). I do not see him himself. I see his "claim," his right, we might even say his "share" in the whole structure. As contrasted with love, justice has this statutory quality, this sense of things fixed.

It is because justice renders to each man his due that it both connects and severs. It connects inasmuch as it assigns to the individual his place in the ordered whole; it severs inasmuch as it allots to each "his" place, which is nobody else's. What belongs to me belongs to nobody else, just because it is mine. Justice binds me to the other by making me bound—*obligatus*—to render him his due. I cannot get free from him; I cannot elude my obligation to him. But at the same time it severs me from him by drawing round about him a circle into which I may not penetrate, or by not admitting me to direct contact with him himself, since it only shows me what is "his," what "belongs" to him. I have to do, not with him, but with his right.

A final point which we have already established as a fact now becomes comprehensible. As distinguished from love, justice can serve as a standard in any question of impersonal relationships, of institutions, laws, ordinances. Since justice is not concerned with the person, but with that share of something which is derived from the quality of being a person, the predicate "just" or "unjust" belongs not merely to persons but to all ordered human relationships in which the shares of the individual members of a social whole are regulated. Hence the idea of justice belongs, not to the sphere of personal ethics, but to the ethics of systems or institutions. Even the virtue which bears the name of justice is one which operates in the sphere of systems. While justice always appears as an inferior value in the ethics of the person, in the ethics of institutions it is the supreme and ultimate standard. The highest requirement of systems, institutions, laws, is that they should be just, while it is required of man that he should meet his fellow men not in justice, but in love.

... Chapter 4 ...

JUSTICE AND LAW

IN THE HISTORY OF THE IDEA OF JUSTICE, THERE
has been a conflict for priority between two ideas as constituting
the basis for justice, namely law and equality. Law is the more
fundamental. For before I can ask *what* is due to each man, an
equal or an unequal share, I must know *whether* something is
due to him. "That is my due, that is your due" simply means—it
is so established, it is already determined. We have given the
name of primal order to this foreordination of what is due. But
where there is order, there is law. Hence the idea of justice is
inseparable from the idea of law.

Just conduct is of necessity conduct which is guided by the
law and directed to the law, which is lawful. Therein lies the
greatness and necessity of justice, but also its limitation. It is
not by chance that in the Gospel, where the nature of God is
revealed as love, a contrast of the utmost sharpness should arise
between lawful justice and love.[1] Once personal goodness has
been recognized, lawful goodness is no longer the ultimate,
supreme value. A fleeting premonition of this fact is expressed
in the old saying: *summum jus, summa injuria.*

It lies in the nature of law to fix, to settle. In many languages
the notion of law is connected with that of settlement. Insofar as
man is regarded in his legal aspect, he is regarded as one who
is settled, as one who is the object of a decision. Further, law
of necessity generalizes, it embraces in one rule a multiplicity
of cases. Every law is a scheme. There can be no such thing as
a law which discriminates in favor of the individual, which
is entirely fitted to the individual, which would admit as valid

[1] Rom. 3: 21 ff; Gal. 3, 4.

the uniqueness of the individual, for that would invalidate the very conception of law. Hence it is precisely justice which can never "do justice" to the single human being as a unique individuality. Only love can do that. In every case the law says: "This happens to many." Law brings, if not all, at any rate a large number under the same rule, and treats those brought under the same rule as equals.

In many respects they may be unequal, but, says law, "that is not the point at issue here. Inasmuch as they are brought under the rule of law, their differences are obliterated." Law always implies equalitarianism, even when that equalitarianism is mitigated by the recognition of differing groups and prevented from attaining its logical extreme by an element of individualism. Within the groups thus differentiated, the differences are no longer respected.

Further, it is part of the idea of law that, since it lays down rules in advance, it indicates events of which foreknowledge is on principle possible. Whether we think here of the natural laws of physics and astronomy, or of the laws of the state, both have in common that what is to be expected in the future has been established in the past and is hence predictable. Law is order by foresight. With regard to human beings, that is the service it renders; it is also its burden and its danger. It offers protection from the arbitrary, it gives a feeling of reliability, of security, it takes from the future its ominous darkness. Yet it menaces freedom, robs it of its spontaneity. In the one sense as in the other it is the factor of stability in human happenings, just as it is the factor of uniformity.

Hence it stands in a twofold relationship to equality. What has been standardized by law will be the same tomorrow as it was yesterday. Law is equalitarian in respect of time. And it equalizes everybody within its sphere; even where it differentiates groups based on different principles, all members of the same group stand under the same law. It makes all equal, or at any rate makes all within the same group equal.

The law to which justice looks is no human code, for it is a law which stands above all human codes as the standard of human legislation, the law which enables us to say of a law set up by men that it is "unjust." It is the law by which lawgivers take their bearings in their endeavor to create just laws and to abolish unjust law. It is, however, the law too on which every man takes his stand, however unwittingly, when he promotes justice or protests against injustice in matters in which no human law exists or can exist. It is an "unwritten law," unless, in the words of the Apostle, it is written in men's hearts.[2] It is the law which the best of human laws strive to express, though they never reach their goal in the attempt. Hence it is the element of perpetual ferment in all human systems. Yet it is foolish and wrong to maintain that justice is a relative thing because no human system can fully express this law of justice. That is as unreasonable as to maintain that the notion of the straight line is a relative one because no human being has yet been able to draw a straight line. It is just *because* we can conceive an absolutely straight line that we can say that no man has ever drawn a straight line. It is just because we have knowledge of the law of absolute justice that we can say that all human laws are mere approximations to the truly just (8).

The illustration of the straight line is not merely fortuitous. There is a curious kinship between the straight (upright) and the just (righteous). There is good reason why the deviation from right is known as delinquency. The straight line is the simplest symbol of steadfastness, because it is the one line in which the direction of progress from point to point remains unchanged. The German word *Recht* which is the root of the word just (*Gerechtigkeit*) is the same as that which denotes a straight line. Right is the straight line, unwaveringly directed to the one point.

But is there no supreme justice which is supreme by the very fact that it stands above the law? Is not the judge just only when he transcends all law? Every serious judge is faced with the question. It arises wherever there is a spontaneous sense of the right. Insofar as law means the law of the state, the non-identity of law and justice is self-evident. Justice is the ultimate standard,

[2] Rom. 2: 15.

transcending all man-made law. But that very justice is inseparable from the idea of legality because it renders to each man his due, because it regards that due as something fixed and fitting. Even when the judge, in his supreme judicial authority, sets aside the law of the state to open the way for a higher justice, in his heart he reverts to that "due," which renders a definite thing to a definite person, and to that ideal order in virtue of which this or that is "due" to him. This is the point at which the supreme standard of justice is differentiated from that love which has need of no law, written or unwritten, which regards man not as placed in an order, not as fixed and "fitted in," but sees him in the freedom of divine love, which gives what is not and can never be, his "due."

... Chapter 5 ...

JUSTICE AND EQUALITY

Between justice and equality, however, there exists not only the relationship established by law. The law which is binding on all creates in the first place a merely *formal* equality. It says: whatever may be due to the individual, all shall be treated according to the law. But that does not tell us what is due to each man by the law under which all stand. The idea of justice, however, has also a relationship of *substance* with equality. It is true that "to each man his due" does not mean "to each man the same." And yet justice is closely akin to equality. Let us illustrate this point by a simple example.[1] At the end of a performance at the theatre, there is a rush to the cloakroom, everyone intent on getting his coat and hat as quickly as possible. It is expected of the attendant, however, that she shall not only hand out the coats and hats as quickly as possible, but also that she shall deal justly by all. How is she going to proceed? Let us assume that five persons have taken up their stand at the cloakroom counter side by side, and that a queue has formed behind each of these five persons. If the attendant were to proceed in such a way that, having served the leading person in one of the queues, she were then to serve the person behind him, who had moved into his place, and so on till that whole queue had been dealt with, before she as much as began to deal with the other four, the people standing in the other four queues would have every right to protest against unfair treatment. She proceeds justly by taking the leading person in each queue from

[1] (This illustration is derived from local usage. In Switzerland the deposit of outdoor clothes at the cloakroom of a theatre or a concert hall is obligatory. The result is that at the end of the performance the counters of the cloakrooms are really besieged by a seething mass of humanity. Tr.)

25

right to left and from left to right. In this way everybody has to wait for the same length of time. Every member of the audience, therefore, has the idea that the just treatment of all means keeping all waiting for the same length of time. First come, first served, last come, last served. Of course the distribution would only be truly just if there were as many attendants as there are queues. Hence, justice is equality. Just treatment means the same treatment for all. An equal wage for equal work, equal praise for equal achievement, equal punishment for equal transgression, equal rights for equal burdens, an equal price for an equal amount of goods. There is good reason why the Latin word for just is *aequum*, and why we express just dealing as "meting with the same measure." It is because of this fundamental relationship between justice and equality that the legal rules which imply of their very nature an equalization of many should be regarded as answering to the nature of justice.

From this standpoint the problem of justice appears at first to be very simple, for what is simpler than equality? Equality and law both satisfy the demands of reason. This simplicity, however, is a mere semblance. Human beings are *never* equal. Equality of treatment is only possible because and insofar as actual inequality is set aside and disregarded as immaterial. Hence equality of treatment always implies a far-reaching abstraction. Without giving reasons, it takes the most vital point for granted, namely that human beings can be treated as equals in certain relationships, in spite of the fact that they and their circumstances are actually unequal. If we consider that the cloakroom attendant is acting justly by keeping all waiting for the same length of time, it is only because we have come to a general agreement that in this case all inequalities are immaterial, or that they cannot be taken into account. If there is an old lady in the crowd who finds it obviously difficult to stand waiting, or if one of the crowd can convince the others that he has a train to catch, the privilege which before was felt to be unjust will or may be felt to be just because the tacit agreement that all should be treated alike is upset by an element of inequality. Equality of treatment is only just if it actually means the same thing to all.

If a schoolmaster were to make the same demands on the pupils of the lowest class as on those of the highest, he would in actual fact be unjust because equality of treatment in this case would in actual fact mean inequality. Hence in many cases, simple equality of treatment must be modified in the sense of equitable treatment, an equal-unequal treatment corresponding to an inequality of fact. Thus the simple treatment of all alike is seen to be an extreme case; it is only just when the inequality of persons may be disregarded in view of the thing to be distributed, or when it is impossible to assess actual inequality at the moment of distribution. "To all alike" is therefore by no means an ideal case of justice; it implies an extreme degree of abstraction which can only be admitted when respect for the inequality of persons is no longer practicable. We might take as an illustration the rationing of food during a war. When this unprecedented measure was first introduced, there was no alternative but to proceed according to simple equality, by the rule of "all alike." Each person received the same card entitling him to the same quantity of certain commodities. In time, however, distribution became more discriminating. Having at first been just in the abstract sense, it became really just when the diversity of persons and their circumstances was taken into account. The heavy labourer, the expectant mother, and so on, received special rations. The rule was no longer "all alike," but "all alike, respect being had to their inequality." And precisely that was felt to be just, and rightly so. Simple equality is as a rule a mere fiction of justice, since it only apparently distributes the same share to each man.

Aristotle[2] was the first to enquire into the nature of justice and to recognize both the close connection of justice with equality and the dual nature of justice. The first, simple justice, which gives the same to each, he called arithmetical or contractual, the second, which gives the same to each according to a scale of actual inequality, he calls proportional, geometrical or distributive. In this way he established a fundamental rule for all time, and we can understand why the theory of justice has at

[2] Nicom. *Ethics*, pp. 5, 7.

all times taken its stand on these Aristotelian definitions. We can even say that the theory of justice has never gone beyond Aristotle, but has always harked back to him. Wherever justice has been demanded, or protest raised against injustice, one of these two kinds of equality is meant, either the contractual, which actually gives the same to all, or the distributive, which, in view of existing inequality, distributes unequally by a single scale and thus in actual fact gives equally. Whether we think of the partial teacher, who does not treat his pupils all alike, or of the unjust judge, who does not mete to all with the same measure, or the unjust polity, which does not grant to all citizens the same right, or again of an unjust tax, which does not impose heavier burdens on the strong than on the weak, or of an unjust granting of leave in the army, which takes no account of special circumstances, such as those of the student or the farmer—what is meant by justice is equality, either in the contractual or in the proportional sense. "This classification is exhaustive—either to all alike, or then unequally, but by the same measure."[3]

The most important question, however, is not yet answered, namely, in what circumstances the one and in what the other kind of equality is just. That means, in what circumstances actual inequality must be taken into account and in what it may be neglected. Equality of treatment, as we have seen, is always an abstraction, a disregarding of actual inequality, on the assumption that the inequality "does not matter in this case." Thus the protagonists of woman suffrage demand the same suffrage, active and passive, for women as for men, since, it is argued, with respect to their place in the state the difference of man and woman "does not matter." Its opponents, on the other hand, regard the difference of sex as essential precisely in this respect, and hence refute the demand as unjust. All, however, agree that it would be unjust to grant the same suffrage to minors, since the difference of age is obviously not immaterial when it comes to participating in the life of the state; on the contrary, it is absolutely essential. Where is arithmetical and where is proportional justice to prevail?

[3] Nef, *op. cit.* p. 89.

Aristotle, the classical master of the theory of justice, made an attempt at answering this question which, though highly remarkable, fell far short of the truth. His theory is that simple equality belongs to the sphere of private law, which deals merely with the exchange of goods. Proportional equality belongs to the sphere of public law, which deals with the personal rights of citizens(9). This distinction is not a practical proposition if only because the two spheres of law are far from embracing the whole range of problems confronting justice. There is extra-legal justice—we have only to think of the unjust or just teacher. The Aristotelian distinction, however, is further impracticable because simple equality enters into public law, while proportional equality enters into private law. Aristotle is thinking primarily of commercial law. Thus, for instance, the demand for equal and universal suffrage is unquestionably based on arithmetical equality, while on the other hand, private law—in liability, for instance—takes account of the diversity of persons and circumstances. Nevertheless, Aristotle's distinction contains an important indication of the right solution.

The arithmetical, contractual kind of justice, which gives to each the same, implies in any case a more thoroughgoing abstraction than proportional justice. It is an extreme case of justice, namely that in which no account is taken of the person in his difference from all other persons, hence where things are more respected than persons. Hence it actually plays a decisive part in the exchange of goods—like for like. The more the person is overshadowed by the thing, the more directly measurable becomes the value of the two things which are to be reciprocally valued, and the more justice coincides with mere equality in the value of things. It is relatively easy to find a common denominator for things—e.g. money value—but not for persons. The more justice is concerned with the relations between persons, the less the differences between the persons can be disregarded, hence the more account justice must take of those differences, so that it is proportional and not contractual justice that must prevail.

But even that is not the last word. The modern democratic movement put forward the demand for equal and universal

suffrage, existing inequalities in legal status being condemned
as unjust. Now this claim for direct equality implied, not a disregarding of the person as such, but a definite conception of the
nature of human beings, according to which what is equal in all
human beings is essential and what is unequal inessential. The
passion of feeling with which this democratic demand was made
in the name of justice shows clearly enough that elements are
involved in the question which can no longer be measured by
purely rational standards. The demand for equal rights issues
from a definite outlook on life, a metaphysical or religious faith
which is not derived merely from the experience of reality, but
rises from the depths of a general religious view of life.

From the strictly empirical standpoint, human beings are both
equal and unequal. The real problem of justice, however, is
always whether it is the equality or the inequality which matters,
or whether, in spite of their actual inequality, men must be
treated equally or unequally. When a jurist of today[4] remarks
in this connection that "there is no objective criterion by which
this question can be settled, since it depends on my subjective
needs, intentions, views, etc.," he is right inasmuch as an element
comes into play here which is not to be apprehended by plain
reason. The jurist just quoted calls it a "standpoint," but con-
cedes in the further course of his argument that "other principles" obtain here by which the kind of justice to be applied
—whether simple equality or the equality which takes account of
inequality—can and must be decided. And if it appears at first
sight as if these "other principles" had nothing to do with
justice, history shows that the very point at which the principles
determining the equality or inequality of men come into play is
the point at which the emotional intensity of the demand for
justice, and the realization that justice is at stake, reach their
culmination. It is the limitation of Aristotle's vast achievement
that he, who has so much to teach us about the nature of justice,
should leave us in the lurch at this critical point. Here the formal
analysis of justice has reached its end. Here questions arise which,
for the sake of justice, we must follow into the sphere of metaphysics and faith.

4 Nef, *op. cit.* p. 106.

... Chapter 6 ...

THE GROUND OF EQUALITY

IT IS NOT ONLY IN THE QUESTION OF EQUALITY and inequality among men that justice points to something beyond mere empirical perception. As we have seen, we cannot even speak of just and unjust, we cannot even imagine the meaning of "justice" without falling back on that primal order which renders to each man his "due," and hence authoritatively determines what is mine and what is thine. It is impossible to discover the ground of mine and thine in any experiential piece of reality. After all, human customs, human agreements and contracts, human laws and constitutions, which render this to one, that to the other, are all subordinated to the criterion of justice. They may be just or unjust, whether they are the one or the other is decided by reference to that primal order which renders his due to each man with truth and final authority. That and nothing else is meant by justice. Without this reference to the primal order, a law may be called unsuitable, harmful, unusual, strange or whatever we like, but not unjust. Whoever pronounces the great word "justice" with serious intent has, by thinking that thought, appealed to the highest tribunal, to the unwritten law which is the standard of all just human legislation and jurisdiction. This primal order is of its nature superhuman, supernatural and eternal.

By calling this order a law, however, we have made a pronouncement of vital import about the equality and inequality of men. Every man of whom we can say that something is his "due," that something is his "by right," is in so far the equal of every other man. In this capacity he stands before the same tribunal, he participates in the order which apportions with ultimate authority. He is raised above the level of mere empirical hazard, he has a claim to justice. He has his place in that ordered structure in which that which is his is due to him. That is the very reason why it is ever possible to regard existing differences between men as "immaterial." At the moment it is not our purpose to discuss in which case it is justifiable to disregard inequality, and in which not. The fact that it can ever be disregarded, and that it can be disregarded with the full consciousness of just dealing, derives solely from the fact that man is regarded as part of that primal order which has power over him as over every other, and which has foreordained his due.

It is a fallacy to believe that the proposition: "The essential in man is equal" is based on perception. Pure perception tells us nothing about the essential or inessential. It tells us only and always that men are equal *and* unequal. But no experience can tell us whether that which is equal in all is essential—essential, that is, in the sense that it alone is taken into account in the distribution of something, so that equal treatment is just treatment. It is, on the contrary, a conviction of faith, hence in the sphere of the will no mere matter of expediency, but a moral obligation. Even the trivial incident of the cloakroom is a matter of faith, i.e. of the faith that every man has as good a right as every other. Let us imagine that incident, *mutatis mutandis*, in a historical setting in which a religious caste system is a matter of faith. We can see at once that the procedure on the part of the cloakroom attendant which we called just becomes absolutely impossible. A pariah cannot take up his stand in a queue with a Brahmin on the ground of equal right. Much less could he expect to be kept waiting no longer than the Brahmin. For him there is no equal right, no justice, by which that which is due to others is due to him. For to him, the outcast, nothing is due. We need not, however, look so far east to realize that equality of right is anything but self-evident. Even for Aristotle, the great theorist of justice, and for his still greater master in philosophy, Plato, there was no such thing. Even for them there were human beings who had no rights at all—namely, slaves. Only free Hellenes had equal rights, and of the free Hellenes only the men of equal rank. And that not merely because that was their kind of political system, but because they regarded that political system as just, thus because, in their view of justice, there was the primal order which renders to each his due, but not a primal order which renders the same to all who bear a human countenance.

To regard actual differences between men as "inessential" is not a self-evident proposition—after all, no man was ever Aristotle's superior in observation and understanding—it is a view dictated by faith. That it is not even the product of philosophical reflection can be seen by the fact that Aristotle, with the genius of his philosophic thought, arrived at a justification of his view of inequality. For he imagined that he could justify the unequal treatment of slaves,[1] of women[2] and of children before the law by pointing out what seemed to him a familiar and self-evident fact, namely that women and children have less share of reason than men, and slaves none at all.

Thus underlying even his theory of inequality there is a conviction of faith, namely that the essential part of men, the part which determines the equality of their right, is based on their share of reason, and on their share of that kind of reason in which—for Aristotle was seldom mistaken in observation—men are actually superior to women and adults to children. In this assessment of the essential part in man, Aristotle fully agrees with his master Plato,[3] and hence they arrive at the same conclusion in their view of inequality before the law. Thus it was not an error of *observation*, no inadequacy or inexactitude of perception with reference to mankind which caused their failure to solve the problem of material justice; it was a mistaken belief(10). They did not believe in that essential equality of men which seems to us, as we stand at the cloakroom counter, self-evident. The fallacy we commit, on the other hand, is to regard our view of essential equality as self-evident. In actual fact, as we can see by a glance at ancient Greece or even the contemporary Far East, it is an event in history, a fresh insight

[1] *Politics*, pp. 1, 4.
[2] *Politics*, pp. 1, 5.
[3] *Republic*, pp. 5, 469; *Laws*, pp. 6, 776 f.

that was once given to men. This is the point at which Christian theology must be called in. For the historical fact which under-lies the apparently trivial incident of the cloakroom is simply the message of the Bible.

That conception of justice by which all human beings, old or young, man or woman, bond or free, have equal rights in the sense that they *ought* to be treated alike, is in essence derived from the revelation of Scripture, according to which God created man "in his image."[4] Not Jew nor Hebrew, but simply man. It is in this sense that one of the oldest laws in the Old Testament, bind-ing all men by one terse clause, runs: "Whoso sheddeth man's blood, by man shall his blood be shed: for in the image of God made he man."[5] The creation of *all* men in the image of God is the deepest foundation of the sense of right in the Bible. This Old Testament doctrine of the dignity of man is not transformed in the New Testament, but it is deepened and generalized. We may even say that it first reached its full force by the faith in Jesus Christ as the Redeemer of all men and all peoples. As Jesus Christ is the goal of all human history, in the teaching of the New Testament the Son of God who became man in him is also the source of all history, indeed of all creation, and the prototype of man. For all men are of him and through[6] him and to him, and the man who believes on him knows "neither Jew nor Greek, neither bond nor free, neither male nor female,"[7] but in faith all are one in One, Jesus Christ, in whom true god and true man were made manifest at one and the same time. That is the tenet of faith which underlies the European conception of the same original right of all human beings.

One objection has, it is true, been raised to this assertion, namely that Stoic philosophy, more especially in the form it later assumed on Roman soil, had developed this universal idea of humanity side by side with the Christian religion and had inferred the equality of men before the law from it much earlier than the Christian church(11). The objection is not entirely

[4] Gen. 1: 27.
[5] Gen. 9: 6.
[6] Rom. 11: 36; I. Cor. 8: 6; Col. 1: 16.
[7] Gal. 3: 28.

groundless. It was more especially the popular philosophers of Stoicism, such widely read writers as Epictetus, Cicero, Seneca and Marcus Aurelius, who actually propounded the idea of the essential equality and unity of men with warmth, emphasis and clarity, and their teaching had perhaps a more direct influence on the later development of Roman law than Christianity. To this objection, however, there are two answers. Firstly there is a difference between the Stoic and the Christian view of the essential equality of human beings which will be discussed later when we come to speak of the inequality of men, and that difference is such that the Stoic doctrine, in its abstractness, its lack of comprehension for the factor of inequality, could never have brought about a revolutionary historical transformation. Secondly, that doctrine was a philosophy, admittedly with a strong religious trend, but it lacked the incomparably penetrative force of the Christian Gospel. Of itself it could never have been a turning-point in history. All it could do was to follow in the wake of the mighty pioneer, the Christian religion, and exercise an influence on history as its companion. How could the meagre ideas of an Epictetus, a Cicero or a Seneca have survived the breakdown of the Roman Empire and the onslaught of the *Völkerwanderung*, and held their own against the dynamic energy of the Germanic peoples? (12).

In any case we must do justice to historical fact. Let us admit that it was the Christian view of life blended with the Stoic which created the European idea of justice, the conception of the equal dignity of all human beings. We shall soon have occasion to point out the specific quality of the Christian as compared with the Stoic conception, and to see not only where they are alike, but also where they contrast and conflict. But Christian or Stoic, one thing is beyond question. The conviction of the equality of the rights of man derived and still derives its force from a religious or metaphysical *faith*.

This idea of justice and the incident at the cloakroom are not only inconceivable in Aristotelian Greece or Brahmin India. Imagine that incident in National Socialist Germany, and let the catchword be the name "Jew," or, in the land of the dictatorship of the proletariat, kulak or bourgeois. The picture of a just distribution dissolves before our eyes.

Modern developments have taught us that what is apparently a self-evident fact is not at all self-evident, but a heritage of history. When the foundations of faith, on which the European idea of justice is based, decay, the idea of equal rights decays with them, to be superseded by a view which can doubtless appeal to facts of perception just as well as Christianity—namely that what is equal in human beings is inessential, and that the essential is unequal, hence that inequality, not equality, of treatment is just. Not only equal rights, but the much more comprehensive notion of justice which claims equality for all who bear a human countenance, because equality is due to man as man— that notion is raised on a foundation of faith. The doctrine of the *imago Dei* in particular is the fundamental principle of the Protestant doctrine of justice(13).

Is therefore the question presented to us by the Aristotelian doctrine of the dual nature of justice unequivocally answered by his arithmetical, contractual form of equality? Does *suum cuique* mean—to each man the same? We have already seen that this is not the case, that not only the equality of human beings must be respected, but their inequality also. Aristotle could give no answer to the question of where this right to inequality is derived from, just as he left us in the lurch with the question of the ground of equality. Shall we discover, even here, the deepest ground in an insight of faith? If not, the most momentous question of the whole doctrine of justice must be left unanswered.

... Chapter 7 ...

THE GROUND OF INEQUALITY

EMPIRICAL OBSERVATION TEACHES US THAT human beings are just as much equal as unequal, but fails to tell us whether or how far that which is unequal is essential. It shows us the difference between man and woman, child and adult, strong and weak, gifted and ungifted, educated and uneducated. It shows us the differences between races, nations, civilizations, and above all the specific differentiation of individual personality. How significant are these differences?

Here two views stand sharply contrasted; one regards the differences as decisive, the other as quite immaterial.

The first view we have already encountered is the antithesis to the Christian and Stoic view. In the Indian caste system it is based on definitely religious grounds, in the teaching of Plato and Aristotle, its basis is also a basis of faith, though expressed in philosophic terms. But it is also axiomatic in the National Socialist theory of the *Herrenrasse* and lower races, as it is in the Russian theory of the proletariat as the only valuable social class. The doctrine of the privileged race or class is, if not a religion, at any rate a definite substitute for religion, with a markedly religious bias, especially in its dogmatism and fanaticism. It is "orthodox" doctrine in all its harshness and intolerance.

Attempts to find rational grounds for such doctrines have constantly been made. Aristotle, who, as befits the detachment of his manner of thought, puts them forward most dispassionately, finds the ground of essential inequality, as we have already seen, in an unequal share of reason, the reason which distinguishes men from women, adults from children and the free Hellenes from slaves. In expounding the institution of slavery, he betrays, it is true, some embarrassment. We can hardly assume that he found the arguments he puts forward completely convincing to himself.[1] We find here a bias that can often be observed in the doctrine of inequality; inequality is simply that which is "given" or desired; its ground must be sought anywhere and anyhow. The Hellenic feeling of cultural superiority to all barbarians may have played its part in the question, reinforced by a lingering echo of the old Greek feeling of superiority as the victors in war. The "noblemen" are, in many nations, primarily those who have distinguished themselves, or at any rate been successful, in war. The ruling caste consists of the descendants of those who triumphed in war. And it is a fact that actual inequality presents a problem that is not easy to solve on rational grounds. The "will to power" (14) seeks an ally in reason, though often with considerable effort.

Hence we can understand that the Stoic philosophers, whose system may be called religious rationalism or rationalistic religion, could denote inequality from the outset as inessential and refuse to draw important practical conclusions from it. In their religious humanism, the specific quality of the individual vanished. Their dogma is the equality of human beings pure and simple. For are not all human beings endowed with the same divine reason? Why should the natural distinctions of sex, race and individuality be taken into serious consideration? What counts is not the physical but the spiritual man, and not even the spiritual *man*, but the spiritual principle in man. That alone furnishes a basis for the dignity of mankind and the unity of the human race. Hence, since it is an impersonal spiritual principle (15) from which the divine, and hence the essential element in human beings springs, personal distinctions are adventitious, insignificant and without consequence.

This Stoic picture of the human race is not only important to us in its historical perspective. On the contrary, it was this idea which re-emerged at the beginning of the modern era and, with a mighty philosophical apparatus, undertook a reforma-

[1] *Politics* 1, 6.

tion of law and human institutions on the basis of a thousand years of Christian teaching and Christian influence on civilization. Nearly all the great thinkers of modern times have drawn from this spiritual source, and it is those who have had the greatest influence on the theory of justice—Locke, Rousseau, Kant, Fichte—whose thought has been largely determined from that quarter. They were, in varying degrees and ways, not only heralds of equality before the law, but also of a curiously individualistic conception of freedom and equality. We shall only understand why that is so if we contrast their conception of inequality as inessential with the Christian view. For the secret of the Christian conception of justice is not equality but the blend of equality and inequality. The blend, however, has exactly the same origin as the Christian idea of equality.

As distinguished from the rationalistic Stoic notion of equality, the Christian view is not based on an impersonal spiritual principle, on a nous or logos pervading all things, a world reason in which all human beings substantially participate, but on the personal will of God.[2] The Christian principle of the dignity of the person is unconditionally personal; the personal God creates the personal and individual human being and predestinates him to communion with Himself. Thus the origin of the dignity shared equally by all mankind is not to be sought in abstract reason, nor in a general order of being, but in the will of the living God, who addresses every man as "thou" and summons him to responsible being, to life in communion, in the love with which He first loved man. Man's right as a person is not founded on the fact of his humanity as derived from a universal reason; every single person is called to a supreme destiny as a human being, that concrete and unique "I." "Thine eyes did see my substance, yet being unperfect."[3] "I have called thee by thy name; thou are mine."[4]

Hence it is not matter which is the principle of individuality, as it is throughout Greek philosophy, but the personal will of

[2] Cf. Emil Brunner, *Man in Revolt, a Christian Anthropology.*
[3] Ps. 139: 16.
[4] Isa. 43: 1.

God which calls the person into being and thereby endows him with responsibility. Individual personality is therefore determined by the will of God just as much as the general dignity of humanity; every human being has his own personal dignity which resides in his predestination to personal being and is identical with the dignity of every other human being. Since it is the divine love which calls him "Thou" and summons him to fellowship, that which makes man man is not different from individuality, but one and the same thing. Hence individuality is never inessential, but is just as integral a part of man's being as that which is common to all men. God does not love mankind in general; he loves the individual in his own nature, created by Himself.

Hence a totally different evaluation of inequality results. God does not create schemes; He creates individuals. By calling a man "Thou" he bestows upon him his own unmistakable countenance, his individuality. The inequality which results from individuality is just as much created and willed by God as that which is common to all mankind. Inequality springs from the same root and hence has the same dignity as equality. In the Biblical story of creation, the same passage, the very same sentence, which speaks of man as God's image expressly includes one of the most cardinal of inequalities, the difference of sex, in the act of creation. "So God created man in his own image, in the image of God created he him; male and female created he them."[5]

In Stoic rationalism, as in its modern derivatives, the difference of sex is, like all individuality, inessential, we might even say insignificant. In Biblical thought it is invested with a consummate dignity, the dignity of creation. It is, however, only an example of all individuality. Not only equality is God's will, but inequality also, the specific nature of every individual human being, and the specific nature of every individual species. He created them "after their kind."

We have not yet reached the end. The personality of man is the condition of his communion with God. Communion can

[5] Gen. 1: 27.

exist only between persons. Where the dignity of man is attributed to general divine reason instead of to a God-created
personality, as is the case with the Stoics and the modern rationalists, communion cannot be the goal of existence, but only union,
the submergence of the individual existence in the universal,
the return of the spark of divine reason to the flaming sea of the
all-pervading reason of God(16). Hence Stoic philosophy and
its religious anthropology does not aim at an ethic of communion
but at an ethic of universality, of an abstract unity of equal
elements. In the Scriptural view, however, man, having been
created *by* love is also created *for* love. Not dissolution in an
abstract All is his supreme and ultimate destiny, but the community of persons. Not the reasonable being of man and the
realization of a general rationality is the goal and meaning of
human life, but the communion with God and fellowship of
man with man based on that communion with God—the Kingdom of Heaven. God reveals Himself as love; in the same way
He reveals true humanity as life in love. Man is only like God
in so far as he truly loves; it is only in that love which became
manifest in Jesus Christ that the image after which and for
which man is created becomes reality.[6] The goal of mankind is
the Kingdom of God, the perfection of community. From this
standpoint the concrete individuality of the human creature
takes on a new meaning: the difference between men is the
condition of the community of natural created beings. Community can only exist where there is difference: without difference, there is unity, but not community. Community presupposes
reciprocal giving and taking, community is reciprocal exchange
and completion. That is the Scriptural standpoint when it comes
to evaluating the difference between individuals. That difference
is in essence the capacity for completion and the need of completion. One has in his individual being what the other lacks. The
man needs the woman in order to be a man, the woman needs
the man if she is to be a woman. The two sexes are dependent
on each other; their union exists not only for procreation—

[6] Matt. 5: 45.

though that, in its turn, creates a new community—but is also a fellowship for mutual completion.

It is the will of the Creator that the individual human being should not be self-sufficient, like the Stoic sage or Robinson Crusoe on his island. It is His will that human beings should be dependent on each other in order to attain fellowship. Creation has so disposed human beings that they must seek and have each other. It is their mutual need of each other which shows that they are predestinated to fellowship. Their individual difference, and the capacity and need for completion which springs from it, is the natural, creaturely condition of the truly personal fellowship of love, just as the married love of man and woman is the natural condition of and preparation for true love after the manner of Christ.[7] The uniqueness of every individual human being is the limitation of that individual, and from that limitation there arises mutual dependence. This dependence is not, as in Stoic rationalism and the modern conception of man derived from it down to Rousseau and Fichte, regarded as a shameful thing which must be overcome, which outrages the dignity of man and must therefore be eliminated or at any rate ignored. We read in Rousseau that men *"vécurent libres, sains, bons et heureux . . . tant qu'ils ne s'appliquèrent qu'un seul pouvait faire, et qu'à des arts qui n'avaient pas besoin du concours de plusieurs mains."*[8] Even the family the only natural *"société, se dissout sitôt que ce besoin cesse. . . . Les enfants, exempts de l'obéissance qu'ils devaient au père. . . . rentrent tous également dans l'indépendence . . . ils n'aliènent leur liberté que pour leur liberté."*[9] In Christianity, on the contrary, this mutual dependence is the goal of creation, the proof of and preparation for the supreme destiny of fellowship. It is a tenet of the Christian creed that no man is sufficient unto himself.

Hence a new conception of justice results. The *suum cuique* can never be interpreted as "the same to all." Human beings are equal, for all have the same destiny and the same dignity; they

[7] Eph. 5: 8.

[8] Rousseau, *Discours sur l'origine de l'inégalité des hommes.*

[9] Rousseau, *Contrat Social, loc. cit.* Cf. Locke, *On Government.*

are equal in that everyone is responsible to God: therefore all have the same right to be recognized as persons. But this equality of dignity is combined with a difference in kind and function, and that is not immaterial, inessential, but an element of the same destiny. Hence to each man is due not only equality but inequality; it is in actual fact "to each his *due*," to each shall be rendered what is indefeasibly his, what is not another's. Both together are expressed in the Scriptural parable of the human community as a body, an organism. Just as every part, every organ in the organism has its own nature and the function corresponding to it, in the body of humanity every man, in virtue of his nature, has his own function, his own service to render to the whole. It is a fellowship of mutual completion by service. But there is a difference between the Scriptural image of man as a member of a body and that contained in the Romantic theory of organism.[10] Man does not derive his *dignity* from his service to the whole. His dignity as a person is anterior to fellowship because every individual is called by God Himself and is personally responsible to Him. The corporate community does not stand above the individual, making him a dependent, subordinate part of a higher whole, but fellowship is only truly personal when it is a community of independent, responsible persons.

Thus the Scriptural conception of equality does not annul individuality and the corporate fellowship of mutual completion. Nor does the Scriptural idea of individuality and membership of a body annul equality. The cardinal factor is the direct responsibility of the individual to God implied in God's call, and the dignity and equality which result from it. The secondary, though not inessential, factor is the mutual dependence resulting from man's predestination to fellowship and its substratum in nature, individual limitation and idiosyncrasy. Hence, in the Christian idea of justice, equality and the equal right of all are primary, while the difference of what is due to each in the fellowship is, though not inessential, secondary.

That is how the Christian faith views the equality and in-

---

[10] Cf. Emil Brunner, *The Divine Imperative, A Study in Christian Ethics.*

equality of human beings; hence that is how it defines the principle of justice. Of the Reformers, it was Calvin who most clearly grasped and expressed this connection between the order of creation and the problem of equality and inequality. His views on the subject may be summed up in the words of an authority:[11]

Men are, it is true, equal by nature. Since all bear the same image of God, the fellowship arising directly from this equality is both a privilege and a duty. But this fellowship in no wise affects differences of status, the hierarchy of the family and society. . . . The incontestable equality of all human beings before God, their equality of value as all being stamped in God's image, does not mean that all are alike in *kind*. Order presupposes difference and adjustment, hence the inequality of gifts and duties, of dignity and achievement within the social body. The antithesis between their natural equality and their inequality as members of one body loses its force when we consider that both, the equality and the inequality, are based on the creative will of God. Equality and inequality are obligations. The privileges and dignities implied in inequality simply mean greater rights for higher duties. This ever-repeated rule, which expresses the balance between rights and duties, corresponds exactly to the principle of equality of value. The unequal distribution of gifts implies unequal tasks and a mutual exchange of capacities.

Luther's (17) thought and teaching were not greatly different, except that he laid the greatest emphasis on the hierarchy founded on difference. The superiority and authority corresponding to it, however, he understands as necessary solely as a service to the community. "It is the aim of all classes of society that each should serve the other."[12] "Rulers have no *raison d'être* save diligently to help their subjects."[13] "The father of the house is its only servant. The mother is its only maid."[14] "The only subject in the state is the government. He who commands is the *servus servorum*."[15]

That is the Christian answer to the question which was left

---

[11] Bohatec, *Calvin und das Recht*, pp. 66 ff.
[12] *Luther, Werke*, pp. 15, 625.
[13] *Loc. cit.*
[14] Pp. 6, 467.
[15] 43, 664.

open, and could not but be left open, in Aristotle's formal theory of justice—namely, what is the cause of equality and inequality, what is the relation between them, hence what is the principle of justice? The Christian religion is the only one in which the idea of justice is inherent, which combines with the recognition of the equal, unconditional dignity of persons the recognition of responsibility to society as a duty and privilege of mutual dependence and service, which emphasizes equally the equality and inequality of human beings and recognizes the independence of the individual as well as his subordination to a social whole as anchored in the will of God. Hence Christianity alone can protect men from the demands both of one-sided individualism and one-sided collectivism.

... Chapter 8 ...

THE DIVINE LAW OF JUSTICE

THE IDEA OF JUSTICE AND THE CONCEPT OF A divine law of justice are one and the same thing. That is not a philosophical theory nor a religious opinion which may be agreed to or dissented from. Whoever says with serious intent: "That is just," or "That is unjust" has, even though unwittingly, appealed to a superhuman, supreme or ultimate tribunal, to a standard which transcends all human laws, contracts, customs and usages, a standard by which all these human standards are measured. Either this absolute, divine justice exists, or else justice is merely another word for something which suits some but not others, which appears expedient to some, but not to others. Either the word justice refers to the primal ordinance of God, and has the ring of holiness and absolute validity, or it is as a tinkling cymbal and sounding brass.

We may doubt justice, as we may doubt truth. But one thing is impossible—to believe in justice and yet reject the divine law of justice. The primitive mind expresses this connection by representing the gods as lawgivers and guardians of the laws of justice. These mythological images reveal a truth, namely that justice is of its nature holy, that it stands above man, that man can no more make arbitrary use of it than he can make arbitrary use of truth. Indeed, there is a close kinship between truth and justice.[1] Man can invent neither, he can only seek them. They stand "beyond" all human legislation or convention. Whoever says: "This or that is just" means: "That is so, beyond the possibility of argument." That is why courts of law have at all times been surrounded by an aura of sanctity. The judge pro-

[1] Cf. Hirzel, Themis, *Dike und Verwandtes*, p. 108.

46

claims, discovers, divine truth. It is a holy thing to hold judgment and pronounce judgment. The pronouncement of a just judgment is a kind of revelation. We meet in it a reality which is absolutely above us, which is binding on all of us, an order which is for all of us inviolable, awe-inspiring, holy. It is not for nothing that oaths are taken in courts of law and that judges are "sworn in." Human tribunals may be concerned with mundane things, with the temporal mine and thine, but the order binding on such things, by which they are just or unjust, is not mundane and not temporal, but superhuman and eternal. We must bow to a just judgment, not by any outward compulsion, but by an inward necessity, whether that judgment be to our joy or sorrow. It is valid and true. A truly just judgment is a divine judgment. The φύσει δίκαιον "is independent of whether it appears good to men or not (Aristotle).² This unconditionally valid thing, this divine primal order transcending all human laws, was called by the Greeks "the law of nature." As they saw the stars revolving in courses which no man could check, they perceived in all the happenings of nature a regularity which awakened in them the sense of a divine order; the order to which just judgment appeals, by which just judgment is distinguished from unjust, appeared to them a cosmic, divine law. To them cosmos meant divine law, a whole pervaded by the divine spirit. That is what Aristotle meant when he distinguished the φύσει δίκαιον the naturally just, as the absolutely just from human legality, from νόμικον, from merely relatively just law. This concept of the *lex naturae* and *jus naturale*, of the law of nature, entered Christianity by way of Cicero, the most influential jurist of the ancient world, and the jurists of the *corpus juris civilis*, whose thought was guided by Stoic philosophy. From the time of the Fathers of the Church to the Age of Reason it formed the basis of European jurisprudence(18).

We may regard it as surprising or regrettable that so many-faceted a concept, originating in pantheistic thought, should have been adopted by Christian theologians and jurists. We shall later have occasion to enquire why this happened, and why the

² *Nicom. Ethics*, pp. 5, 10.

idea dominated Christendom for fifteen hundred years, even for thinkers who had no great interest in the synthesis. But one thing is beyond question, that within the sphere of Christian thought the concept "law of nature" was given a new meaning. Within the Christian faith there is no room for a pantheistic conception of the cosmos. While the ancient Greek thought of the law of justice on the analogy of the law of nature, the Christian thinks of the laws of nature on the analogy of the law of justice. For the believer in the God of Scriptural revelation, the orders of nature are creations of the divine will. They are as and because God "called" them into being. "And God said let there be— and there was";[3] "For he spake, and it was done; he commanded, and it stood fast."[4] God is not an immanent world logos but the Legislator of the world. The law of the world is the manifestation of a creative will. And the law of justice is also the law of a divine will. Underlying the *suum cuique* there is the order of creation, the will of the Creator which determines what is each man's due. The law, the order of creation is that primal order to which every man appeals, even though unwittingly, who thinks the thought of justice. What is dimly apprehended by the plain man's sense of justice—Everyman's sense of justice—is revealed in divine revelation as the order established by the Creator.

But why, it may be asked, do we relate the law of justice to God's will as Creator? Why not simply to his moral commandment? The law of justice is certainly a divine imperative for the human will, it is a moral precept, a standard, a rule of action. But the law of justice is a special case, and quite different from the commandment of brotherly love. It not only expresses what ought to be; it expresses what *is*. The law of justice points to an order of being in virtue of which there is allotted to every creature its sphere, its scope, its freedom and its limitation. To every creature, along with its specific individuality, God the Creator gives the law of its being thus and not otherwise. By the act of creation, he determines what is due to it. "The mountains rose, the valleys sank down, into the place which thou hast

[3] Gen. 1: 3.
[4] Ps. 33: 9.

founded for them."⁵ "Who shut up the sea with doors, when it brake forth."⁶ Creation is primal allocation, the precept of material life. Every creature *must* be what God created it to be, and insofar as freedom is given to it, i.e. in everything that is not the fulfilment of the law of creation in itself, every creature *must* respect the order of creation established by the Creator. It *must* respect every other creature as a thing created, willed by God.

Hence to every creature, there is given at its creation, with the mode of being manifested in it, its law of life. Its right is given, its scope delimited, what is due and what is not due to it is determined. Hence in creation there takes place that "settlement" to which the *suum cuique* refers.⁷ The fact that man has not only moral duties, but also a claim, a right to something, that something is his "due," is based on creation.

The fusion of equality and inequality, which is of such momentous importance for justice, is only comprehensible from the standpoint of the order of creation. God created all men equal by creating all in His image, by calling each one into existence as a creature responsible to Him and predestinated to communion with Him. The fact that every human being, without prejudice to his specific mode of being, is, like every other, a creature who must give an account of himself, who is endowed with freedom and responsible for the use of that freedom, that he is a creature predestinated to human being and summoned to the supreme vocation—therein every human being has his dignity as a human being, which is identical with that of every other human being. It is that which vests in him his primal right, the right he must and may uphold against any other man. That is the equality of men founded in creation, the source of the eternal inalienable rights of man.

At the same time, however, every human being is endowed by the Creator with a specific mode of being—for instance that of man or woman—and even this which is his in distinction

⁵ Ps. 104: 8. (R.V.).
⁶ Job. 38: 10.
⁷ Cf. *supra*, p.?

to others must be respected. What is due to the man is not the same as what is due to the woman, although what is due to both as human beings is equal. Both their equality of dignity as human beings, as persons, and their inequality in kind and function are established by creation. Both must, as it were, be acknowledged, both are due and must be taken into account in the allocation of rights and duties. The law of creation demands the mutual recognition of that which is allotted by the act of creation, these primal rights. Thus the law of justice refers to a primal allocation, to the act of creation, whereby each man receives what is due to him. That is the reason why, wherever this creative will is not known, there is in the principle of justice neither equality nor inequality nor the right relation between them. It is only by comprehending the order of creation as the basis of all justice that we can understand why both the humanity shared by all and the specific nature of the individual constitute a claim, a right which must in justice be acknowledged, and in the acknowledgment of which justice consists. No one who sets aside the order of creation can find a relationship between the rule of justice and the specific nature of the creature.

For that same reason the commandment of brotherly love cannot form the basis of justice. The command to love in itself recognizes no claims or rights, no delimited areas(19). It says nothing of what is due to all, and above all, nothing of what is specifically due to each. The command to love neither differentiates nor delimits. Here "there is neither Jew nor Greek, there is neither bond nor free, there is neither male nor female."[8] Love in itself establishes no order; on the contrary, when it is about its own business it transcends all orders, all laws. It enquires neither into its own rights nor into those of others, for to all it gives itself, whole and undivided and beyond all limits. But it always presupposes justice and fulfils the claims of justice before setting about its own business, which consists in transcending those claims, in the more than just, in the free gift of what no man can justly lay claim to. In presupposing justice, it admits that it is not itself capable of fixing the bonds which justice implies. But the bounds which mark out

[8] Gal. 3: 26.

special rights and duties are established in the order of creation, which renders to each man his due.

Let us take an example to make this clear. In Marx and Engels' famous account of conditions in England in the early days of capitalism,[9] what arouses the greatest indignation is the wretchedness of the children who were forced into industrial labour. Why are we indignant when children of ten are herded into factories and forced to work twelve hours a day? Because we feel that it is unjust to the child, that it is being robbed of its childhood, that it is being outraged. Its right to its childhood is being stolen, burdens are being laid upon it which are not its due. We call it unnatural when a child is thus labelled as an adult. Thus our sense of justice appeals to the order of creation. This is not the will of the Creator. He who made the child thus and not otherwise has given it, with its specific mode of being, as a creature, the law, the right to be thus and not otherwise. By placing a child among us, He has endowed it with a right that we may not violate and must respect. The child has a sacred right to be treated as a child and not as an adult. Its specific nature as a child implies *ipso facto* the right to be *treated* as a child. This connection between creaturely being and creaturely right can only be founded on the order of creation. The order of creation is the protection of the rights of the creature against the wantonness of men. The protection is sacred; it is the divine law of justice.

The precision in differentiation of the divine commandments in the Bible arises from this differential order of creation which renders to each man his due. As we shall see later, the Bible itself founds that differentiation on the divine order of creation. Wherever a special commandment is laid upon man, woman or child, the order of creation is involved. No such differentiation is implied in the commandment of love. The commandment of love presupposes it, but does not create it. Justice pronounces what is "due" to each human being, and can do so because it takes its stand on the primal order, the order of creation. The order of creation is that delimitation of areas in virture of which man is part of a whole, and in virtue of which justice exists.

[9] Fr. Engels, *Die Lage der arbeitenden Klassen.*

A last point will make this fully clear. The order of creation not only renders to each his due, but also places him in definite relationships, institutions or systems. The order of creation does not only render to man and woman their due—equal as human beings, unequal in their special kind and function as man and woman—but it also binds man and woman together in a special relationship, marriage. Marriage is that relationship between the sexes in which man becomes a husband through the woman and the woman a wife through the man, so that the bond between them is truly human and personal. Thus not only does the order of creation stamp man as man and woman as woman; it creates marriage itself, joins man and woman together in a personal bond.[10] It is only when this bond is understood as a divine creation and ordinance that the difference between the sexes is seen to be human, personal and moral. Marriage alone makes it possible to understand the male nature and function of the man and the female nature and function of the woman.

God, however, created not only human beings but marriage also; not only the personality and individuality of human beings, but the bond between them called marriage. We rightly call marriage a "divine" ordinance. Marriage can also be understood in its biological, sociological and historical aspects. In doing so, however, we do not grasp it as a moral obligation but as a pure fact, a thing which has grown in one way or another. In the revelation of Scripture marriage is recognized as an ordinance of God, of the Creator. Thus according to the teaching of the Bible there exist not only rights of human beings and rights of men and of women, but also rights of marriage. It is not only the man who has claims which the woman must respect, nor the woman rights against the man, but marriage has a right and a claim on man and woman. Not only is the human being thus bound founded on the order of creation, but the bond itself. There is a sacred, divine institution of marriage, sacred and divine because it is founded in creation, and that institution cannot be arbitrarily altered by human beings unless human life is to decay. Marriage as a divine institution has its divine law. The main cause of the modern decay of marriage is that

[10] Mark, 10:9.

marriage is no longer recognized as a divine institution but only as a mere contract between human beings which can be dissolved as easily as it is concluded, and whose substance can be determined by their own free will.

It is only when we have understood marriage to be a divine institution of fellowship that we can truly grasp the rights of husband and wife as husband and wife. The special rights and duties derived from the difference established by creation must all be realized as relating to the relationship, as based on it and deriving their meaning from it. All the differences between man and woman established by creation are, as we have seen, differences which call for their complement, and all relationships established by creation, such as marriage and the family, are relationships whose object is completion, and which are formed by individuals capable and in need of completion. All individuality established by creation means "belonging to something." As the key belongs to the lock and the lock to the key, so that the lock is useless without the key and the key without the lock, the man, as man, is created for the woman, and the woman, as woman, is created for the man, and the man, as man, and the woman, as woman, are unintelligible without the whole which they form together—marriage. Their inequality acquires meaning through this relationship, this fellowship of completion. It is from the fellowship that the specific right of the man and the specific right of the woman are derived. Only when marriage is understood as founded on creation can justice in the relationship of man and woman be defined. But while the key is useless and worthless without the lock, the same cannot be said of man and woman. For their *humanity* is not exhausted by their function as husband and wife. On the contrary, in the order of value, they are *first* human beings, *then* husband and wife. Their dignity as persons, as human beings, transcends the creaturely distinction of kind and function on which their union is based. Hence the rights of the human being as such take precedence of all rights which arise from the differentiation of human beings and the fellowships of completion based on it. To those rights, therefore, we must now turn our attention.

their equality before the law—the Christian faith on the one hand, and Stoic religious thought on the other.

However widely these two spiritual powers may diverge in their view of the human being and his destiny, at this point they agree, and at this point their historical influence has always acted in the same direction. Both admit a unity in the human race, an essential likeness, on which the inalienable dignity of all who bear a human countenance rests, which implies certain primal rights to freedom. Those rights may be asserted even against the political order and are dependent on no concession from the state. We shall have to show later that in the more exact definition of this freedom, the Stoic doctrine of the law of nature and the Scriptural doctrine of the divine order of creation diverge, that in the former, the doctrine of freedom is based on rationalistic individualism, in the latter, on the Christian conception of fellowship. What we have to do now is to elucidate the Christian conception of freedom.

In the Christian understanding of man, the cardinal fact is not freedom, but man's relation to God, the sovereignty of God. The first thing to be said about man is that he belongs to God, his Creator, that the sovereignty of God is meant to find, and does find, real expression. But the inevitable inference from this premise is freedom. For the sovereignty of God must find expression in man in a way which corresponds to the nature of God—in love, by love, for love. The root idea of the message of Scripture is that man shall be the expression of God's sovereignty through faith and in love. Faith, in the Christian understanding of the term, is simply the acceptance of the love of God which revelation has made accessible to man. But that acceptance, like its earthly form, brotherly love, must be a free act. Hence it is that freedom to which man is called; the very word of God which subjects him to God's rule bestows that freedom upon him.[1] Thus freedom belongs of necessity to the destiny of man. God can only have communion with a free being. Like all fellowship, this supreme communion is only possible in freedom. It is only in freedom that man can do God's will as a loving

[1] Gal. 5:13; II Cor. 3:17; John 8:36.

creature who obeys of his own free will. Love, like faith, is an activity of freedom. The free response of man to the voice of God, which calls to him and calls him, faith as supreme personal responsibility and personal responsibility as communion with God—that is the Scriptural conception of man and the dignity of man. All are called to this freedom, to this obedience, hence all participate in this one dignity which pertains to the pre-destination to human being.

This freedom, however, does not come within the scope of the theory of justice; it stands above it. For justice is concerned with that "due" which may be rendered or not rendered, thus with a freedom which may be refused to man or stolen from him. But the freedom of faith lies beyond what men can refuse or steal. No slavery, no imprisonment, no coercion by the state, no threats of punishment can destroy this freedom. The *libertas christiana* is raised above the sphere of justice because it does not allot anything. Its subject is the person *qua* person, not the person in relationships. In it man stands face to face with God, and there no man can intervene. This freedom can only be bestowed by God Himself, and only He can take it away. That is why the question of liberty, as an integral element in the rights of man, is incidental, and not central, in the teaching of the New Testament, which is supremely concerned with that most intimate relationship. Where the most personal kind of freedom is in question, the slave and the prisoner can be free men.[2] The freedom of faith is so profound and so anchored in the centre of the person of God and man that no injustice or tyranny of this world can touch it, let alone rob man of it. Hence the right to liberty cannot be inferred from the *libertas christiana*. For the right to liberty, like all justice, has its origin in the structure of created order.

The slave can, in the sense of religious freedom, be a free man—that is the clear teaching of the New Testament and an incontrovertible fact of Christianity. But that does not mean to say that slavery or any other form of human bondage is *per-*

[2] For the solution of the problem of slavery in the primitive Christian community, see inf.

missible. The right to liberty is an integral part of that order in which God the Creator has placed man, which God gives to man within the world. What is usually called "religious toleration" is not the freedom of faith—that is a thing which the state can neither give nor take, which it neither can or needs to guarantee. But human injustice and tyranny, and the power to enforce them, can deprive man of the free practice of his faith, the freedom of the cultus, of religious activity, and can, on the other hand, force upon man a religious practice which is against his conscience. Hence we might call this particular right, the right to the free practice of a religion, "religious toleration," the most fundamental of all rights to freedom, since it approximates most closely to the true freedom of faith, even though it was not the first to appear in history. It is nevertheless significant that the state guarantee of *this* right should have been the starting-point of the general recognition of the rights of man by the state (21). It certainly took the church a long time to realize the error into which it had fallen during the growth of the Church of the Roman Empire, namely that of attempting to achieve religious uniformity by force, and to become converted to the principle of religious toleration. For more than a thousand years, the church believed itself bound to protect the true faith by state coercion. It had tried to do better than the Creator himself, who gave to man, with his freedom, the right to fall into error. Where man does not possess the outward freedom to throw in his lot with error, he cannot in true freedom throw in his lot with truth. When a mistaken zeal robs man of the outward freedom of choice by forcing on him a particular form of worship and punishing any expression of a faith which deviates from ecclesiastical rule, faith is at once endangered, the very faith which was to be safeguarded by this mistaken compulsion. It took many centuries to struggle against a tyranny which had become intolerable before man secured this most vital right. The church which today protests, and rightly so, against the oppression it suffers at the hands of the totalitarian state, would do well to remember who first set the state the bad example of religious intolerance by using the secular arm to safeguard by force what can only spring from a free act of the will. The church should always bethink itself with shame that it was the first teacher of the totalitarian state at nearly every point(22).

While the right to freedom of religious practice comes first owing to its close proximity to the real freedom of faith, which no man can abolish, looked at from the standpoint of human life, the primary right is the right to physical freedom. "Freedom means more than half of life" (Calvin)(23). It runs counter to the order of creation that man, on whom God bestowed not only freedom to turn towards Him, but also freedom to do His service, should not have the free use of his body and limbs(24). Man has a right to his life, not against God but against his fellow men, a right to his body and limbs. It is notable that one of the first formulations of the rights of man is called the Habeas Corpus Act. It is a guarantee of the personal, physical freedom of the Englishman insofar as the state can only imprison him in quite definite and circumscribed circumstances. It is the awful delusion of the totalitarian state that its subject belongs to it body and soul. By the divine law of creation, man belongs to no man and no system. When the community overrides this primal right, as in capital punishment or military service, it can only do so lawfully because and insofar as the individual has either violated the rights of others by his conduct, and hence forfeited his own, or insofar as a general good is at stake which each man must regard as more important than his own life.

Above all, a human being can never lawfully become the property of another human being. Slavery, the power of another to dispose of my life, my body, my limbs, is iniquitous. It is contrary to the order of creation. For while the inmost freedom, the freedom of thought, faith, love, is not destroyed by it, it destroys the freedom of action which, in the order of creation, follows from free will. Slavery abolishes the unity of the outward and the inward man, of soul and body, established by creation. It is not a man's own soul, his own will, which commands his body and moves his limbs, but the will of another.

The will of the Creator, however, has allotted to every man his life, his body and limbs as his most primordial, most direct "due." The Creator created man for responsible action, not only for responsible faith and will. It is true that no slavery can destroy the inmost dignity of the person—the finest things that were ever said on this subject were said by a slave, Epictetus. But slavery violates the dignity of the human being, treats him as though he were not a person and possessed no human dignity. Human dignity is refused him by human beings. Hence slavery is the primal wrong(24).

It was not only the power to dispose freely of his body and limbs, however, which was given to man by creation, but also "property." The man who has nothing at his disposal cannot act freely. He is dependent on the permission of others for every step he takes, and if they so wish, they can make it impossible for him to carry on any concrete activity. Without property there is no free personal life. Without property there is no power to act. The man who treads on strange ground, touches strange property at every movement he makes is not a free man. And the word "property" must be taken literally as own—ership, or as we say today, private property. Without private property there is no freedom(25). Collective ownership can never replace the value of private property in terms of freedom. Where I have no right of disposal, I have no free scope. For somebody who is not myself has the right of disposal over collective property, be it the corporate body, the union I belong to, or the state. The fraction of right in state property which I possess as a citizen of the state cannot outweigh the dependence to which I am bound by the general will of the state. It is just as easy to be a slave of the state as a slave of a single master. Where the state is sole owner, and I am not an owner at all, even though the state be a democracy in every other respect, I am a slave of the state, a slave of the general will which gives my own will no free scope. Nor can corporate property replace that free scope which is given by private property. Without private property I may become a slave of the corporation. For in this case too an alien will, the will of the corporation, tells me what I have to do and leave undone. All that collective property means is that in a certain domain— the domain of the collective property—certain incontestable rights are granted to each individual. But it gives him no actual right to dispose of that property[3] Yet without something over which he has the right of free disposal, man cannot be free. We shall at once realize this if we take as an example the most immediate kind of necessary private property—clothing and household goods. The man who can never put on his own clothes, sleep in his own bed and eat at his own table is not a free man. The more closely a sphere of life is connected with our person, the more necessary it is that it should stand under the same law of freedom as our body. The lack of personal property is largely responsible for the reduction of the proletariat to an impersonal mass. Neither the tenant farmer, nor even the man who merely tills corporate land, is a free man, but only the farmer who is as closely bound to *his* land as he is to his clothes and household goods.

Thus everywhere in the Bible private property is presupposed as normal. Not even the communism of love practised by the primitive community at Jerusalem was an exception to this rule, for all were free to place their property at the disposal of the community or not. Yet even within these limits the communism of love of the primitive community was not imitated by the other communities of primitive Christianity. It cannot serve the purpose of a public order of justice. Man cannot really "subdue the earth" unless some fragment of it belongs to him. Over the space he must have real dominion in free will, in it he must have full power to do all that the measure of his creative gifts allows. It will be shown later that this does not exhaust all that there is to be said on the subject of property, that on the contrary, corporative and state property have an important part to play as a check on private property. Hence it is not maintained here that everything must be private property, but only that without private property no true freedom of action is possible.

In fulfilment of the Creator's gift, man is also, by divine ordinance, granted freedom in the use of his sexual faculties. It is true that this freedom is, in virtue of the divine law, limited

[3] For a more detailed consideration of private and collective property, see inf.

by certain conditions, though not by such as men may impose as they like, but by those which *are* imposed. The power to use his body and limbs as he will is due to man as a personal right, and the same is true of his sexual powers. The abolition by the state of his personal freedom in favor of eugenic planning is one of the most terrible forms of despotic injustice. There is, of course, a limitation of the right justified by fact, where the sexual power on which the continued existence of the community depends has degenerated, so that its effects would be detrimental to the community. But this interference in the right to freedom of sexual activity must operate within the narrowest limits. Every system of eugenics, regulating human procreation by definite human plans is a violation of a primal human freedom which must result in a devastating destruction of personality and dignity. At no other point does human, rational planning so directly infringe the rights of the Creator, who, by human procreation, creates human beings. If: "Be fruitful, and multiply, and replenish the earth"[4] is a divine command to man, that command implies the freedom to obey which must not be violated by any ruler or state. No state has the right to prevent man from doing what God has laid upon him as a duty.

Further, man has a right to obtain his livelihood from the earth by the work of his hands. He is so made that he must draw his sustenance from the earth. Hence that right must never be withheld from him by other men and their alleged lawful claims. But man is not only created to work; he has a right to work. The right to work is implied in creation and any condition of law and society which is of such a nature that men— even masses of men, as in our time—are deprived of that right must be called unjust. And that injustice calls for redress by the very community which has created or tolerated such conditions. Any rights, no matter how well founded or acquired, which stand in the way of this primordial right must be opposed and abolished as fictions. We shall later have to show that this cannot be taken to imply a constitutional guarantee by the state of the right to work.

[4] Gen. 1: 28.

There is, however, a further primal right established by creation, namely every human being's right to an adequate development. Every child has the right to a healthy childhood, to an education befitting his dignity as a human being and to a normal development of his powers. We regard it as unnatural, as an unjustifiable interference with God's order of creation, if an absurd custom cripples a healthy child's feet. In the same way, every interference with a child's healthy growth, physical and mental, which "cripples" it, is an injustice against it. When it comes into the world, the child brings with it certain rights which no state, no society, no family may withhold from it. "What God has created, he will preserve." No human law is justified in curtailing that sense of life which God has given to every child. A "law" which does so is an unjust law. The Roman *patria potestas*, which allowed a father to kill, expose or sell his child, was an unjust law, however much the Romans, in their blindness, may have regarded it as just. The right to grow is a primal, indefeasible right.

The measure of education, however, to which every human being is entitled in virtue of his natural predisposition, is quite another question. The possibilities of education and development for every human being are in themselves unlimited, or in any case indefinitely wide, but the means a particular society can apply to the education of its members are, of course, limited. No society can justifiably be expected to provide every one of its members with access to every imaginable educational opportunity, for no society, no state would be in a position to do so. On the other hand, it is obviously the will of the Creator that every new-born child should be given proper care, and every growing child an education which will fit it for life. Yet as soon as we try to find a mean between the unattainable, abstractly conceived maximum and this obvious and indispensable minimum, we find ourselves in difficulties. Here there is clearly room for a great diversity of historical developments. The same measure, and still more the same kind of education, or aid to development, is not necessary in every state of society. The solution of this special problem will have to be sought later in connection with what we shall have to say on the social order.

Under the heading of the "rights of man," however, many things have been claimed which have nothing to do with these primal rights; they correspond rather to certain political or social ideas which are not only controversial in themselves, but involve consequences which can only have a meaning in connection with the rights of the community, and above all with the needs of the family and the state. Not all human rights are primal personal rights conferred by creation. They may be in themselves important, significant or even, in a certain condition of the social and constitutional order, necessary—for instance, the freedom of trade and commerce, the freedom of the press and so on—but they can be deduced from the primal rights only indirectly, and with the aid of certain historical assumptions.

In conclusion, we understand by primal rights such rights as we have discussed as being due to man in *all* circumstances, and hence may *never* be withheld from him by the community; on the contrary, it is incumbent upon the community to protect them at all times. These rights, however, comprise only those which are of such a nature that, should they be withheld, man could not fulfil the end to which the Creator created him, which He appointed together with man's concrete creaturely nature both as a privilege and a duty. The freedom of the press is a very valuable thing, but no one would venture to pronounce it one of those primal rights based on the will of the Creator, while the claim to be treated as a human being and not as a chattel clearly bears the mark of its divine origin. There are certain liberties which are correlated to a certain state of society; there are others which are primal and not dependent on the state of society. The only rights based on creation are those which we denote as "primal rights of man." They are due to each man in virtue of an immutable, eternally valid order of creation. Without them, man is not man in the full sense of the word, that is in the domain of visibility, of the concrete human community of action. To say that he can fulfil his inmost destiny as the child of God in prison or as a slave is no argument, for the rights of man, like everything else which we call justice, are not concerned with man in his invisible personality, but with man in his visible position in the visible fabric of order, and hence designate a personal dignity which *can* be taken from him, but *must* not, which on the contrary *must* be respected. This latter is one of the most vital tasks of social communities, above all of the state.

... Chapter 10 ...

THE INEQUALITY OF MEN AND THE RIGHTS OF THE COMMUNITY

THERE IS HARDLY A GREATER CONTRAST between pre-Christian and modern thought than in their attitude to the problem of equality and inequality. In classical philosophy, it is the inequality of men which stands in the foreground. It is inequality which determines the position of the individual in the nation and the state. The social order is unmistakably hierarchical, not to say a caste system. The individual is a dependent member of this ordered whole. For the modern mind, on the other hand, the determining factor is the equality of men. The rights of the individual as such, the equal rights of human beings are constant; indeed they are—or were till recently—accepted as self-evident, the only question being how a social order could be formed on that basis and the existing order understood. Understanding is mainly reached by the theory of the contract. In this view, human communities are based on a contract. Thus the individual is not a member of a structure which exists independently of him, a given social order which allots to each individual his place, but the social order originates and exists through the will of the individual persons, who are essentially equal and hence equal before the law. Between these two extremes there stands, not only historically but substantially, the Christian view.

As we have already seen, Christian teaching presumes a primal equality of men and hence a justice which, corresponding to this primal equality established by creation, confers on each man equal dignity and equal rights. But the inequality of man is just as firmly anchored in the teaching of Scripture as equality. The equality of personal dignity is balanced by the inequality of

65

kind and function. This inequality however, is not understood as being purely irrational, as a capricious, hence inscrutable decree of the Creator's will, but as a pre-condition of the natural community of men. By these inequalities, men become mutually dependent; each needs the other, they are predestined to mutual exchange and mutual completion. The individual is not the self-sufficient entity set up as an ideal by the Stoic doctrine of autonomy; he is dependent on the other. Human life should be a mutual give and take. For the ultimate meaning of human existence is not the rational existence of the individual, but life in love(26). Hence fellowship is not a thing which may form part of human life or not, as man thinks good; fellowship is the thing for which he was created. Thus the natural forms of community are not established by man in view of their expediency; they are primal ordinances of the Creator, institutions which are preformed in the diversity of each man's natural gifts. As man, as a sexual being, is created for woman, so that he cannot decide at will whether he will give effect to sexual fellowship or not, marriage, as the really personal sexual community is no contract, no union for the sake of expediency, based on the will of the contracting parties; it is a creative ordinance, instituted by the Creator who, in view of it, created man as man and woman as woman(27). Both man and woman, as man and woman—not as persons—are dependent members of a whole which stands above them. It is not they who determine the form of fellowship, neither whether it shall be nor in what manner it shall be. This form of fellowship is, on the contrary, a primal institution, independent of the will of the individual human being, an institution whose "foundation statutes" are from the outset established, which man cannot create, but only enter. In the Christian terminology "he entered the holy estate of matrimony." The law of marriage is not an agreement, a man-made convention, but an institution given to man which he has to recognize and realize.

Let us return to the metaphor used in the last chapter. As the key belongs to the lock just because they are unlike, just because their inequality is the pre-condition of their unity—the key "fits" the lock, it was made for the lock and the lock for the key, their unity of function being based on their diversity of form—we must regard the diversity of men as the basis of their community of function. Through the community of function, man receives the law of how and for what his diversity of kind is to be used, "what it is meant for."

Hence not only individuals but forms of community such as marriage and the family have their own intrinsic rights with respect to individuals, and these rights are of such a nature that they enable the diversity of human beings to serve the functional whole. They are, so to speak "directions for use," by a divine authority, of certain constants in natural life. Man is not master of marriage, but marriage of man—not, it is true, absolutely, but only in the mundane sphere, in the world of systems, for as a person, a human being is neither man nor woman in the face of God. Here lies the limit of the domain in which the earthly institution of marriage has authority. Forms of community, insofar as they are orders of creation, are not dependent on the will of man, but confront him as independent powers with their own laws and claims and their own rights. While the exercise of his sexual faculty is one of the primal human rights of every individual, it is one of the primal rights of the marriage community that the divine law of matrimony should regulate that exercise.

Through the community, the individual receives his due, though that "due" differs in every case. What is due to the man is not due to the woman; indeed, it is as the Apostle once said: "The wife hath not power of her own body, but the husband: and likewise also the husband hath not power of his own body, but the wife."[1] The individual marriage partner is not master of himself, but belongs to the other partner, because it is only through that partner that he or she becomes an active, functioning member of the marriage community and hence fulfils the destiny of his or her different nature.

From this point of view we can recognize the objectivism of the ancient world and the subjectivism of the modern world as

[1] I Cor. 7: 4

two antithetical half-truths. Objectivism was right in part: the individual *is* part of an embracing whole, he *is* placed in a whole whose law is in itself and is not derivable from the will of the individual. The communal whole is *not* the product of a social contract. It is not the individual who bestows the law upon the whole, but the whole requires of him, the individual, subordination to the law of the whole which was prior to him. The subjectivism of modern times, however, is also partially in the right. The individual is never simply and solely a member of an inclusive whole, a dependent organ of an organism, the organism ranking higher. The individual stands rather *above* the whole as a person just as much as he is subordinated to it as an individual with a specific mode of being. He never derives his dignity from the whole; he does derive it from his concrete destiny, which gives his specific nature room to develop. To each of these partial truths there corresponds a partial untruth. The objectivism of the ancient world did not recognize the intrinsic freedom and equality of men, the intrinsic dignity of the person, which is bestowed on every human being by the divine predestination of persons; but modern subjectivism fails to recognize man as innately unequal, as predestinated to fellowship. Hence there is in the ancient community a bias towards totalitarian autocracy, while the modern structure of state and society shows a bias towards anarchic individualism. In the ancient world, the right of the individual is submerged in the right of the community, above all of the state; in modern times the right of the community yields to the right of the individual, above all in marriage.

Marriage is not the only primal form of community established by creation. The relationship between parents and children is equally primal as regulated in the family. Parents have an inherent right as against their children, children as against their parents, and the difference between the marriage partners is expressed in the family in the difference between the rights of father and mother. This fundamental order must therefore not be held up to ridicule or doubt because the roles are often reversed by abnormality of character or unhappy social conditions.

Any normally conditioned human being knows perfectly well what is the right structure of the family and what is a reversal of roles. It is not right when the woman takes the lead in the family, when the father looks after the children while the mother goes out to work. Fortunately, nature speaks clearly enough here in spite of all the distortions due to an over-intellectualized culture and social mismanagement. But what is for the man in the street simply a fact of nature with a very vague claim to legality is in the Christian faith an order of creation, a natural difference ordained by God as a criterion. We can always rediscover the substance of that criterion, of the right which the community— the family, for instance—always possesses as against its individual members, by taking full account of the predestination of the human being to personality on the one hand and of the diversity of natural disposition and function in view of the community on the other.

Every member of the community, father, mother and child, has a right as against every other member. It is precisely the right that springs from the community on the one hand, from the predestination to personality of each individual member on the other. We must not, of course, leave out of account here the historical mutability of all human relationships and systems. Above all, we must not lose sight of the immutable constants. Men have never borne and never will bear children. In spite of all intellectual development, men and their specific function have remained clearly and characteristically distinguishable as a species from women. A certain type of female emancipation, now fortunately on the wane, which put forward a claim to equality with men, is one of the forms of the rationalistic individualism of modern times. On the other hand, the man's brutal presumption as lord and master, which deduced from the difference of function a difference of dignity and hence an inequality before the law, was a corollary of the autocratic objectivism of the ancient world. The Christian faith, the Bible as a whole, has always conceived the constants of creaturely life as ordinances of the Creator, hence not merely facts but criteria.

Marriage and the family alone are, so to speak, primal and

plastic forms of community whose structure is manifest and clearly outlined. But they by no means exhaust the ways in which the intrinsic differences of men and communities are blended according to the order of creation. Labour is another such community. Primarily, work for a livelihood establishes a relationship between the individual and nature—for instance the soil he tills. Man is so made that he must live by drawing his sustenance from the earth. That is ordained in creation, it is a natural activity grounded in the will of the Creator. Yet it establishes no relationship with the community. Work for the purpose of livelihood is at its origin an individual process. In actual fact, however, what happens is that such labour is carried out in co-operation, that the medium of labour and its produce on the one hand, the character of the natural human endowment for work on the other, demand co-operation in labour. The diversity of the natural gifts of individuals, combined with the problems and difficulties presented by the object, points to community of labour. What one man can do the other cannot; one man prefers this kind of work, another that. Labour requires thought to guide it and hands to labour. It requires from one man great muscular strength of limb, from another sensitiveness and delicacy. Here too there is a natural dovetailing of the functions to which men are predisposed by nature. Owing to its exemplary combination of diversities, the family forms the original, most natural co-operative economic unit, a domestic economy. But the family is only *one* example of such co-operation. Hence organized labour is intended by the Creator to be a communal and not merely an individual activity. The natural order established in creation and the reciprocal relation of man and nature require a co-operative organization of labour. In this sphere too, creation has ordained an unmistakable interdependence, a need and capacity for mutual completion. The one needs the other, is dependent on the other; that is not a shortcoming, a reason for shame and ground for complaint, as it is regarded by the Stoic with his ideal of self-sufficiency, or by a modern rationalist like Rousseau. It is a positive good, intended by God because it is a natural form of community. God has so created men that they must be together, not only in marriage and the family, but in work too, in mutual give and take, in the co-operation of "each according to his kind." Thus if private property is a demand originating in the equality of men, the right of the union or corporation as against the individual is a demand originating in the diversity of men and leading them to community. Independence of the individual *and* membership in a whole, free assent *and* submission of the individual to the purpose of the community, the rights of the individual over the community *and* the rights of the community over the individual—these are the inevitable conclusions of reflection on the order of creation. One does not only *need* the other; from the standpoint of the community he has a *right* to what the other has and he lacks. From this standpoint every purely individualistic attempt to understand economic life, every attempt which takes the rights of the individual as its point of departure, is demonstrably unjust, as unjust as the collectivistic standpoint which reduces the individual to an element without rights of an abstract, inclusive community. None should be strong for himself alone, none weak for himself alone. The creator has created strong and weak so that the strong may serve the weak and the weak give the strong the opportunity of service. Their diversity is the basis of the fellowship in service which has its own rights over the individual. This mutual adaptation is not merely an act of charity, a gift of love, but always and primarily a demand of justice. These are just claims, rights and obligations.

A great deal of theological controversy has turned on the question whether the state may be denoted an order of creation (28). This question by no means concerns theologians only; as we shall see immediately, it is not without its significance for constitutional law (29). The controversy, in which, characteristically, the two main Christian confessions stand in opposite camps, arises from no lack of clear principles, but from the fact that the nature of the state itself includes two antithetical elements which can be differently evaluated. Insofar as the state is the most comprehensive of institutions, the form of community which includes all others, it is doubtless a necessity lying in the God-created nature of man, an ordinance of the Creator. For God has so created man that he must endeavour to establish a form of community which shall embrace all others, and that he has need of it. Neither the "must" nor the "need" is a thing which of itself has its root in evil, in that which is contrary to creation. Both are in conformity with creation. Nothing which is necessary merely as a consequence of evil belongs to the order of creation. Insofar as the state is not only a form of community, but a mode of force, and organization which, like the modern state, is equipped with the monopoly of coercive force, it cannot be understood from the standpoint of creation, for coercion assumes that the good, the thing which is in the interests of all, is not done willingly, but must be enforced. From this standpoint the state presupposes evil and is, as a system of coercion, necessary on account of evil.

But whether we regard the state in its beneficent or in its sinister aspect, it is in any case an unconditional necessity for man as he now is, for man in whose being selfishness and the asocial, anarchical instinct play the great part we all know so well. Without the coercive system of the state, peaceful human life would fall victim to the destructive powers of anarchy. Hence the critical problem confronting justice is whether we should regard the state predominantly as an order of creation, or rather as a system of protection, necessary on account of evil, secondary with respect to the one decisive fact that it is an ordinance of God,[2] a divine institution. This assertion legitimates no particular form of the state, no divine right of kings, but merely the state as such. It is a moral necessity, yet at the same time a reality, a divine gift, in spite of the fact that, like the bread for which Christ prayed and thanked God, it comes into being by natural means. But since its existence is a necessity, the fundamental law of its being is given by Him who founded it. Its prime duty, however, the duty which takes precedence over all others, is to exercise authority, to have power to command.[3]

[2] Rom. 13:1-7.
[3] John 19:11.

Thus in the state we become aware of an element which is, less clearly perhaps, but not less necessarily, inherent in all the orders of creation, the hierarchical element, the element of authority necessary to its purpose. This exists even in the family and is called there "parental authority." It lies in the God-created nature of the individual members of the family that the father should be the head of the family, and as such should have an authority not conferred by man. In the economic community of labour too there must be, of necessity and in virtue of the diversity and co-operation of men, a gradation of competence with a directing head at the top. But in the state, in conformity with its special function, this hierarchical structure takes on a new and more emphatic sense. Here we have governors and governed. How some come to be governors is of secondary importance in comparison with the fact that there must be governors if the state is to fulfil its purpose, especially its fundamental function, the curbing of anarchy. Thus the ruling power of the state is not a matter of human will but is, like the state itself, a divine ordinance. That is the meaning of Paul's assertion that "there is no power but of God." The state with its authority is also a divinely ordained entity which is, in respect of the individual human being, independent, existing in its own right. The state can no more be derived from the will of individuals, from a social contract, than marriage and the family. It does not at all lie within the will of man whether he will have a state or not, nor does it lie within his will whether the state shall have authority, power to command. Both take precedence of the will of the individual as a divinely instituted law. The state is independent with respect to the individual, not merely in actual fact, but morally, in virtue of its right. That is the answer to the individualism which attempts to derive the state from the human rights of individuals.

The answer to be given to the collectivistic view, however, is equally important. The state certainly enjoys inherent authority over the individual, but the individual enjoys, in the moral sense, inherent rights in respect of the state. Insofar as man is a person in relationship he is bound by the authority of the state, but insofar as he is a person before God, he is bound by no state. The state has never had rights over his soul; man never "belongs" to the state. Man never receives his human dignity *through* the state, but prior to the state and independently of it.

The state certainly has a moral right to a human being, but that right is limited by the right which the human being has to the state. As the state can require of a man that he should submit to its ruling power, man must require of the state that it shall protect his primal rights. If it does not do so, it is unjust. That does not release the individual from his duty of obedience, but he is morally justified in criticizing the injustice of the state and in demanding and endeavouring to bring about the cessation of that injustice. We shall have to deal later with the question of the right to resist.

On both sides, therefore, the individualistic and subjective and the collectivistic and objective, the foundation of the state in God's creative will becomes significant, indeed decisive. The state is God's ordinance, therefore its basic law is independent of the will of man. The state is God's ordinance, therefore its limitation is God's will. Where the former is forgotten, the menace of anarchy arises; where the second is forgotten, the menace of the totalitarian state arises(30). It is not for nothing that, in modern times, the concept of sovereignty has been applied to both errors. Sovereignty is a concept which cannot with impunity be transferred from God, to whom alone it belongs, to men or human things. Nor is it by chance that Frederick II, the great mediaeval sceptic, was the first to use the concept of sovereignty. The theory of sovereignty, even when it is not so intended, is the beginning of political atheism with its double potentiality, individualistic anarchy or the collectivistic totalitarian state. If we seriously believe in the sovereignty of the people, then, as Rousseau, the most eloquent advocate of this fallacy, noted, we proclaim thereby the *révolution permanente* (31). There is no limit to the caprice of a people which feels itself sovereign. And if we speak seriously of the sovereignty of the state, as modern legal positivism does, then, as recent times have shown, the totalitarian state already exists. Neither state nor people is sovereign. Both stand under a law which is binding upon them, which sets limits to their rights. Sovereignty belongs to God alone. To bear that in mind and never to forget it is the first commandment of truly wise government and political maturity in a nation. It is not mere mediaevalism, nor a relic of past times, if the charter of the Swiss Confederation opens with the words: "In the name of God Almighty." For without the limitation in the will of God, a people declines into anarchy and mob rule or the state into totalitarian tyranny.

. . . Chapter 11 . . .

INDIVIDUALISM AND COLLECTIVISM

WITH THESE TWO TERMS WE HAVE ARRIVED at the central problem confronting society in our day. It is easy to see that it is at the same time the central problem of the theory of justice. In the name of justice, some condemn individualism in its economic form of capitalism; in the name of justice others declare war on the tyranny of collectivism in its political form of the totalitarian state. The man who, as a member of the proletarian working class, has experienced the curse of an economic order mainly directed by private capital will tend to see salvation in communistic collectivism; he will thereby run the risk of overlooking the cloven hoof of the totalitarian state of which it is an integral element. The man who has lived in fear of the totalitarian state will long for the return to individualistic freedom and forget that it was the anarchy it bred which provoked reaction in the form of the totalitarian state.

The thoughtful man knows that salvation lies in neither of these extremes. He is necessarily driven into an Aristotelian mean, yet as a rule when he considers the two systems whose power resides in a single idea—in the one case order, in the other freedom—he feels great perplexity in attempting to find rational grounds for his efforts to attain the mean. He has no alternative but to take an unsatisfactory and unimpressive refuge in compromise. He will remain in this painful situation until he recognizes that the two extremes are partial truths, half-truths, torn out of a real, creative truth and unity, out of that knowledge of the individual and the community which is established in Christianity alone.

Modern individualism, as we have seen, has its source in that

Stoic rationalism which regards the divine reason dwelling in all men alike as the ultimate foundation of all human dignity and all justice. Yet we can only understand the force with which the individualistic principle of the metaphysical unity, equality and freedom of man came to bear on subsequent history if we recollect that its first and greatest protagonists believed their doctrine to be based not only on the wisdom of the late classical world, but also on the Christian doctrine of revelation. Even Locke, who has perhaps a greater right than anyone else to claim the title of founder of this modern individualism conceived his ideas to lie well within the scope of Scriptural religion. Absorbed in the elements common to Stoic rationalism and Christianity in their explanation of the dignity of man, he quite overlooked the antithesis between them, and the confusion has had disastrous consequences down to our own day(32). The logic not only of Locke, but of Rousseau, Kant and Fichte, far removed as it is from Christian thought, is fired by Christian feeling.

For the "idealism of freedom" (Dilthey), man is a rational being, and this essential element of all things, this rationality, is the divine element. It is that which gives every individual his personal dignity and predestinates him to freedom, but since it is the same rationality which resides in all men, it is the foundation of the equality, independence, autonomy and self-sufficiency of the individual. For as a rational being, everyone bears the essential in himself; his need of the other is not "essential" but "incidental"; the need arises only because and insofar as he is a natural and not a rational being. That is as much as to say that the meaning of life lies entirely in the rational development of the *individual*, that in comparison the community is inessential and can give him nothing essential. Communities can be nothing but utilitarian organizations created by the free consent of individuals in order to give effect to a definite purpose to which the individual could not give effect himself. Hence the original form of all communities is the contract, freely entered into and only to be dissolved by mutual consent (33). The community is therefore a mere expedient, a product of necessity. Since the individual is too weak, individuals must—unfortunately—cooperate. Hence the community finds its purpose only in what it has to give to single individuals for the attainment of their own rational, personal purpose. The community therefore, having been brought into being by free agreement, can be dissolved by free agreement like any other contract.

That is how individualism regards, in particular, the state. The state is the product of the social contract, if not historically, at any rate actually. Its legality, its human significance, is based solely on that contract. That is what the state *should* be. That is its justification, its very essence. Its *raison d'être* lies in those aims which individuals as such are not capable of realizing, primarily the security of life and freedom. Hence the state is to be understood entirely from the standpoint of the free rights of individuals, has to serve them and is only just insofar as it serves them. The justice of the state is identical with the protection of the free rights of individuals.

The way in which rationalistic individualism regards marriage is not substantially different, although in this case the development of its bias was checked partly by the facts of nature and partly by Christian tradition, so that its consequences developed less obviously and more slowly. But in the last resort marriage is in this view a contractual union, necessary, like every other form of community, for the fulfilment of a purpose. That purpose, however, like all communal purposes, lies outside of essential humanity. Man as a *natural* being requires it; the *natural* substratum of human existence here asserts its claims. Marriage, like the state, is only possible because each party to the contract foregoes part of the freedom due to him in order to fulfil the common purpose of procreation and the satisfaction of the sexual instinct. The parties to the contract themselves determine the substance of the marital union. They are bound to each other because and as long as their contract holds good; they are, however, free to dissolve it as they were to conclude it. Divorce is not a catastrophe destructive of the very sense of marriage, but a possibility existing from the outset, such as exists with any consensual contract. The steady increase in divorce has its main source in this individualistic conception of marriage, though many people may not be fully aware of the fact.

It is in the economic sphere, however, that the individualistic conception of man has developed with least let or hindrance. The starting-point in this case is on the one hand the notion of private property as implying the absolute right of disposal, the conception of private property in Roman law carried to its logical extreme—"I can do as I like with my own." It is only, however, when economic individualism is allied with political individualism in the radical sense of the term that it can develop its ultimate consequences in the form of capitalism. It demands from the state firstly the guarantee of unlimited freedom of trade, commerce and residence. But its main demand is a negative one —non-intervention by the state in the economic process, absolute self-determination of economic activity on the basis of free competition, free exchange, *laisser-faire, laisser-passer*. This radicalism, however, would hardly have developed into capitalism proper had not chance brought another factor into play —the mechanization of production and transport, whereby private property in the form of ownership of means of production in the present-day sense of the term, was first enabled to become capital and to attain its enormous economic ascendancy. When private property, on the legal basis provided by liberalism and combined with the modern technique of production, transport and finance, can develop in the sense of unconditional right of disposal as capital, when, under the fiction of the free contract, it can employ the labour of the propertyless while regarding that contract as terminable at any time, when, on the other hand, without any restraint on the part of the community, it is free to formulate that contract as it pleases, and when production and sale are governed solely by the law of supply and demand, we have in its pure form that economic system which is called capitalism. Thanks to the speedy intervention by the community, this purely individualistic form of the economic order only became historical reality in the earliest stages of capitalism. Nevertheless the liberal and individualistic idea has left its mark on modern economic life down to most recent times. The economic system of modern Europe and America is capitalistic and individualistic, though not, perhaps, in the strictest sense of the term. Its achievements in respect of economic technique were vast and unprecedented, but its social consequences were appalling. The reaction could not fail to appear. It appeared in the full tide of capitalism as its extreme, collective antithesis in the Communist manifesto of Karl Marx.

In itself, collectivism, as the subordination of the individual to a social whole of which he is a dependent member, is much older and more primitive than capitalism. It lies in nature, from which man has sprung, to preserve the species but not to develop the individual. Thus collectivism is the starting-point of all historical life. Not only the primitive clan, but also the pre-Christian and non-Christian societies and states are collectivistic. Even in ancient Greece, where we can discern the first stirrings in history of a radical individualism, the conviction that the right of the state takes precedence of the right of the individual was axiomatic and beyond controversy. While the individualism of the Sophists regarded every form of community as controversial, not so much as the idea of primal, individual rights of man ever entered Greek legal thought. Even in Plato and Aristotle we find only the right of the state as against the individual, but never the right of the individual as against the state. A construction of the state on the basis of individual rights of man would have been unimaginable to the Greeks; this possibility first made its appearance at the end of the ancient world in the rationalism of the Stoics. Collectivism, the subordination of the individual to the social whole, is historically the primitive form.

While in individualism the freedom of the individual comes first, in collectivism the order of the whole comes first. While individualism as the *révolution permanente* has a bias towards anarchy, towards the dissolution of society into its constituent atoms, collectivism aims at an authoritarian social order supported by power. The individual has no independent rights, no independent significance; his business is to submit. His impor-

tance is measured by his service to the whole. The societies of
ants and bees are the perfect patterns of collectivism. The individual exists for the sake of the whole; he has to sacrifice himself to the whole. With respect to the whole he has nothing to
say. This collectivism may appear in three different forms—
organic, mechanistic and universalist.

1. Organic collectivism is most nearly akin to that existing in
nature. Hence it is the most primitive form of collectivism, although in modern history it emerged last. The ruling scheme by
which it interprets life is the organism. It gives full effect to the
proposition that the whole is more than the parts. The individual
is *nothing* but a subordinate part, an organ of the whole. Between the individual and the supreme whole there is inserted
a gradation of intermediate wholes, as in the organism the aggre-
gation of cells in the finger, the hand, the arm, the trunk, are
intermediate wholes between the individual cell and the bodily
whole. The whole, however, which includes and dominates all
the organs, is the state.

This structural gradation is at the same time a principle of
valuation. The individual as such is rated lowest, the whole of
the state highest. Indeed, since there is no principle to limit the
state, there is in the nature of things no value higher than the
state. The state assumes a mystical and religious significance.

2. Mechanistic individualism can only be understood from the
standpoint of radical individualism; it is at once its product and
the reaction against it. So long as the notions of freedom and the
rights of men inspired radical individualism with religious feeling, it regarded itself as a radical opposition to all collectivism.
But when it loses the link with its transcendental and religious
source—we may here recall what was said above on the religious
character of Stoic rationalism—when it becomes purely secular,
by atomizing society it creates the conditions in which mechanistic collectivism can come into being. Liberal capitalism, which
acts as a solvent on the community, is in every sense the forerunner of Communism and the soil from which it springs. Communism is only conceivable if we assume the proletarized mass
created by capitalism. Radical individualism looses the organic

bonds of society, grinds mankind into shifting sand which can settle nowhere, and this pulverized mass of humanity is subsequently welded by mechanistic collectivism into the artificial unity of the proletarian, totalitarian state.

It is true that the fiction of the equal rights of all still subsists. Echoes can still be caught in phrases of the ideology of freedom and equality underlying the revolution of individualism. In actual fact there are no individuals left. The mass-state is everything, the individual nothing. This is seen most clearly, and comes to its most powerful effect, in the fact that the state is the sole owner of property. Private property is abolished; thereby the individual has lost the true basis of his freedom; he is delivered, bound hand and foot, to the sole employer, the state. For all its ideology of freedom and equality derived from equalitarian individualism, there is no individual left. The *volonté générale* has absorbed him into the "collective." Freedom has become an illusion which may be sustained for a time by a pseudo-democratic state machinery, but sooner or later it is unmasked as an illusion, and then it is too late.

3. In universalist collectivism—Plato—Hegel—the individual is sacrificed to the abstract ideas and values of the "general mind." The ruling principle is mind, and mind is understood as that which is common to all. Once again the individual is deprived of independent meaning, and has value only as a vessel of the general mind. This general mind, however, takes on concrete form in the state. What arises, therefore, is state absolutism based on idealism. The function of the state, however, is to organize general intellectual activities—science, art, culture. Man exists for culture, not culture for man. Man exists for the state, not the state for man. The state is the great ego, the individual the small ego. The small ego must submit unconditionally to the great and sacrifice himself to the aims of the great. The state grants to the individual the scope and rights it thinks fit. Here the individual has no primal rights.

In historical reality, these three forms of collectivism merge; none has appeared pure, with all its consequences, if only because the heritage of nearly two thousand years of Christian tradition cannot simply be blotted out by atheistic movements and ecclesiastical controversies. Of the three, however, it is mechanistic collectivism which has unquestionably developed most consistently in the form of the communistic totalitarian state, while National Socialism was from the outset a compromise dominated by the theory of organism.

Opposed to all these forms of collectivism, as well as to individualism, there stands the Christian conception of the individual and the community in all its inward consistency and completeness. It is not a synthesis, still less a compromise, but the original unity. The other conceptions stand revealed as fragments torn out of it. For the Christian understanding of the individual and the community is not human wisdom, but the wisdom of God manifested in creation. It is the justice which befits the human being as an individual and in community because it is in accordance with the creative plan of Him who created individuals and communities alike. Thus justice is identical with the principles set forth in the previous chapter, in which the relation of equality and inequality is conceived as founded on the divine creation of persons. Hence all we need at this point is a brief summary of what has already been said, though with special reference to the contrasts presented to left and right.

In the Christian understanding of man, a communal structure based on a contract is neither necessary nor possible. Communities are just as much established in the divine order of creation as the independence of the individual. They are innate in the God-created individual with his capacity and need for completion. Their prototype and standard is the family founded on marriage. Hence the Christian view of the community is in principle patriarchal in the sense that diverse individuals are naturally united in a community in which they find completion.

The absorption of the individual in the collective whole, however, is just as impossible in Christian thought as the construction of the community on the basis of a social contract. The independence of individuals is just as much God's creation as the community founded on their diversity. The dignity of man, which is his by reason of his creation in the image of God, is not bestowed on him by the community. He brings it with him, so to speak, into the community. It is given him direct by God, by that divine call which makes him, the individual, a responsible person. It is because the individual is directly responsible to God that he possesses an independence transcending all community. A human being is more than marriage, more than the state. There will be human beings when marriage and the state are no more. Man alone, not marriage, not the family, not the state, is predestinated to eternity. The state, marriage, and all institutions are there for man, not man for them. If there had to be a choice between individualism and collectivism—fortunately there need not be—the Christian would have to choose individualism. Even though it is the distortion of a half truth, he would none the less have in it the larger half of the truth, as long as the passion for freedom is alive in him.

The Christian view of the relationship between individual and community may be formulated thus: fellowship in freedom, freedom in fellowship. The concrete form of such free fellowship is federation. The federative principle, however, must not be taken to mean a community based on a contract or a union.

The federation meant here is the form given to an a priori fellowship not derived from the consent of individuals to a contract. Hence it includes within itself that element which modern liberal federalism no longer knows nor understands, a genuine, original, undelegated authority. The ideal is not the modern democracy, derived from the principles of Rousseau and based on the social contract and the sovereignty of the people, but a community such as the family, where there is an a priori fellowship, a primal law not set up by men and a primal authority not first instituted by delegation on the part of the individual members of the community. Christian federalism must not be confused with the rational democracy of our day. The difference between them is as great as the difference between Epictetus, Rousseau or Kant and the Bible—and that is considerable.

. . . Chapter 12 . . .

JUSTICE AND THE LAW OF NATURE

As a result of the breakdown of the positivistic, historical theory of law, the law of nature(34) has of late come into the foreground, but all modern discussion of the subject is vitiated by the ambiguity of the term. It is not sufficiently realized that there are at least three different conceptions of the law of nature—firstly, the objective and collective law of nature of the pre-Christian world, secondly the subjective and individualistic law of nature of modern times, which has its roots in late classical Stoicism, and thirdly the Christian law of nature.

In the pre-Christian, objective type of the law of nature, "nature" means the rational order of the cosmos, the logos pervading and ruling the cosmos, on which all true justice is based. In the law of nature of modern times, nature is almost equivalent to human reason, though only insofar as divine reason rules in it. In the Christian law of nature, nature is the divine creative ordinance of God, of the God who revealed His will to mankind in Jesus Christ. It should be immediately clear from what has already been said that widely divergent views of justice arise from these different conceptions of nature, so that unless we clearly distinguish what is meant in any given case, it is impossible to say in detail what "the law of nature" represents and what consequences ensue from views based on "the law of nature."

One thing is, it is true, common to all three forms of the law of nature. All mean a justice which transcends human caprice and convention, a principle and valid standard of sacred authority. To this extent all natural law stands opposed to positive law insofar as positive law means those standards by which all positive law of the state is to be judged, those principles to which positive law at its best endeavours to give effect, and which are therefore the source of all just order, action and judgment. The law of nature means "that which is in itself just," that law of justice which is inherently just, which is eternal and immutable, transcending all men and all times. Hence in every view, in every idea which presupposes a supreme standard of justice, and has not fallen an uncritical victim to historical fact, there is a vestige or a germ of "the law of nature." The "law of nature," however, in all its three main forms is distinguished from the mere general "idea of justice" (35) by claiming not merely to be a formal idea of justice, but also to contain within itself certain fundamental standards of an actual just order. The "formal idea of justice" merely means that every legislator, every judge, every critic must endeavour to do justice. His eyes must be fixed on that point "justice," and he will then discern what is actually just. But the "law of nature" means: there are certain basic principles, such as, for instance, the primal rights of man, which are a final canon of appeal whenever it has to be discovered what has to be rendered to each man as his due. Above all, that very proposition, namely that justice consists in rendering to each man his due, is the fundamental principle of all natural law. We find it as the underlying principle of justice in *all* forms of the law of nature, whether classical and objective, Stoic and rational, or Christian, and we find it *only* in connection with the law of nature. Wherever the law of nature has been surrendered, the principle of the *suum cuique* has been surrendered too. We can even say: the law of nature is the *suum cuique*. Whoever admits the *suum cuique* has in principle admitted the law of nature.

What is generally meant by the opponents of the law of nature, however, is that modern law of nature which claims Grotius as its father and was developed on the one hand by the more or less rationalistic school of Pufendorf, Thomasius, etc., and on the other by the English and French philosophers of the Age of Reason. Many of those who have launched learned polemics against the law of nature have had no inkling, or have at any rate ignored, the existence of the Classical and Stoic, and above all of the mediaeval Christian forms of the law. This is the more surprising in that they themselves, in their opposition to the law of nature, set out from a view of law which, like that of Kant and Fichte, is itself rooted in the law of nature. To complete the confusion, in modern times the law of nature has meant a view of law which, in naturalistic fashion, takes the "laws of nature" as its starting-point and guiding principle and is hence diametrically opposed to the two thousand-year old tradition of the law of nature. For at all times what has been meant by the law of nature is a *moral* principle of justice which subjects and regulates the natural instinct of man, whether it be the instinct of power, of gain, of sex. It has never acknowledged that instinct as a principle of action or of judgment. The doctrine of the law of nature in the European tradition, whether that of Aristotle, the Stoics, the Church Fathers, the Schoolmen, the Reformers or the Rationalists, is not naturalistic but anti-naturalistic. The concept of "nature" upon which it is based has always been a theological, religious and moral principle, and the concept of the *lex naturae* underlying it has nothing in common with what is known today as natural law.

There are, however, in the history of language and ideas fateful mutations which cannot be reversed. Anyone who attempted in our day to revive and apply the old doctrine of the law of nature in any of its forms would find that no definition, however precise, of his conception of nature and the law of nature would safeguard him from the misunderstanding that he wishes to subject law to the forces of nature. The man of today, whether jurist or theologian, seems incapable of eliminating from the concept, "the law of nature" the association "the laws of nature," "natural instinct" and so on, and that misunderstanding will flood away all the barriers of definition, no matter how securely erected. Hence on account of its later history the term must simply be abandoned. The European conception of justice, incorporated for two thousand years in the idea of the "law of nature," will have to be renewed without the use of the term.

The renewal is the more necessary since that inevitable mis-understanding is not the only one which besets the law of nature. On the contrary, as we have just seen, the concept suffers by being contaminated with no less than three different views. The opposition of modern jurisprudence is almost exclusively directed against the rationalist and individualistic form of the law of nature. Since, as a rule, no other is recognized, those who reject that form of the "law of nature" reject the law of nature absolutely. The disastrous, but inevitable result of that rejection is that jurists have no alternative but to resort to the positivistic and historical view of law, that is, to the existing law of the particular state in question, the actual power defining the state. The opposition to the law of nature has not only prepared the way for the totalitarian state, but made it possible. That is why so many jurists of our day are finding a new interest in the law of nature.

We may ask, however, how Christian theology came to appropriate the term "the law of nature" which, after all, took its rise in a heathen and pantheistic manner of thought quite alien to it. That came about because there was a very close kinship between the Scriptural conception of the order of creation and what the Greek philosophers and Roman jurists meant by the law of nature. It was not by chance that so fearless a creator of language as the Apostle Paul, who intentionally coined new terms and avoided common, familiar ones, should have adopted this Stoic conception of the law of nature as a standard,[1] that, on the other hand, the Reformers, whose breach with a thousand years of tradition was achieved precisely by a new understanding of "divine justice," unanimously and unhesitatingly applied the concept of the law of nature presented by the Church Fathers and the Schoolmen, as an integral part of their social ethic. There is an obvious analogy here to the use of that other Stoic idea adopted by St. Paul, the idea of conscience. Though the *term* "the law of nature" might be avoided, Christian thought could not but assimilate its substance.

---

[1] St. Paul uses φύον three times in the sense of a divine standard of creation: Rom. 1: 26; 2: 14; I Cor. 12: 14.

The Christian conception of justice is, as we saw, determined by the conception of God's order of creation. What corresponds to the Creator's ordinance is just—to that ordinance which bestows on every creature, with its being, the law of its being and its relationship to other creatures. The "primal order" to which everyone refers in using the words "just" or "unjust," the "due" which is rendered to each man, is the order of creation, which is the will of the Creator made manifest. When we say that it is "unjust" to treat a child in the same way as an adult, or "unjust" to deny to a human being the respect due to his personality on account of his race, the ultimate, deepest reason for such a verdict is the fact that God, the Creator, has created every human being in His image and that it is His will that the child should be respected as His creation in the way befitting its specific mode of being. Behind a fact of nature—the nature of a man, of a child, there stands therefore the sacred will of God, which requires from us that we should respect that specific form of creation. Thus the will of God sanctions a natural entity as a thing to be respected by us. An order which the unbeliever simply calls an order of nature, a thing which "simply is like that," is recognized by faith not as a thing which "simply is like that," but which must be, because God created it so and wills it to be so. We cannot be just, our laws cannot create an order of justice, if these natural facts are not acknowledged and respected as lying in the will of God. The rights of man are rights which, so to speak, God gives men at their birth. The rights of communities are rights which go back to a definite relationship between men based on the order of creation—for instance, that of man and woman in marriage. In the last resort all justice means these constants of creation as a basis on which every human being receives his due.

It was this connection between nature and the will of God, firmly rooted in the faith in creation, which enabled Christian theologians and jurists to appropriate the conception of the *lex naturae* and the *jus naturae*, of the "law of nature." That is why, for Christian as for Stoic doctrine, the word nature is a theological concept and a criterion. By "the law of nature" Christians meant

simply and solely the order of creation. They did not reject it as
an idea derived from classical tradition, although they knew
perfectly well that their theological interpretation of this divine
primal order was not the same thing for them as it was for a
Stoic philosopher or for Aristotle. They did not reject it because,
although it stood in a different theological connection, it seemed
to express the heart of the matter; the right which proceeds
from the God-created nature of man. Even the Reformers, who
laid far greater stress on the depravation of human nature by
sin than the scholastic theologians, were not afraid of using the
concept "the law of nature," because in their opinion sin does
not destroy the constants of creation or alienate them from their
original significance. They regarded it even as a proof of God's
goodness that He had preserved these constants of creation in
spite of the sinfulness of man.

That is the objective or ontological meaning of the Christian
term "the law of nature." It has, however, a subjective or epistemological meaning which nevertheless is closely akin to the
first in substance. Christian teachers, taking their stand on clear
pronouncements in Scripture, believed at all times that even
the "natural man," that is, the man untouched by the historical
revelation of God, was well aware of these orders of creation,
though without knowing the Creator. Since they are orders of
nature, man cannot but become aware of them in one way or
another. The "functioning" of the orders of creation is not necessarily dependent on knowledge of the Creator. The stars move
unwittingly in accordance with the will of the Creator; so do
plants and animals, so, in a larger measure, does man. The
divine order of creation is effective in him from the first moment
he lives—how could he live else?—and long before he is capable
of knowledge. It is not surprising, therefore, that, as soon as
he can observe and reflect, he should become aware of the divine
orders of creation or that his awareness of them, and the respect
he feels for them, insofar as it lies within his will, should be
closely connected with the requirements of justice presented to
him by conscience. The Christian theologians could not close
their eyes to the fact that the idea of justice, or the sense of

justice, was a thing common to all men, and that the best of the pagan philosophers, especially Aristotle, had pronounced great truths on this kind of justice. They were of the opinion that all truth comes from God, but not that all truth comes from Scripture alone. Since they freely and gratefully accepted the teaching of the masters of classical philosophy in matters of rational science, mathematics, physics, astronomy, since they did not imagine that there must be a specifically Christian mathematics or physics because Christians derived from Holy Scripture a special knowledge of the divine design of salvation, in questions of law and the state they accepted with gratitude the teaching of Plato, Aristotle and the Roman jurists, and in particular esteemed the *Politics* of Aristotle as a masterpiece of wisdom in social ethics. Even the Reformers did not act otherwise, in spite of their doctrine of the sinful state of man, and Calvin in especial never concealed his admiration for Roman law, on which he was an authority, and for the Aristotelian doctrine of justice and the state. In spite of all the modifications brought about by the Christian concept of creation, the Platonic and Aristotelian basis of the Christian theory of the state, including that of the Reformers, must be plain to every thinker.

None the less with regard to the second, subjective and epistemological principle of the law of nature there is a not inconsiderable difference between Protestant and mediaeval Catholic doctrine which corresponds to the difference in their assessment of the sinfulness of rational knowledge. The Reformers lay far more stress than the mediaeval and Catholic teachers on the fact that sin obscures the capacity of human reason even in spheres which are accessible to rational knowledge. From that they deduce that we cannot dispense with the specific divine revelation even for the comprehension of mundane justice based on the knowledge of the order of creation. Although they believed that the orders of creation are not hidden even from those who do not know the Creator and His creative will, they argued that secure and clear knowledge of the principles of mundane justice can only be obtained from the knowledge of the Creator and His creative will as it is revealed to us in Scriptural history and doctrine(36).

In form and substance, the present volume may be taken as a confession of this Protestant faith. What was said by Aristotle, the master of the ancient doctrine of justice, is widely valid and forms for all time the basis of the theory of justice. Yet as we have already seen, the Aristotelian doctrine is quite inadequate to a clear and fundamental grasp of the nature of justice. It is only from the Scriptural idea of creation that we obtain access to the solution of the problems which Aristotle had perforce to leave unsolved, and which were solved in an erroneous and one-sided fashion in later times on the basis of purely rationalistic thought. How right the Reformers were in their sober, critical estimate of man's capacity for rational knowledge in matters of secular justice can be seen most clearly in the history of the later, rationalistic conception of the law of nature.

What was taught in later times by rationalistic consideration of the essentially just under the title "the law of nature" proved to be one-sided and dangerous in proportion as thinkers abandoned the Christian law of nature in favour of a purely rationalistic conception. For this rationalistic law of nature is none other than that of individualistic liberalism. The farther removed it is from Christian faith, the more one-sided it becomes. And that, in its turn, is the reason why even jurists who were certainly not blind to the significance of the law of nature came to the conclusion that they must, in the last resort, reject it. What they missed in it—I am thinking in particular of the greatest of them all, Gierke(37)—was the comprehension of the idea of the social body as the basis of all true social justice. But as we saw, this very conception of the social body is an integral element of a genuinely Christian theory of the law of nature. For in the Christian doctrine of justice, the principle of inalienable rights of the individual human being is blended with that of membership of a social body; not only the equal dignity of men, but also their natural inequality and the fellowship of completion based on it, are derived from God's creation. If the idea of justice had remained faithful to its Christian form, to the Christian theory of the law of nature, the great breach in the development of law and the state would not have been necessary. We can even go further: wherever this Christian doctrine of the law of nature was maintained even partially, as in England, Scandinavia, Holland and Switzerland, the breach either did not occur or was far less profound. All these countries are characterized by the fact that the "mediaeval" or rather the Christian pre-rational element has remained a potent factor in their political, social and intellectual structure because the Christian law of nature was not ousted by the rationalistic law of nature.

If, however, we nevertheless decide to abandon the *term* "the law of nature," there is a third reason for doing so. It was not only the individualism already discussed, a feature only of the rationalistic law of nature, which led a number of leading jurists to oppose the notion, but the legal ambiguity which every law of nature seems to involve. If, as was fully the case in the mediaeval world, the "law of nature" implies that a law of the state must not be obeyed if it conflicts with the law of nature, and hence is unjust, the law of nature means an intolerable menace to the system of positive law(38). What enabled the error to arise, and to become more and more dangerous in its effect, was the development of the law of nature into a complete system of law which entered into competition with the positive law of the state; this has been increasingly the case since Grotius. No state law can tolerate a competition of this kind presented by a second legal system. The laws of the state actually obtaining must possess a monopoly of binding legal force; the law of nature must claim no binding legal force for itself if the legal security of the state is to remain unshaken. That is the point at which the Reformers diverged most widely from the view of mediaeval Catholicism. They took their stand clearly on the side of positive law, only granting to the law of nature the function of a criterion.

There is only one point, though it is of momentous importance, in which the law of nature retains more than its significance as a standard and takes on a directly positive significance, namely in the "right to resist," that is, the right of the citizen to resist a political power which has degenerated into tyranny, and it is precisely at this point that the problem of the law of nature has, of late, taken on a quite unforeseen urgency. At the beginning of the modern era the modern constitutional state gradually emerged from the demands of the law of nature and the right to resist implied in it. The more the constitution of the state provides means whereby its political and legal order can be adjusted to the people's sense of and desire for law, the less it stands in need of the very dangerous expedient of the right to resist. Hence the right to resist, which played so great a part in earlier legal and political history(39), could be regarded as obsolete in the modern constitutional state. But that was no longer possible when the totalitarian state created a new legal situation in a twofold sense. In revolutionary fashion, the totalitarian state abandoned the historical tradition of law and created a new law of its own, which stood in crass opposition to the legal sense of the mind of today. Further, in establishing a dictatorship, it abolished the modern constitutional machinery, which had been forged with endless toil and struggle in order to guarantee a lawful adjustment of the law of the state to the people's sense of right. This safety valve, which had been preserved even in the constitutional state, has been choked, and the danger of explosion has hence grown acute. The right to resist implied in the doctrine of the law of nature, which had lost its moral justification, once more became a moral necessity. How else shall a people, deprived of the lawful means of altering an intolerable state of the law, give expression to its natural lawfulness if not by resistance? How else can the rights of man, not only outraged but contemned by the totalitarian state, be asserted save by resistance? Hence in the conflict with the palpable injustice of the totalitarian state and its positive "law," the idea of the law of nature was revived.

In their profound respect for the authority of the state and positive law, the Reformers had only made use of the right to resist with the utmost caution. They pointed the way to the modern constitutional state by basing the right to resist on positive law and the constitution. This foundation on positive law of a principle inherent in the law of nature was the germ of the modern constitutional state. Their theory of the right to resist is hence as it were absorbed and at the same time fully developed in the modern constitutional state. This fruitful and beneficent development was rudely checked by the totalitarian state. A political system so minutely organized and so rigidly centralized can leave no room for a right to resist based on positive law. Anyone who is not prepared to come to terms with the legal monstrosity of the totalitarian state has no alternative but the right to resist based solely on the law of nature. Hence wherever peoples are suffering under the rigours of dictatorship, it is on the law of nature and the idea of the rights of man that they have set their hopes. The law of nature, the eternal unwritten laws of the Creator, are nerving their will and convincing them of the divine righteousness of their resistance against a tyranny which is devoid of any foundation in law and can in no way claim the obedience due to the "powers" because those powers do not attend upon what is, in the words of the Apostle, the *raison d'être* of all powers—they do not attend upon lawful order as, after all, the Roman state did. On the contrary, by their lawlessness, they destroy all law, and by their very existence outrage all sense of law. Hence the totalitarian state, which arose on the ruins of the law of nature, has been the means of bringing it to life again.

. . . Chapter 13 . . .

STATIC AND DYNAMIC JUSTICE— HISTORICAL RELATIVITY

As WE HAVE SEEN, THE MODERN POLEMIC against the law of nature implies much misunderstanding and in particular ignores the fact that there are different forms of that law. Yet there is an ultimate reason for the opposition which is inherent in the law of nature itself and even lends a certain justification to the assertion that all justice is relative. Every law of nature, every theory of justice which takes its stand on an absolute, divine law of justice, is of its nature static. The very immutability of the divine law is decisive in this connection. Justice, in this acceptance of the term, is that which is firmly established, at all times unalterable. This immutability, however, stands in a certain opposition to the eternal flux of history. Anyone whose thought is directed by concrete, ever-changing human reality, feels *any* kind of law of nature, hence any form of immutable justice, as an outrage on life. What was yesterday just may be crass injustice today. The dress which fits the child perfectly will cramp it intolerably when it has grown. The very law, the very order, which once protected and guarded the life of individuals in the community becomes, since both individuals and communities change, a hindrance and a danger. Hence justice must change with changing life. The πάντα ῥει—the universal flux—claims its rights. The man who does not respect it loses touch with life and becomes a doctrinaire or a despot. His activity presents that picture of justice which is enshrined in the dictum: *fiat justitia pereat mundus*. The dynamics of history are not an invention of a rootless modern world; properly understood they answer to a reality of historical life. Not only the

96

egalitarian and individualistic form of the law of nature, but *any* form of the law of nature must, by its static quality, come into dangerous conflict with the living reality of history. Again we find inequality side by side with equality—not only the inequality of human beings living in community, but the inequality of times, the inequality of yesterday and today, in which every man and every community participates and which is inseparable from living growth and the law of the transitoriness of all earthly things. That equality of times, that equalization of yesterday and today, which we noted as an essential feature of law, is an abstraction which, if it is rigidly maintained, either destroys or is destroyed by life. Here we encounter the actual dialectic of being and becoming, of permanence and change, of the static and the dynamic. Without permanence, no truth, no faith, no justice; but the converse is equally true: without change, without constant transformation, no actual truth, no actual faith, no actual justice. The man who only respects the law, and not with it the irrational growth which no law can embrace, cannot create a justice which really serves life. This connection between law and equality on the one hand and growth and inequality on the other makes a certain divergence at once clear. Where justice is taken to imply the equality of the rights of man rather than the diversity of the claims of the community on individuals, the static quality of the law is more strongly stressed than the dynamic quality of history; where justice is understood rather from the standpoint of the body social based on inequality than on the equality of the individual rights of man, the dynamic quality of history takes precedence of the equality of the law of justice. We might even say that the spirit of Roman law tends to the static, that of German law to the dynamic, and that each bears within itself its specific danger. The antithesis of static and dynamic in law is only an enhanced form of the dialectic of equality and inequality. Hence it is only to be expected that in the Christian view of justice, which admits both equality and inequality to a share in the idea of justice, the dynamic quality of history finds its place side by side with the static quality of law. And we may expect this to come about through the same subordination of inequality to equality as in the solution of the problem of the rights of individuals and the rights of the community.

Of all religions, Christianity is the one which takes most account of history, indeed which gives history so central a place in its doctrine that we might even call it the religion of history. The God of the Bible is a God of history, a God "Who makes history," Who manifests Himself in history and makes the existence of mankind and the individual historical. The Scriptures understand life not as unchanging being, but as a drama, with beginning, middle and end.

It is true that this history is not primarily related to earthly life as such. This history, which moves forward to its goal, is the specific history of the salvation of man, and not history in general. Nor does the fact of existence of itself imply participation in this history. That participation is won by faith. Hence it would be exceedingly misleading to transfer the dynamics of the history of salvation *in toto* to general history, as Hegel did. Those dynamics are not of the kind that can find expression in the sphere of mundane justice.[1] Yet the sphere of mundane justice is seen from that standpoint and seen in a new light. The secular world, the life which justice has to rule, is not merely the world created by God, but a world which has fallen away from the order of creation. Human nature as we all know it is not simply the human nature created by God, but a nature whose core and centre has fallen away from God. Hence the concept of nature in Christian teaching is twofold,[2] in that it denotes both the original order and that which has fallen away and violated that original order. This point must necessarily be of importance for the Christian conception of justice.

There are two kinds of justice. Firstly, that which "is in itself just" is based on the divinely created nature of man and presupposes it; it is the absolute justice of the order of creation. Secondly there is relative justice, which is just in reference to a reality which has fallen away from the order of creation (40).

[1] Cf. Emil Brunner, *Offenbarung und Vernunft.*
[2] As in Luther; cf. Lau, *op. cit.* p. 100 ff.

This distinction between the absolute justice of the order of creation and the merely relative justice of human order emerges in exemplary form in that passage of the New Testament where the Pharisees put to Jesus the question of divorce.[3] Jesus answered: "What did Moses command you?" They replied that Moses suffered "to write a bill of divorcement and put her away." Thereupon Jesus said: "For the hardness of your heart he wrote you this precept. But from the beginning of the creation" it was not so. In the order of creation man and woman were joined together by God to form a unity and "what God hath joined together, let not man put asunder." What is truly just is clear—indissoluble marriage. "Whosoever shall put away his wife, and marry another, committeth adultery against her."[4] It is equally clear that this absolute justice is based on the order of creation. Does Jesus mean to say that the law of Moses is a perversion, a frivolous alteration of God's order and hence not to be acknowledged? Does Jesus mean to criticize the law of Moses? On the contrary, he justifies Moses. He indicates the motive which forced the concession upon him—the "hardness of heart" of human beings. In the sphere of civil law, God's creative ordinance cannot be simply set up as the law. Here the actual condition of man must be taken into account if more harm than good is not to be done by an abstract fanaticism for justice.

Jesus has no intention of criticizing the law of Moses, but he confronts a relative system of law with the absolute law of God, which is binding upon the conscience of every individual. For the Christian conscience there is no divorce; for the state there must be a possibility of divorce—however strictly regulated and limited—because the state has to reckon with human beings whose hearts are hard.

The most important consideration which ensues from this consideration of man's falling away from the order of creation is the recognition of the necessity of an order of justice established by the state, of the just in the form of coercive law. We have already seen that the state can be understood in two

---

[3] Mark, 10: 1 ff.
[4] Mark, 10: 11.

aspects, as part of the order of creation in the sense of the most comprehensive ordering of the community, and as an order of preservation in the sense of coercive law and the curbing of anarchy by the use of force. The greater the weight that is attached to evil in the reality of human life, the greater will be the importance conceded to the coercive law of the state. It lies, however, in the very nature of coercive law that it cannot be identical with the pure justice of the order of creation, that it must differ from the "law of nature" laid down in the order of creation. "Because of the hardness of your hearts he wrote you this precept" which is not the law of creation. The modification in the status of man due to evil necessitates a modification of the order of justice, not only in the sense that it becomes a coercive system of positive law, but also in the sense that the substance of this positive law cannot coincide with that of the law of nature laid down in the order of creation. That is why there *must* be a difference, if not an antithesis, between positive law and the law of nature. Hence the notion of justice necessarily undergoes a modification in its application to the positive law of the state. We might for the present define this modification as a mitigation due to its adjustment to actual reality. Relative justice comes into being. And not only does relative justice exist, not only is that relativity inevitable, but the system of positive law becomes serviceable only by reason of that mitigation. It would only be just in the abstract sense if it were not adapted to the actual facts of life. The adaptation of the Mosaic law to "the hardness of your hearts" was not the product of a moment of weakness and false forbearance, but an inward necessity. Absolute justice would not be just, but unjust, as a system of state law within given reality. It would not serve the end which justice has to serve, namely, submission to God's law of life, but would have exactly the contrary effect. In the system of positive law, relative justice is superior to absolute justice because absolute justice would, from the outset, be no more than a fiction, a lie, and an outrage on life.

But does that not overset our whole previous argument, put us in danger of losing all solid ground under our feet? Who is to tell us what form this necessarily relative justice is to take in given reality, once absolute justice can no longer function there? Does it not mean opening the door to arbitrariness and lack of principle? What multitude of sins would not be covered by the appeal to the mere relativity of all justice based on positive law! An immense uncertainty now invades the whole theory of justice which, by its very relation to the immutable order of God, had achieved definite pronouncements, a clear distinction between just and unjust. One thing, however, has been brought home to us by the realization of the menace to clear standards which relativity implies. It is a good thing that our starting-point was absolute, not relative justice, for to begin with relative justice is to lose all solid ground under our feet before we have taken the first step. But the question is whether we shall not be overtaken by the same fate if we once quit the ground of absolute justice. A profounder consideration of the matter will reassure us.

Once we have seen the realization of the truly good to be impossible, to create the best that lies within our means does not imply the surrender of absolute justice. For, in seeking earnestly for the best possible adaptation to the given situation, we shall be guided solely by the question of how the truly good may be preserved and find expression in that necessary adaptation. The creation of the "best possible" is guided by the will to give expression, as far as possible, to the truly good within the framework of existing limitations. Every positive system of justice is a compromise between the truly just and what is possible. But it must be noted that the best solution is not an abstract maximum of approximation to the absolutely good, but that adaptation which best responds to the *sense* of the demand for justice in the given circumstances(41). The rigorism of abstract legality is in all cases alien and dangerous to life. Real life, as we know it, requires beyond the rigour of the law a certain flexibility and adaptability to the individual case.

Hence the adaptation of justice to the concrete event will be the more successful, the more individual its verdict can be, the smaller the range of cases it comprehends. The greater the circle of persons or things covered by a law, the more abstract, schematic and hence unjust must be the order it creates. Hence a system can approximate to absolute justice in inverse ratio to the range of persons whom it covers. Thus marriage and the family can approximate to the order of creation, but a just order of the state must be far remote from true justice. A just order in the real sense of the word can be established in a small state, still more in a parish, far more readily than in a great state. The greater the domain in which order has to be established, the greater the abstraction, the greater the violence done to individual concreteness. The greater the actual deviation of a human situation from God's order, the "more evil" a state of things, the more widely must the system of positive law deviate from the creative ordinance of God. Where the whole state is out of hand, the forces of order must be more massive and authoritarian than where long and energetic training has created a condition of moral reliability and balance. Where sexual immorality and the decay of the community are far advanced, a marriage system attempting to enforce, in all its rigour, the indissolubility of marriage by the law of the state would have the contrary effect to that intended. Only by a wise and conscientious consideration of present and historical fact is it possible to achieve an order which is, in the given circumstances, the most just. That is the factor of truth in the historical and relativistic view of law.

What that view overlooks, however, is the other side—namely that the best possible system can only be created where the truly just has not been lost sight of, where every deviation from it is extorted by the compulsion of reality, where the truly just is grimly defended against the second best for fear of a third best taking its place. The optimum of the relatively just lies between overreadiness to adapt to reality and excessive rigour in maintaining the abstract idea of absolute justice. It is difficult to say which deviation from this rule is worse—a feeble opportunism or a fanatical dogmatism. The greatest measure of justice will only be found where there is neither dissimulation nor evasion of reality, but where, in full awareness of actual and present reality, men search for the closest approximation to the sense of true justice which it admits.

In determining what is just, the weight of actual circumstances will be the greater in proportion to the multiplicity of men and conditions which have to be ordered. It is like tilling a field which must, at the given moment, be taken as it is and can only be changed gradually by steadfast effort slowly taking effect. Social institutions have something of the perdurableness of nature about them. They are difficult to change; their inertia is the greater the more impersonal they are, the more they are concerned with things. The injustice they incorporate is for all practical purposes irremovable by the just will of the individual. To change them requires the co-operation of many, and requires that co-operation in proportion to the number of persons they embrace. But not only that. The value they have for the community as a system and a service is dependent on the fact that they function at all. The determination to improve them may, instead of improving, throw them out of gear altogether. Anyone interfering in such a system because it seems at isolated points to conflict intolerably with justice must take thought in many directions if his interference is not to do more harm than good. A few blind fanatics of justice can ruin a state, a custom or a social order more thoroughly and more expeditiously by their fanaticism for absolute justice than a host of ill-intentioned revolutionaries.

Hence the demand for adaptation to existing historical conditions does not spring from laxness, lack of moral courage or readiness to follow the line of least resistance, but from the realism required by morality, a realism which allows no confusion of wishful thinking with reality, which must act for order and cannot rest content with the feeling that it has "stood up" for absolute justice, though in vain. Fanaticism for justice, the mind in blinkers and cut off from reality, is not the proof of a strong feeling for justice, but a symptom of a not very laudable self-centredness. On the other hand, realism in justice must not be confused with the attitude of the Blimps of this world who, at every demand for change made in the name of justice, rise in their wrath and shout "Impossible." The greatest measure of justice will be realized only where men are so loyally devoted to the truly just that for its sake they will carefully study the ground on which it is to be planted, so that it shall yield that greatest measure. Their readiness to adapt, their apparent relativity, turns out to be true love for genuine justice, as can be seen by the fact that they infinitely prefer the smallest realization of the truly just to any resounding but utopian program of justice, and that, having once been able to give effect to the smallest measure of true justice, they restlessly seek to do more. They stand perpetually as middlemen of true justice between the absolutely just and reality, always on the lookout for business to be done for justice in reality. They are aware of how necessary it is to know what true justice is because possible justice can only be put into action in reality through the knowledge and love of true justice.

Anyone who really cares for justice must suffer deeply from the enforced acquiescence in a great deal of injustice because it forms part of a system which, even with its great weaknesses and imperfections, is nevertheless better than the disorder which arises when men attempt to improve an imperfect system with inadequate means. Hence the attitude of the Christian faith to justice and reality is essentially a conservative one because the scope of fruitful individual interference in a given system is relatively narrow in comparison with the vast distance between the individual and the system. Any man who cannot appreciate the beneficence of an even relatively just system as compared with anarchy both overrates his own powers and underrates the power of evil. For every system has been won by struggle from evil, as coast land is won from the sea by dykes. The paradigm of this Christian conservatism is the attitude of St. Paul to the state, to the pagan Roman Empire of Nero. He does not hesitate to call it an ordinance of God, a tool and minister of God "for good," in spite of its very imperfect justice. He enjoins the members of the Christian community to be obedient to it and to recognize it as God's servant. We can form a reliable judgment of a man's knowledge of Christian justice by whether he accepts or resents

St. Paul's judgment on this point. It is not the true Christians who are offended by it, but the fanatics of justice, who love justice less than themselves, who never put justice into action but, relishing their own protest against injustice, carry it on their life long and get no further. In the short and far too neglected Epistle of St. Paul to Philemon we have a classic testimony to what is meant by this Christian conservatism, and to how little it has in common with an untroubled acquiescence in the unalterable, to how mightily the passion for the truly just burns in it, even when it looks from the outside like approval of an unjust system. We may conclude this chapter with a short exposition of this Epistle. Its occasion and contents are as follows:

A short time before it was written, a slave, Onesimus by name, dreading punishment for some transgression, had escaped from his master Philemon, the head of a small Christian household in Colosse. In some way unknown to us this slave came into contact with St. Paul, then a prisoner, and was converted by him to Christianity. St. Paul then kept him for some time as his assistant. An opportunity later arose for St. Paul to return Onesimus to his master by a courier who was to take an epistle from St. Paul to the community at Colosse, and the Epistle to Philemon is the letter he gave Onesimus to take with him. This Epistle is therefore an authoritative testimony to the attitude of the great teacher and leader of the primitive Christian community in a concrete case of slavery.

The first impression it will make on a reader of today who approaches it with this enquiry in mind will be one of surprise and disappointment. He may already have felt some uneasiness that St. Paul should return the slave, who had succeeded in liberating himself from the most inhuman of human relationships, that of slavery. He will be further astonished that St. Paul acknowledges a certain right to compensation on the part of the slave's master for the loss of his work. Above all, he will be surprised that St. Paul has not one word of censure for the slave's master for participating, though a Christian, in an institution so degrading and unjust as slavery by keeping a slave, or presumably a number of slaves, instead of emancipating them. On the contrary, St. Paul speaks in the highest terms of Philemon's exemplary Christian conduct, hence he does not require the emancipation of this slave as a necessary consequence of the Christian knowledge of the just. Above all, he will be surprised that St. Paul does not make use of the occasion to launch a solemn protest against the iniquity of slavery. He will infer that slavery presented no problem to primitive Christianity and hence will find no matter for surprise in the failure of Christianity to solve the problem of justice, since justice is totally incompatible with this denial of the most elementary right of man. His conclusion will be that the Christian church should think shame of this Epistle and might do well to seek another basis for a doctrine of justice than that to be found in Scriptural revelation. He may find a solution of the historical riddle in the fact that, "as is well known," primitive Christianity, owing to its belief in the approaching end of the world, regarded all worldly institutions, including slavery, as of no consequence, but by reason of that very indifference, may raise no claim to throw light on the problem of justice in this world. What meaning could a faith have for the problem of justice which tolerated in silence and without question that scandal of human injustice, slavery.

Our reader has entirely missed the point of this Epistle. If we read it as it is meant, we shall realize that St. Paul was by no means restoring his *protégé* to slavery. He had quite a different fate in mind for him, and was striving to obtain it. But what he wanted, he wanted not only for the slave, but for his master Philemon too. The new thing was only to be achieved by a transformation in both. He calls on Philemon to receive his slave as he would receive the Apostle himself, to whom, like his slave, he owes his Christian faith. He wishes to see the relationship between Onesimus and his master based not on justice, but on love, on the love by which St. Paul is bound not only to the slave Onesimus (he calls him his "son," whom he has "begotten," "his own bowels") but also to his master Philemon (whom he calls his "brother" and "fellowlabourer"; he is convinced that Philemon will do more than is asked of him). Philemon is to re-

ceive Onesimus as "a brother beloved," since St. Paul and Philemon on the one hand, St. Paul and the slave Onesimus on the
other, are brothers. The whole style and tone of the letter show
that no rule of justice is concerned here, but the much sublimer
rule of love. Nothing is demanded, no principle laid down, but
in the love of Christ an appeal is made to the free response of
love. Although the Apostle would feel justified in "enjoining"
Philemon as his Apostle and spiritual father, he does not do so.
"Brother," he writes, "let me have joy of thee in the Lord."
The new relationship is to spring from Christian love, the love
which unites all three, the whole household, the whole Christian
community. That is why St. Paul offers to meet any claim for
compensation out of his own purse. The debt must be acknowledged, it must not be repudiated. But even this question is to be
solved in the memory of the love of Christ by which Philemon
owes his own self to the Apostle. What rises before our eyes is
the picture of a Christian fellowship of love, which leaves far
beneath it anything that can enter into systems of justice. The
institution or order of slavery is dissolved from within and replaced by the order of fellowship in love without any appeal to
a just mundane order. The problem of the injustice of slavery
fades into the background. Without even being mentioned it
has been solved by something which no claim for justice can
achieve, by fellowship in love, by brotherhood.

Yet we are still faced with the question why the Apostle
neglected to deal with the problem of slavery in all its implica-
tions, considering that it was a matter of importance not only
in this concrete, personal instance, but for the whole of humanity.
It was because the Apostle's business was not to set up a general
doctrine of justice but, as a missionary and a spiritual father, to
place concrete instances in the supreme light, that of Christian
love. If the Apostle had been asked why he had not spoken of
slavery, he might well have answered that it was not his business
to teach worldly justice, but to proclaim to the world that divine
justice which is identical with the love of Christ. But if he had
been asked whether he did not regard slavery as an unjust institution, indeed as the acme of all human injustice, and whether

Christianity should not be called upon to protest and revolt against it, he would, we may imagine, have replied that he and the Christians had more important things to do than to protest against the unalterable, and that an open struggle against the iniquity in the given situation might increase the wrong, but could not put a stop to it. Slavery was an integral element of the economic and legal system of that time, as money and the machine are integral elements of our economic and legal system. The protest of a tiny minority must perforce remain purely academic. Should it, however, be adopted as a program of action, it could have no other effect than to throw the whole legal system of the time out of gear. For the Christians there was no alternative but to behave differently themselves, in such a way that the legal system did not come into play, that the whole question of law and justice was left out of account, or rather that the legal system was recognized, just as the Roman state was recognized as the minister of God, and Roman law as a service for good against evil. This relative justice was acknowledged for the services it rendered to order, in spite of the fact that it contained an element of such extreme injustice as slavery. That is why St. Paul sent the slave back to his master, that is why he admitted a possible claim for compensation, that is why he gave no order for the slave's emancipation. That is all exactly on the same lines as the famous thirteenth chapter of the Epistle to the Romans with its recognition of the state and its power. The order which exists in actual fact, which is only relatively just and in part extremely unjust, is to be acknowledged as long as it cannot be superseded by an order which is equally effective and more just. To intervene high-handedly at any point and set up postulates of justice is not the business of the Christian community.

The situation was, of course, radically altered as soon as Christianity became a predominant factor in the shaping of public order, as it was from the time of Constantine onward. In this new situation, the Christian was no longer a mere object of the law; he was at the same time its source. Hence he was partially responsible for its substance. Even at this juncture Christianity renounced the attempt to put the entire program of a doctrine of justice into action at one blow because it realized the fruitlessness and danger of a fanaticism of the kind. What it did do was to work with all its might for a progressive realization of better justice. Hence it never lost sight of the two sides of the question—the true justice of the divine order of creation and the necessary modifications imposed upon it by existing reality. For it knew that the realization of justice is not to be attained by evading reality, but by understanding it and making full allowance for it, while abstract postulates of justice, even when proclaimed with what is meant to be prophetic fervour in the name of God, have never brought about any least realization of justice. It is one thing to awaken the conscience of individuals as a preacher of God's word, and he who does so cannot be absolute enough in his challenge. It is quite a different thing to set up postulates for the form which a system of justice is to take, and he who does so cannot be realistic enough. But the only true realist is he who, in his grasp of given reality, never forgets the principles of true justice laid down in the order of creation.

... Chapter 14 ...

JUSTICE AND THE REVELATION
OF SCRIPTURE

1. THE NEW TESTAMENT

I T MAY SEEM SURPRISING THAT A THEORY OF justice conceived from the standpoint of faith in the revelation of Scripture should not take the document of revelation as its starting-point. We must enquire why. This question, which was touched on at the beginning of the present volume, can only be properly answered now that the specific nature and sphere of the idea of justice has been defined. The question is the more urgent in that the "righteousness of God" is not only frequently spoken of in the Bible, but is its central theme, so that the Bible might be called the book of God's righteousness.[1] If we look at the matter more closely, we shall see that righteousness in this sense means something which is not only far remote from what we mean by justice, and must mean when we speak of just law, just wages, just punishment, but is its direct antithesis. It is, however, a dialectical antithesis, in which each term retains its antithesis as its own ground.

When the Apostle Paul, in that cardinal passage of the Epistle to the Romans in which he sums up his message,[2] denotes its substance as the "righteousness of God," he means neither distributive nor contractual justice, neither that which gives a just reward for labour nor inflicts just punishment for transgression, hence not the justice which renders to each man

[1] Rom. 1: 17 and 3: 21 ff.
[2] Cf. *Theologisches Wörterbuch zum Neuen Testament.*

his due, but an activity of God which, as he distinctly says, must be understood "without the law," and as directly opposed to merits and claims. It is the love of God, bounteous and forgiving, revealed in the atoning suffering and death of Jesus Christ. This use of the idea of justice, so paradoxical not only to our use of language, but to any use of language at all, can only be understood on the whole background of Scriptural revelation. It may be that a summary of the cardinal points of the Scriptural doctrine may help to elucidate it.

God's will and God's law can only become effective in man through the reconciling, merciful gift of the love of God; man, in the faith that his salvation is undeservedly bestowed upon him by God, renders to God the honour due to Him as the sole Saviour, and himself takes up the position which beseems him, namely that of one whose function it is simply to receive.

This paradoxical reversal of the notion of justice comes out probably most clearly in St. Paul, but it is not confined to him. The natural sense of justice is violated in the same way by Christ's parable of the labourers in the vineyard.[3] All those who came first and those who came last to the labour receive the same hire, and their "just" protest is answered with the words: "I will give unto this last, even as unto thee. Is it not lawful for me to do what I will with mine own?" Once more it is love, the incomprehensible gift, bound to no law of retributive justice and standing in absolute contrast to what we must call just in the things of this world, which is shown here as God's manner of action. It is obvious that the parable is not meant to lay down rules for the payment of wages to labourers. The point at issue here has nothing to do with mundane arrangements and their justice. What stands revealed here is the order of the Kingdom of God. The substance of the parable is not the *justitia civilis* but the *justitia evangelica* which consists precisely in the cessation of all deserving, in the denial of all lawful claims, and is hence the antithesis of the law of worldly justice.

The same point is again made clear in the exceeding right-

[3] Matt. 20: 1 ff.

eousness of the disciples by which they are to be distinguished from the Pharisees.[4] This exceeding righteousness consists precisely in the fact that they shall not rest content with satisfying the just claim of the other; the free gift of their love shall exceed anything which is due to the other "by right"; they are even to forego their own good right. Their conduct is not to be guided by the rule of law or justice, but by the example of the loving God, who maketh His sun to rise on the just and the unjust,[5] Who gives the heavenly reward without any regard to just claims for wages. In this total setting aside of all that is and must be called justice in the things of this world, the Gospel is revealed as the teaching which does not regulate earthly things but proclaims the Kingdom of God, and the justice which it proclaims is not the justice which is applicable to the circumstances of this world; it is the nature of the new aeon.

This was stated by Jesus directly and explicitly. When a man came to Him asking Him to arbitrate in a dispute over his inheritance, Jesus refused with the utmost sharpness: "Man, who made me a judge or divider over you?"[6] He does not say that there should be no judges and no just division of inheritances, but that is not His business. He is He who brings the Kingdom of Heaven, not the arbitrator in matters of earthly law. The well-known parable of the tribute to Caesar[7] has the same meaning. The Pharisees were trying to force Jesus to commit Himself on a burning question of political ethics, namely whether taxes were to be paid to a foreign army of occupation. Jesus solved the problem by asking for a coin. It bore the image of Caesar. Therefore let Caesar's business remain Caesar's business: do not confuse the Kingdom of God with problems of earthly justice. The antithesis between the earthly sphere and the Kingdom of God even takes on a programmatic significance in the conversation between Jesus and Pilate.[8] To Pilate's question whether Jesus is the King of the

[4] Matt. 5: 20.
[5] Matt. 5: 45.
[6] Luke. 12: 14.
[7] Matt. 22: 15, 15 ff.
[8] John 18 and 19.

Jews, He answers in a manner which may mean yes as well as no, but makes it unmistakably clear in which sense He is, and in which He is not. "My kingdom is not of this world"[9] The sphere in which there are just claims, rights, debits and credits, and in which justice is therefore the supreme principle, and the sphere in which the gift of love is supreme, where there are no deserts, where love, without acknowledging any claim, gives all—these two spheres lie as far apart as heaven from hell, and that which shall endure from that which shall pass away. The Kingdom of God is the Kingdom in which marriage and the family, law and the state, have ceased to exist, and its principle, love, is what remains when all law, even faith, hope and the knowledge which finds utterance in human speech shall be no more.

This Kingdom of God and its righteousness, the free gift of love, is the substance of the New Testament message. That is the point at issue in Christian faith. But it does not imply that the Christian community can remain indifferent to earthly justice. It is true that Jesus himself taught practically nothing about the justice of this world, since he had only one thing to teach and to incarnate—the righteousness of the Kingdom of God. The Apostles, on the other hand, had to instruct their communities how, being citizens by faith of another world, they were to behave with regard to the earthly institutions in which, after all, they had to live—marriage, the family, the relationship of master and servant, the state. But all these things are, as it were, only incidental to the New Testament message and appear for the most part in special passages, clearly distinct from the real message, the so-called *Haustafeln*, or household words. It has always been noticed that these passages contain a kind of ethical instruction which differs from that contained elsewhere in the apostolic teaching. Attention has been drawn to their prosaic, homely tone and the suggestion made that their substance has been taken over from Rabbinical and Stoic ethical sources.[10] What has not been really understood is that the

[9] John 18: 36.
[10] Cf. Werdinger, *Die Haustafeln.*

questions treated in these passages are of such a kind that they can only be treated in homely, prosaic fashion, and that it is no matter for surprise if Christian teaching in such questions should coincide with the conclusions of Jewish or Stoic morals. For these passages do not deal with the essential message of the New Testament, the Kingdom of God, the *agape*, but with the ethics of mundane systems and their principle, legal justice.

This is to be seen first of all in the fact that the injunctions contained in these passages vary according to social and civil status. Love, in itself, is the same for all; justice discriminates. For love there is neither master nor servant, man nor woman, child nor adult. Love gives the same to all—itself. But justice renders to all their "due".[11] Hence in these household words different injunctions are given to men and to women, to children and to parents, to servants and to master. And each is enjoined in accordance with his status. The duties which the Christian is here exhorted to fulfil are such as arise not from his quality as a Christian, but from his place in a civic system, and hence are clearly delimited and defined. They are duties of the justice of this world. The ethics of these passages, insofar as they deal with these various obligations, are ethics of worldly order, not of love. The Christians are called upon to render to each man his due, honour to whom honour is due, tribute to whom tribute is due, custom to whom custom is due, fear to whom fear is due, just as the men are called upon to render to their wives "due benevolence"—clearly marital duties are meant—and wives to submit to their husbands.

What the Apostle has to say in this connection about the civic duties of the Christians is particularly instructive.[12] They are to be subject to the "higher powers," to do what is required by the justice of the state. The state, the imperial Roman state, is the "minister of God" as the administrator of a legal order, although it cannot be aware of the fact since it does not know the God whose minister it is. This civic justice is simply and solely Roman law. The Apostle says of the system that those

[11] I Cor. 7: 3; Rom. 13: 7.
[12] Rom. 13: 1.

who do good shall "have praise" of it, but that he who does evil shall be punished. This good and evil, therefore, cannot be what Jesus' disciples learned from the Master as good and evil, what they alone know, the free gift of love, but that "good and evil" which is incorporated in Roman law,[13] a certain familiar civic legality, a legal morality. Christians are to do this good also, and not to do this evil, and that not outwardly, but "for conscience sake." That is the New Testament doctrine of the *justitia civilis*. The Apostle concludes his instructions with the characteristic phrase that Christians shall "owe no man anything," that is, that they shall, in all these various spheres, do what is required by the order, the law of justice, of each.

What is, then, the basis of this doctrine of justice according to which every man shall be given his due? What does this "due" refer to? The dominant idea in St. Paul's observations on the state is "the ordinance of God" τάσις. In the first, most important clauses, this idea occurs four times. The Christians are to be "subordinated," for the powers are "ordained" of God; whoever "resisteth" (is insubordinate) resists the "ordinance" of God. These clauses deal with the ethics of order, and of an order "ordained" by God. It is to be understood that there should be here no mention of an order of creation. Wherever the duties of married people and the members of a family are discussed, on the other hand, the order of creation, or "nature," always comes into the foreground, for instance in the classic passage where Jesus was called upon to pronounce upon the permissibility of divorce.[14] Jesus contrasts the law of Moses, which sanctioned and regulated divorce, with the order of creation—"from the beginning of the creation"—in which the indissolubility of marriage is an integral element of its very nature. By divine creation husband and wife are one flesh in marriage, "and what God hath joined together, let not man put asunder." Marriage is a union of human beings founded in divine creation. The vital corollary of that fact, the first and most essential duty of justice, is unconditional fidelity, inseparability. In the same

[13] Rom. 13: 3.
[14] Mark 10:1 ff.

way, in a passage in the Epistle to the Romans, the proper and improper use of the sexual organs, the unnaturalness of homo-sexuality, is derived from creation, here called nature.[15] Again, the functional superiority of the husband over the wife in marriage and the corresponding subordination of the wife to the husband, is derived from creation, just as certain moral imperatives are given in "nature." The basis of the differentiation of the duties of justice for each social class is a divine ordinance, whether it be the power of the state[16] ordained by God for the curbing of evil, or the order of creation, or nature. The commandment of God, insofar as it draws distinctions, is ontologically based on the order established by God. The commandment of God simply reveals the eternal will of God already incorporated in creation. The ethics of justice in the New Testament are the ethics of order.

This duality of instruction, this distinction between the justice of this world and the spiritual, heavenly justice, makes it suspect to a certain kind of theological monism, which strives to reduce everything to a single formula. It scents a false dualism which rends heavenly and earthly asunder and destroys the unity of obedience. The fear of such a dualism, which has been rendered only too familiar by the most recent of political slogans—heaven to you, the earth to us—and which has actually played a disastrous part in Christian history, is absolutely justified. No Christian can concur in a separation which proposes that God should command in spiritual things and a temporal ruler in earthly things. But there is no possible question of a dualism of such a kind here. It is one and the same God who gives us the law of justice by which earthly systems are framed and the law of love for our relations with our fellow men. For it is one and the same God who established the orders of creation as orders for our time, and gave the promise of the eternal life in which those orders shall pass away. It is one and the same God who commands the Roman Christians to obey the state and the law of Rome, and to fulfil the duties laid upon them, and who

[15] Rom. 1: 26.
[16] Rom. 13: 4.

commands the same Christians to requite evil with good, hence to do what no law can require. But the unity of the order of justice with the order of love which is so radically different from it, goes still further.

It is not only one and the same God who gives and requires both, but, as we have seen, the ultimate purpose of the order of creation is the purpose of community. Their meaning, their reason and their goal is love, even though their specific nature, being of the order of justice, cannot be of the order of love. These orders are not ultimate things, but they serve the ultimate, they preserve, protect and educate for the ultimate, just as they have their deepest, primal cause in the love of God. Even the state with its coercive law, its "sword," that most outward, wide-meshed of institutions, the nature of which is most remote from the nature of the community of Jesus, the fellowship of love, serves love because it preserves man from anarchy and its horrors. The harsh law of the state is, it is true, quite a different thing from love, but it serves love. Its sense is "the good",[17] the welfare of the community.

Hence the deepest motive which should move Christians to fulfil the duties imposed upon them by those institutions is simply love—that love which is freely given by Christ—so that the Apostle can write that they shall be subject in the love of Christ and render each other their due.[18] Thus wherever the order of *justice* is concerned, the motive power of love which comes from Christ is concerned also. Hence Christians do not cease, when they have fulfilled the duties of justice in the civic order of the state, to be servants of their Master. He who commands is One, but the substance of the commandments is different in each case. Their deepest meaning, however, is one and the same—the love of God.

Although the New Testament contains the outlines of a doctrine of earthly justice, it contains but scant indication of a Christian doctrine of mundane institutions, nor is that in any way surprising. For firstly it was to be assumed that the basic facts were

[17] Rom. 13: 4.
[18] Cf. Note 19 and Rom. 13: 7.

familiar to everybody, secondly, the message of Christ and his Apostles, and the primitive Christian community, were concerned with greater things than the framing of worldly systems, and thirdly, for the Christian community at its foundation, since it formed a tiny minority in the Roman Empire, and had no voice in public affairs, the shape of worldly systems was of no immediate interest. What good would it have done to teach them what they had to do *if* they had anything to do? The situation of the first Christians was radically different from that of the Israelites at the time of their national independence.

2. THE OLD TESTAMENT

For this reason the Old Testament presents a totally different picture from the New Testament. Here we find in the state, law and economics systems which are as magnificent as they are unique. Above all, in the Prophets of the Old Testament the demand for justice in the name of God is put forward more urgently than anywhere else in history. For the people of Israel were to be and wished to be the people of God, and the will of their Lord was to be and had to be made manifest not only in the personal, inward life of individuals, not only in the life of the community serving God, but also in the public institutions of the people as a whole. That is why we find here what we so painfully miss in the New Testament, a detailed social ethic ruled by the commandment of God, a more or less complete ethic of social institutions and justice. Hence we can understand that Christian theology tends to seek beyond the social ethic as laid down in Christian faith and to turn to the Old Testament. To do so, however, cannot but give rise to the gravest misgivings. Nor are those misgivings personal to us, and hence due to a more critical attitude towards the Old Testament. On the contrary, the greatest teachers of the Protestant church and theology (42) —not only Luther, but Calvin too—who had at heart on the one hand the unity of the Old and New Testaments, on the other the shaping of public life according to the will of God, have expressed those misgivings with the utmost frankness. They all warn us against taking and applying the Old Testament dispensation in law, the state and the economic order as criteria for ourselves (43). Their reasons are clear and hold good even today. With the enrichment of knowledge due to critical research, we may today formulate them as follows:

1. The divine revelation in the Old Testament is a preliminary stage of the revelation in Jesus Christ. That is to be seen firstly in the fact that the order of the Kingdom of Heaven and the order of this world, the fellowship of faith and the community of the people, were not yet clearly distinguished. Israel was a theocracy. The law of the state was at the same time the law of the religious community and the law of the religious community was the law of the state. The laws of religion and the synagogue were enforced by the same coercive means as those of the state, and transgression of them punished in the same way as transgression of civic laws. To belong to the nation was to belong to the fellowship of Jehovah; national unity and the unity of the religious community were one and the same thing. The children of Israel were born into the synagogue as they were born into the nation. Only he who belonged to Israel belonged to the God of Israel. Membership of the fellowship of Jehovah independent of membership of the national unity was unknown. The distinction between these two powers, the fellowship of faith and the national community, and the liberation which that distinction operates of the fellowship of faith from the element of coercion by the law of the state, was first fulfilled in the New Testament, above all by St. Paul.

2. The theocratic community which makes the covenanted people of Jehovah a phenomenon unique in history finds perfect expression in the nature of its public order. The moral and religious law is blended in one indissoluble unity with the liturgical law of priest, temple and purification on the one hand, and with the law of the state on the other. Hence the law of justice underlying social and political institutions can never be separated from the liturgical laws. If we wish to take over from the Old Testament standards of social and political order, we must take over with them the standards and institu-

tions of the cultus, hence the whole apparatus of priest and temple and the laws governing them.

3. Further, the law of Israel, although it set itself up as the law of God's immutable will, varied considerably at different times, and these variations lie before us in the Old Testament. The political and juridical order of the epoch of the Judges is totally different from that of the Kings, and again from that of the post-exilic period when Israel had lost her national independence and was a province of some great state or other ruled by heathen kings.

4. In all its different phases, the Israelitic order of justice and law confronts us as that of a national community of the ancient world, which is utterly different from our own. To transfer any element from its system to our own circumstances would, even if such a theologian's dream could come true, probably be as devastating in its effects as a transfusion of blood between different blood groups. Healthy blood so transfused is mortal.

Not only the political order in the narrower sense of the word, but the economic, social and family order of the people of Israel is unique in history. Hence any possibility of revival, of direct borrowing, is ruled out. What is apparently alike would become quite different in a different setting. Hence when theologians expect us, for instance, to regulate the problem of interest on capital according to the twenty-fifth chapter of Leviticus, they are no less ridiculous than the Swedish Puritans of the eighteenth century who demanded that a lady seen riding in men's clothes should be stoned.

3. THE TEN COMMANDMENTS IN PARTICULAR

But should not the Ten Commandments, at least, as the authoritative summary of the divine imperative of the Old Testament, form the basis of a Christian doctrine of justice? In actual fact the important jurist Oldendorp (44) based his Lutheran jurisprudence on the Decalogue as late as the mid-Reformation. There can be no question of the incomparable catechetical importance of the Decalogue for the instruction of a Christian congregation, especially in the Protestant church. But the very element which makes the Decalogue the Christian text of instruction par excellence renders it unsuitable as the basis of a scientific doctrine of justice. For this same summary of the law of God bears the unmistakable stamp of the Old Testament phase of revelation. It is all one; the purely religious commandments which lay down the conditions of communion with God (first and third), the liturgical law which sets apart a holy day, the Sabbath (fourth), the purely inward, moral law, which condemns false covetousness (tenth), and the remaining five, which may be taken in part as the interpretation of the one commandment of love, and in part as a law of justice. This thoroughly Israelitic blend of the most heterogeneous domains, so characteristic of the Old Testament, could not but reinforce, again and again, that bias towards theocracy which has been native to the church from the time of Constantine and Theodosius onward, which supports the true faith by the secular arm and formulates as a rule of law what can only be heard as a free resolve of faith. It is the appeal to the Decalogue which has repeatedly led to the confusion between the personal world of faith and the institutional world of justice. It was one of the main reasons why the principle of justice was never distinguished in its peculiar essence from love. The modern world, in which the existence of the various creeds, side by side, religions and philosophies in one and the same nation, makes the return to theocracy as impossible as it is inadmissible for reasons of faith, imperiously demands that distinction between what holds good in the world of institutions and what holds good in the relationship of persons: it demands a strict distinction between the justice of the *suum cuique* and the love which knows nought of rights and claims.

But even apart from this radical rejection of the Decalogue as the basis of a doctrine of justice, there is the objection to it which must arise in face of any Christian exegesis of the Old Testament code. The exegete always reads into these simple laws —more especially into those now under consideration, the fifth to the ninth commandments—more than they actually contain.

That means that he is drawing their substance from another source, whether it be the "law of nature" or the doctrine of love as set forth in the Sermon on the Mount. In themselves, the five commandments cannot be interpreted as a doctrine of justice. In spite of Luther, the fifth commandment makes no pronouncement concerning the state and other social institutions, but only concerning the relationship of children to father and mother. The sixth commandment makes no pronouncement concerning the power of the state over life and death; it does not envisage capital punishment nor military service nor euthanasia nor abortion; it speaks solely of murder. The seventh commandment has nothing to say of the nature of marriage, but merely condemns crass adultery. The eighth commandment has nothing to say of the rights and wrongs of private property, of unearned income and so on; it merely condemns theft, without stating what is righteous and what unrighteous property, or what is lawful and what unlawful gain. And finally the ninth commandment has no regard for "the property of a good name," the right to personal honour and the duty of rendering to each the honour due; it makes the simple statement that no false witness shall be borne in a court of law. To use the Decalogue in the exposition of the Christian ethic is, of course, not prohibited; indeed such use will always be an aim of Christian instruction. The Decalogue is eminently fitted to such use by its selection of the essential, by its incomparable arrangement and pregnancy. Hence it will always remain for us an unrivalled text for instruction, but not a source of insight into the truth of social ethics. When we wish to know what is just in the state, in economics, in society, marriage and the family, we receive no help from the Decalogue but can only attach to its commandments what we have learned in other ways. Since our present business is not didactics, however, but an enquiry into our special theme, the Decalogue cannot be taken into account here. Luther's assertion, explicitly repeated by Calvin, that the Old Testament law can have no direct meaning for us as a rule of conduct remains in principle true.

This implies no denial of the importance of the Old Testament as a source of knowledge of social ethics, as a mine of instruction for all Christian teaching on the justice of this world. It means that such teaching cannot be direct and legal, but only indirect. In actual fact the will of God in the shaping of society is powerfully manifested in the Old Testament, though in the manner which befitted its own stage of revelation, the theocracy of the people of God, the contemporary stage of culture attained by that people and its situation with regard to its heathen neighbours. Hence we must always seek, *behind* the individual laws, injunctions and institutions, the principle underlying them, the divine imperative which is binding on us today; we can at no point take them over as the letter of the law. In so seeking, however, we shall find the simple principles laid down in the order of creation which we have elucidated in the previous chapters, and hence remain in line with our leading Christian teachers.[19] Anyone who can find a greater wealth of teaching in the Old Testament is free to do so and to reveal it; we shall gratefully learn from him. But he will not be able to bind us by Old Testament laws under the banner of truth to Scripture in the literal sense "as it is written." For there is obviously a great deal written in the Old Testament as divine law which no Christian can regard as binding upon himself unless he ceases to be a Christian.

The law of the Old Testament may be regarded on the one hand as an interpretation of the commandment of love, as Jesus himself interpreted it in the Sermon on the Mount; here, however, we have in the New Testament an insight which goes far beyond anything the Old Testament can give. Or, on the other hand, the Old Testament law is a law of justice, which imposes duties upon men according to their status; in that case the definition "the code of the Israelites" holds good; it is a formulation of the justice established in the order of creation, which renders to each man his due, and holds good only for that time and situation. It would not, however, be difficult to prove that both in the Old Testament and the New, this law of justice goes back to the order of creation and is founded on it, hence that

[19] This is also Calvin's view. See Note 44.

. . . Chapter 15 . . .

JUSTICE AND LOVE

I F EVER WE ARE TO GET A CLEAR CONCEPTION OF the nature of justice, we must also get a clear idea of it as differentiated from and contrasted with love. The contrast, however, does not present a plain alternative to action. One and the same man who, as a Christian, has become a citizen of the other, heavenly kingdom, and holds his πολίτευμα,[1] his citizenship, in Heaven, belongs nevertheless, as *cives romanus* or *Eidgenosse*, to an earthly state and hence is subject not only to the heavenly law of forgiving love, but also to the earthly law of even-handed justice. In the same way, the nature of justice is radically different from that of love, yet, deriving from the one God, is very closely akin to it. The antithesis does not sever the bond between them, nor the bond annul the antithesis.

As might be expected, Aristotle, the master of the classical doctrine of justice, has nothing to say about this kind of love, for he does not know it. He too speaks of love, but in the form of φιλία, friendship, and he rightly places it in a certain contrast to justice. Friendship too, in its own way, goes beyond justice, and is hence akin to what is proclaimed in the Bible as love. Yet φιλία is all the same widely different from love, for φιλία, friendship between noble minds, is given to a noble mind for its deserts. "Only what is worthy to be loved can be an object of friendship"[2] says Aristotle, in so many words. But love asks no questions about the nature of that which is to be loved.[3] That is precisely the miracle of the love of God, Who

[1] Phil. 3: 26.
[2] *Nic. Ethics*, 8, 1155 b.
[3] Matt. 5: 44 ff.

loves not only the man who is worthy to be loved, but also the unworthy. It is always love all-the-same, never love because.[4] It is a loving born simply of the will to love, not of the nature of the beloved. It is not a love which judges worth but a love which bestows worth. Neither Aristotle nor any other pagan knew this love; it is identical with the message of Scripture.

It was the Prophet Hosea who first spoke of this incomprehensible, divine love. His own human experience was for him a parable, indeed the means of knowing divine love. He loved, incomprehensibly, his own faithless wife, who had given herself up to whoredom and whom he had turned away according to the law. And then he had to love the creature that was unworthy of his love. That was God's way of revealing to him the nature of divine love. God too loved a "whore," Israel itself, which had fallen away from him and was running after a strange God. God loves those who have become utterly unworthy of His love. He loves them not for their goodness, beauty, lovableness or worth, but *in spite of* their being what they are, without a reason and simply and solely because it is His will to love them, because it is His will to bestow His love upon them. That is *agape*, the love born of the lover, the freely given, incomprehensible love of God.

It is above all this love to which the New Testament bears witness. This love was revealed in Jesus Christ as the love of Him who loves sinful mankind. It is neither $\varphi\iota\lambda\iota\alpha$, which sees and loves the worth of the friend, nor the love of the mother who is bound to her child by the bond of blood. Its source is not natural but supernatural. It is the very being of God, to such a point that we say: "God is love," and again: "He that dwelleth in love dwelleth in God and God in him."[5] This love is known only where God is revealed as He Who does not judge the sinner according to his deserts, but incomprehensibly forgives his sin and so heals the breach in communion. This love is therefore only to be comprehended and won by faith. For to possess this love is the same thing as to possess God—the God who "first

---

[4] Cf. *Eros und Agape* by Nygren, the authoritative work on this subject.
[5] 1 Ep. John 4: 16.

loved us,"[6] and reveals Himself as that loving God in His acts of revelation and reconciliation. The faith of which the New Testament speaks simply means to be opened to and for this love, to receive the love of God.

Justice is a totally different thing. When we are just, and deal justly, we render to the other what is his due. Justice makes no free gift; it gives precisely what is *due* to the other, no more and no less. Its basis is strictly realistic, sober and rational; there is nothing super-rational, incomprehensible about it. On the contrary, justice is that which is comprehensible to all. But love is not comprehensible, not rational. It is super-rational, it does what would appear like madness to an Aristotle. For it loves the unworthy. This love is only to be comprehended by him for whom the "foolishness of the Cross" is no folly, but who recognizes in it "the power of God."[7] This love is inseparable from faith.

Justice is rational because it views man in a rational system. Justice exists where something is rendered to man which is his due. It is insofar sober and realistic as it is impersonal. It is not for nothing that justice is represented blindfold. It does not regard the person, thereby differing both from Christian love and the φιλία of Aristotle; it sees only the lawful right and the man who possesses it. Whoever that man is, this or that is due to him. He bears his lawful right in his hand. Even where it is a question of the rights of man, hence of a lawful right which entitles to no object but is entirely based on the nature of man, of the dignity of man which must, in justice, be recognized, it is impersonal and realistic. For even this personal right is a right, something due to everyone who is a person, a general thing. Justice does not even then say "thou." It knows no "thou"; it knows only the intellectual value, the intellectual thing—the dignity of man. The just man recognizes in the other the same dignity which he finds in himself, the same quality as a person, the same general law of being. Even this strictly realistic justice is an occasion of feeling, the feeling of the general dignity of man, but that feeling is not love. For love loves that particular

[6] 1 Ep. John 4: 19.
[7] 1 Cor. 1: 18.

being; it says "thou," it is directed to the concrete person in his uniqueness, even though it does not love because that person is what he is, but because he exists. It loves him, this particular person, not a human being nor humanity in his person, which cannot be loved, but only respected in justice. It loves because God gives that love, because it loves that person as the beloved of God(45).

Justice can make no use of this love, nor does it need to. Justice is never concerned with the human being as such, but only with the human being in relationships. Justice belongs to the world of systems, not to the world of persons. But because the person is higher than all the systems in which he is placed, because all systems are there for persons but never persons for systems, love transcends justice. Yet in its own place, justice is supreme. Within the system as such there can be nothing higher, for love knows nought of systems.

This often leads to misunderstanding. It is taken to mean that the loving human being, the true disciple of the church, must cease to be a loving human being in the world of systems. He can never do that if he is a true Christian. But in the world of systems he cannot give effect to his love except by being just. He remains loving none the less, but as long as he is active in the world of systems, his love compels him to be just. Within the world of systems, he must, so to speak, change his love into the current coin of justice, since that alone is legal tender in the world of systems. He does not cease to be a loving human being, but he can only find an object for his love when he is no longer concerned with the world of systems, but with the individual human being in it, detached from it, where, so to speak, he can look through the meshes of systems to see and grasp the human being himself.

Hence justice, as compared with love, is not an inferior thing, a thing which should not be. As long as we human beings live in this world, where there are systems, justice is as indispensable as love. This can be seen by the fact that the man of love, as soon as he has to act in the world of institutions, turns his love into justice. He knows that if he did otherwise, he would ruin, destroy, the world of institutions. Love which is not just in the world of institutions is sentimentality. And sentimentality, feeling for feeling's sake, is the poison, the solvent which destroys all just institutions.

The more closely an institution approaches the personal sphere, the smaller the number of human beings it embraces, and the less things in it predominate over persons, the greater is the scope it gives to love. "The state, the most impersonal because the most comprehensive of institutions, knows nothing of love" (Karl Barth). The man of love can only serve the state with justice. He must transform his love entirely into justice for as long and insofar as he acts in the state. And vice versa, marriage, the most personal of all institutions, which comprises only two persons, in which the natural purpose is closely interwoven with the fellowship of persons, is so accessible to love that the marriage is perfect in proportion as its ruling principle is love and not justice. Yet even in marriage an element of justice comes in. What the husband owes to the wife is not the same as what the wife owes to the husband. Even the most perfect of marriages is an institution, which is made visible in it. Between marriage and the state there lie the manifold institutions of social life which, according as persons or things predominate in their purpose, are ruled more by justice or more by love. But because no man, as a member of an institution, is *only* a member of an institution, but always and only a person, there is room for love even in the most impersonal of institutions, not in the actual activity of the institution itself, but "between the lines."

Justice, however, is always the pre-condition of love; justice must never be neglected by love. Love can only do more, it can never do less, than justice requires. A citizen who falsifies his income-tax return in order to practise charity cannot appeal to love in exculpation; love of that kind is sheer sentimentality. True love is always more than just; it fulfils first the impartial law of actual justice. There is therefore no such thing as love at the cost of justice or over the head of justice, but only beyond justice and through justice. Love is always more than the recognition of the rights of a human being, but, for that very reason, it can never deny that the other has a right to this or that on the assumption that there can be no more talk of justice where love is. That is only true when the other has *first* got his rights, when he has been given his due, not out of compassion but out of justice. The labourer has a right to a just wage; he is therefore right to protest when the wage to which he has a right is offered to him as alms, as a gift of love. The real gift of love only begins where justice has already been done, for it is that which is beyond justice.

It has already been suggested that only love can be perfectly just. That is true in the sense that we can only fill a glass quite full if we are ready to let it run over. It is above all true with reference to action. Love is the only guarantee that all the motives which stand in the way of justice shall vanish or become ineffective. Love fulfils all the commandments of justice because it knows that its real work only begins when justice has been done.

The mediaeval doctrine of the "work of supererogation" is not erroneous if it merely serves to bring out the distinction between the obligations of justice and the obligations of love; it is erroneous if it places love outside of the commandment of God. For love is the supreme commandment of God, indeed, properly understood, the sole commandment of God. But this love always does more than man is bound to do by justice, which establishes the various distinct and fulfillable obligations. The obligations of justice can be fulfilled because they are distinct, but love is never fulfilled; it is always in debt[8] for it is not to be perfected. The demand of justice can be satisfied, the demand of love never. Its measure will never be full, while the measure of justice, as a measure of the world of systems, of the mundane sphere, is full. Love can fulfil justice, but cannot itself be fulfilled. It is always at the beginning. Only the love which is without measure fulfils itself—the love of God.

[8] Rom. 13: 8.

...PART II...

PRACTICE

...Foreword to Part II...

The special character of this second part renders some explanation necessary. To ascertain principles is not the same thing as to apply them in practice. In this second part we are confronted with the multitudinousness of facts. Facts, however, are not only multitudinous; they are also complex, and both multitudinousness and complexity make it impossible to devise a single and convincing method of application even for principles which have been clearly and securely established. Yet the application cannot be neglected, for what is the use of principles which are not applicable in practice? It would be well if theology could hand over this part of the work to other sciences. It will do so as soon as they are available to do what has to be done—namely to apply the principles of the Christian conception of justice to the problems of sociology. Instead of that two things happen: firstly, theologians and other Christian teachers rest content with amateurish improvisations which have, of late, taken as their watchword: "The Church as Sentinel"; secondly, jurists, sociologists and economists entrench themselves behind the neutrality of a science which they allege to be free of philosophic bias. The unsatisfactoriness of this situation, which is just as calamitous in the secular field as it is in the Christian church, is the only reason why theology is justified in making a first attempt, and, so to speak, throwing across an emergency bridge to hold until those equipped with wider knowledge advance and make it secure.

Hence all that is said in this second part must be regarded as tentative. Only the order of God is infallible. Even human knowledge of the divine order is subject to error—how much more so its application to the particular problems of the social order! There will even have to be further discussion of principles although the main lines are clear. In any case it would be folly and arrogance to claim any finality for the application of the basic principles to the concrete problems, especially those of economics and international relations.

... Chapter 16 ...

JUSTICE IN THE POLITICAL ORDER

THE MONSTROSITY WHICH BEARS THE NAME OF the totalitarian state has at last succeeded in reminding us that there are not only primal rights of individuals and of communities, but that there is a just and unjust order of the state itself. The totalitarian state is not, like a dictatorship, a form of the state. It is the absorption of all institutions and all rights by the state. The totalitarian state is the inevitable consequence of the view that the state is sovereign, that it is not subject to law, but that it can establish as law whatever it likes and approves, and that all rights obtaining among the people issue from the state. The totalitarian state must of necessity come into being wherever political thought is centralistic, and all organization is regarded as issuing from above, from a state centre, wherever federalism, the building up of the community from below, has vanished. Indeed, it is already potentially present where the state is held to be the supreme value. Hence its antithesis is not democracy but the federally organized commonwealth of nation or state. The bulwark against the totalitarian state is not democracy, but federalism.

Federalism is the just order of the state, and federalism is the state built up from below. That is the order of creation. All institutions exist for the sake of man; man never exists for the sake of institutions. Hence the primary datum is the individual human being. That is the view of things entailed by the Christian belief in creation. The call of God goes to the individual. Only the individual can hear it, only the individual has a conscience, only he is, in the true sense of the word, a responsible person. Whenever people speak seriously of "collective persons(46)" the way to the totalitarian state lies open. The primacy of the individual over all collective factors—that is the principle of the individualism and liberalism which are deeply rooted in the Christian faith.

This individualism, however, at once finds its limitation. The individual is called to fellowship. He is called by love to love. Love is the true substance of life and love is fellowship. Hence both individual existence and existence in fellowship are based on the relation to God in which there is as yet no question of rights or systems. But as soon as we enter the realm of justice and institutions, man, as an individual, at once becomes the man in his place. Just as every man owes his creaturely existence to the fact that two individuals, a man and a woman, became one, every man, at the root of his existence, is part of a community. This community, however, is not the state, but the family. The one community without which human life cannot be imagined in any circumstances is the family. Hence the family is the primal community and its rights take absolute precedence over the rights of any other natural community, even the state. The family is the root and prototype of every community. In the order of creation, its right is primal. No state can formulate the law of marriage and the family according to its own will. The state is just only when its legal system lays due stress on the law of marriage and the family, which are independent of it. As we can see by the totalitarian state, the state has the power to outrage and misuse this primal institution, to abolish it by its system of positive "law," but thereby it merely exhibits its own injustice. The state is just only when it recognizes that the law of marriage and the family takes precedence of all laws of the state, that it cannot be created by the state, but only recognized and embodied in a system of positive law. Hence the monstrosity of the totalitarian state appears most clearly where it takes upon itself to abolish the institution of marriage and the family, which is founded on creation, and to replace it by some other institution which it regards as preferable or expedient, whether it be the anarchy of free love or the human stud or barracks.

It is, however, an element of the law of the family that the family, and not the state, has control and custody of the child. This right is, of course, limited, though not by the state, but by the right of the child itself, and the state must, in certain circumstance, act as its advocate and protector. It cannot, however, act as the master of the family, but only as the protector of a right which the child possesses in itself as a human being, as a person. The right to educate belongs primarily to the family. Since the family, and not school, is the true place of education, since it is the family alone that *can* educate, the family has the primal right *to* educate. The rôle which the state has to play here is only representative and subsidiary. If, in our day, the state is expected to take charge of education, that is only because the family can no longer discharge its duty of education; the state can only take the family's place by doing what should really be done by the family. The state exists for the sake of the family, not the family for the sake of the state. The family is an incomparably superior form of community to the state, for the family is true community. The state can never be a true community; it is, and must be, far too devoid of personality.

The family, however, is not the only community whose rights take precedence of those of the state. Between the family and the state there exist, in the order of creation, a host of intermediate links, all of which, on principle, take precedence of the state, namely all those forms of community which are an integral part of human life. The state is only an integral part of human life in that there must be a supreme, encompassing union of all the primary forms of community, and insofar as the state, with its monopoly of coercive force, must take charge of everything that men do not do of their own free will, but only under compulsion. In itself, human life is conceivable without the state, but it is not conceivable without the family in the wider sense of the word or the community, hence without the organization of the "wider family" growing out of the family. Before the state exists, there exists this concrete community of those who are more or less kin to each other; but before the state exists, there exists also a host of communities of labour. It is not essential to human life that the state should exist, but it is essential to human life that man should work with other men, because he cannot cope as an individual with the problems presented by life and his mind. The association of men for the purpose of coping with material life, and the association for the purpose of intellectual and personal intercourse, are an integral element in the social nature of man, inherent in him and not acquired. Aristotle's term, ζῷον πολιτικόν, a political animal, a term which has perhaps influenced European jurisprudence more deeply than any other, pronounces a great truth in a very dangerous form. It should be, man is a ζῷον κανωνικόν (47), a being predestined to community. In his being as laid down in creation, the need for mutual completion, that is, social community, is an integral element. That is true not only of the sexual community, which finds its fulfilment in the family, but of community in the economic, technical, purely social and intellectual spheres. Work in common is not man's only duty and desire. He is obliged, and desires, to carry on intellectual intercourse, to laugh and weep with others, to play and to argue with them, to act before them and be a spectator with them, to have and be an audience. All these things are antecedent to the state, have their rights which take precedence of the state, are necessities prior to the state. The state is only the last link in the chain of these associations.

Hence the standards of justice obtaining in these forms of community are antecedent to the state; they are formed in manners and customs, agreements, contracts, rites and ceremonies, established rights to which, in the first instance, no state pays heed. It is not the state which sets this life in motion, not the state which determines by which rules it shall proceed, not the state which can pronounce on its justice or injustice. That all lies "in the nature of the thing," the nature of the circumstances and of the men living in them. The state, in all this, comes later, protecting, preserving, regulating, but not as a creative or constitutive agent. Its function is co-ordination and protection, support by its coercive power. As the individual is antecedent to marriage and the family, the family to the community and the manifold communal forms of economic, social and intellectual life, all these things are antecedent to the state, and the manner of their organization, like their standards of justice, are prior to the law of the state. As the trunk of a tree grows in concentric circles, with the outermost the last and biggest, human life grows from the individual by way of the narrower to the wider community.

The wider the circle, the more impersonal the community becomes, the more abstract, the more remote from the personal meaning of life is its "concern." Every wider circle is formed because the narrower one is unable to face a definite, urgent task. The expansion of the circle always means the calling in aid of others for the performance of a task which is beyond the capacity of the individual and the small group. Hence the expansion is always proportional to the comprehensiveness of the concrete task, which, because it is more comprehensive, is more external, less concerned with the personal sphere. In the case of the state, however, another factor enters—the monopoly of coercive power extending to the extreme case of power over life and death. The elements of danger—force, the means of coercion —are, as it were, expelled from the inner circles of the community and collected in the outermost circle. The state is the widest, most embracing circle of organization; in it is vested the monopoly of force. Its legitimate function is hence unique in these two features—its comprehension of all other organizations and its monopoly of coercive force. The state must only do what it alone can do in virtue of the fact that it is the most comprehensive form of organization and is equipped with coercive force. The more vital human life is, the more vigorous the individuals and the smaller, more personal, the communities, the fewer will be the tasks committed to the state and the more will be performed by the communities antecedent to the state. The state has only to take charge of such tasks as are beyond the capacity of the other communities, and of such as arise from unwillingness and from the destructive, anarchic and antisocial tendencies existing in man. The importance of the state grows with the elements of destruction and evil; the more evil men are, the more they need the state; the less the power of evil in them, the more is done that should be done without the state. The coercive law of the state is only a substitute for the lack of voluntary justice.

This federative, organic picture (48) of the structure of human institutions stands in contrast to that which is familiar to us today and has found its terrible consummation in the totalitarian state. The totalitarian state did not first come into being in 1917, 1922 or 1933; it grew gradually out of the modern conception of the sovereignty of the state and the breakdown of individuals and communities, and the deepest cause of that failure is the atrophy of the Christian substance. The more families and communities fail to do, the more the state must do. The state becomes the general servant. It is called in aid for everything because what is needful is not done of men's own free will. The overburdening of the state proceeds in exact proportion to the decay of the communities antecedent to the state, to the structurelessness of human society. A natural, organic structure based on free will is replaced of necessity by the artificial structure of the state, which is imposed by force, and which works from above downwards, from the most comprehensive to the smallest communities and to the individual. What comes into being is the modern centralistic state which fills the void between the central power of the state and the individual with its artificial forms of organization, its departments, districts and sham communities—structures without personal life, mere units of state administration. The state thus created is the substitute for the lost community of the people, and, as such, is the last step towards the totalitarian state. This last step from the centralized to the totalitarian state is achieved by the abolition of the independence of the individual, by the non-recognition of the primal rights of men, the prestate communities having already lost their vitality and their dignity. This inversion of the structure of the state which, instead of being built up from below is organized from above, is the one great iniquity of our time, the iniquity which overshadows all others, and generates them of itself. The order of creation is turned upside down; what should be last is first, the expedient, the subsidiary, has become the main thing. The state, which should be only the bark on the life of the community, has become the tree itself.

The consequence of this inversion is the idea that there are and should be no rights but the rights of the state: we shall deal with this point later.[1] The law of the state is only a just law insofar as it protects and preserves the rights both of individuals and communities, which exist independently of it and are founded on the divine order of justice. And that is the very thing which is so widely contested, or has at any rate become so insecure today. But where it is seriously contested, the idea of the totalitarian state already exists. For the totalitarian state is nothing but the absorption of all rights into the law of the state, that is, the complete freedom of the state to call what it will right, and to recognize no legitimate primal claims, whether of individuals or of groups. The state has become master of everything and everybody, and man, with everything he possesses, has become a slave of the state, without property, without dignity, without freedom. For he is only free insofar as he is entitled to an activity which is not commanded nor permitted by another. But in the totalitarian state, individuals and groups have only as much free play as the state allows. On principle, everything belongs to it—life, strength, freedom, ability, the work of the men living on its territory. Whether the state takes the form of a dictatorship, or plays the farce of democracy, it is all the same, even though the individual citizens who have surrendered to its power are fully convinced that they are masters of this state because they all have the same right to create the state which enslaves them all.

The totalitarian state or federalism (49)—that is the burning issue of justice in our time. But it must be grasped in all its depth, and that means that the totalitarian state must be recognized even in the states and nations which imagine themselves to be democracies and hence immune against the virus of totalitarianism. No *form* of state renders any country immune against totalitarianism, for the totalitarian state has nothing to do with constitutions. It is the "omni-competent state," the turning of all life into a

[1] See inf. Chap 20, section on *Just Law*.

state affair, a phenomenon which only becomes possible when the prestate groups and individuals have been deprived of power. It is true that the omni-competent state has a certain affinity with the dictatorship, but its historical roots are to be found in the republic of the French Revolution, in Rousseau's *Contrat Social*, in his principle of *aliénation totale*, and there is no state which has not suffered, more or less, from this contagion. And one thing must never be forgotten: the totalitarian principle found its most logical expression in Russian communism, for slavery to the state is only consummated when private property is abolished.

... Chapter 17 ...

JUSTICE IN THE FAMILY ORDER

MARRIAGE AND THE FAMILY ARE COMMU-
nities whose practical purpose is most readily permeated by the
purely personal purpose of the personal community, hence in
which justice lies most open to the influence of love. In true
marriage and the family, a synthesis of three highly heterogeneous principles becomes possible—natural love (*eros*), justice,
and Christian love (*agape*). Justice is represented on the subjective plane by faithfulness to the marriage fellowship, or to
the institution of marriage as such. These subjective factors
belong to the sphere of ethics, but not to that of the theory of
justice. What we have to deal with is the justice of the institution itself.

1. JUSTICE IN MARRIAGE

The idea that there is such a thing as a just institution of
marriage is alien to modern, subjective individualism which sees
in marriage only the "bond of love" and can therefore only
recognize justice in marriage in the form of the free contract,
which, freely concluded, can be just as freely dissolved. The
Christian view of marriage, as we saw, is based on the recognition
of the divine "union"—"what God hath joined together, let not
man put asunder." Marriage is an order of creation, that is, man
is so created that, his personality being embedded in a sexual
nature, he can only fulfil his double purpose as a sexual being
and a person in a union which is monogamous and lifelong.
God has so created man that only marriage which is strictly
monogamous and in principle indissoluble can fulfil nature's
purpose of sexual union without prejudice to the purpose of the
person, and the personal purpose without prejudice to the pur-

pose of nature. Only strictly monogamous marriage, being a sexual community of this type, does justice to the claims of personality; any other sexual union is sub-personal. Justice therefore appears in marriage as indissoluble and strictly exclusive monogamy. In this, as in every other fellowship based on the order of creation, the factor of personal equality—equality of dignity and purpose of the person—is united with unlikeness of function. Only where husband and wife recognize absolute equality of worth in each other, and strive to express that equality in all relationships, is the law of justice fulfilled in marriage. That, however, is not the whole of marriage, but only the first step. The next step is: only where the husband gives the wife her due, and the wife the husband his due, is the law of justice fulfilled. What the husband owes to the wife is not the same as what the wife owes to the husband. How closely this form of community approximates to a purely personal relationship we can see by the fact that both husband and wife owe themselves entirely to each other within the sphere of the sexual community. The Apostle expresses this in the following way: "The wife hath not power of her own body, but the husband, and likewise also the husband hath not power of his own body, but the wife."[1] The one *belongs* to the other. The husband has a *right* to his wife, the wife has a *right* to her husband. Hence "let the husband render unto the wife due benevolence; and likewise also the wife to the husband."[2] Where a marriage is good, this precept of justice will not make its appearance as such; both natural and Christian love will render this due "of itself," spontaneously, without the intervention of an imperative of justice. This obligation appears much more often in its negative form, as the claim that that which belongs to the marriage partner shall not be diverted to a third party. Justice appears in marriage as the prohibition of adultery in any form.

In spite of the fact that the husband owes himself to the wife with the same entirety as the wife to the husband, the nature of that entirety is totally different in the two sexes—not different in degree, but different in kind and function. The equality of

[1] I Cor. 7: 3.
[2] *Ibid.*

dignity does not do away with a certain hierarchy of organization. "The husband is the head of the wife."[3] That too, like the principle of monogamy, is founded on God's order of creation.[4] The modern mind, permeated with rationalistic individualism, naturally revolts against that fact and sees in it a degradation of the woman, while in actual fact the true dignity of the woman requires this order, which is inherent in the nature of man and woman, so that any marriage partnership on a different basis is unnatural, and therefore degrading. This hierarchy, which in no way implies an inequality of dignity, will take effect primarily in the family community. It is the patriarchate, not the matriarchate, which is founded on the order of creation; it is, however, safeguarded from degenerating into tyranny and absolutism by the stipulation of equal mutual obligation, in which the equality of personal dignity finds expression.

Marriage, indissoluble and exclusive, is the law of the order of creation, the divine, sacred ordinance. It is the unqualified and divine standard for the recognition of good and evil. It is, however, not unconditionally valid as a law within the compulsive legal system of the state. Jesus does not contest the law of Moses, which was given "for the hardness of your hearts." He merely alludes to it as the antithesis to the ordinance which is primal, and hence morally binding. Nothing else counts for the man who is ready to bind himself by the will of God, but the legal order of the state is a totally different matter. Here, as everywhere else, it is a necessary accommodation to actual reality. Hence "for the hardness of your hearts" the legislator of the state will be obliged to admit the possibility of divorce, but if he knows what true justice is, he will reduce that possibility to the absolute minimum required by the circumstances. A legal system which, for all practical purposes, does not concern itself with adultery, will never be able to maintain a strict order of divorce.

On the other hand, every state will learn by experience that it cannot allow the divine order of creation to be infringed with impunity. All political anarchy in the state begins with anarchy in marriage. The state in which adultery and divorce are the order

[3] Eph. 5: 23.
[4] I Cor. 11: 7 ff.

of the day is also ripe for political decay. No house can be built with mouldering stones; no sound body can grow out of diseased cells. If the social basis, marriage, is rotten, the whole community is rotten. Modern individualism, which has no comprehension of the order of creation, is the solvent of all national community.

2. The Family

The foundation of the family is monogamous marriage. Indeed, it is the family, the child, from which the rule of exclusivity and permanence in the sexual union derives its profoundest meaning. Divorce is a catastrophe for the children, just as adultery on the part of the parents is an utter confusion of their existence. The sexual union must be strictly monogamous, not for the child's sake alone, but primarily for the child's sake. For the objective sense of marriage is the child.[5] Sexual differentiation in creation has no other meaning. It is only in respect of the child that we can understand the fact that we are created different in sex; this, the religious view, tallies with that of biology: the sexual apparatus "serves" procreation.

There is in the family too a justice answering to the order of creation. The difference between the Christian and a naturalistic or rationalistic outlook here becomes clearer than ever. Because the child is the meaning imparted to marriage by creation, the question of marital fertility does not lie within the free will of the parents. The command of creation says quite unequivocally: "Be fruitful and multiply."[6] It is not by chance that this is the first of all Scriptural commandments. Procreation, the root of all human life, is withdrawn from private judgment. All capricious, self-seeking prevention of procreation in marriage is a destruction of the divine order, in which marriage and the family are joined together. Here too, "what God hath joined together, let not man put asunder." Childlessness in marriage, if undesired, is a misfortune; if desired, it is a wrong. The foundation of a family is not a matter for human agreement.[7]

---

[5] Cf. E. Brunner: *The Divine Imperative. A Study in Christian Ethics.*
[6] Gen. 1: 28.
[7] But moral regulation of natural fertility is not excluded thereby. Cf. *The Divine Imperative*, p. 368.

The second point in which the Christian view of justice in the sphere of the family is distinguished from others is once more the fusion of equality with difference. The dignity of the child is equal to the dignity of the parents; the primal right of the child as a person is equal to theirs. The child has a sacred right against its parents which in some cases must be protected by the community. We can infer the fundamental iniquity of divorce solely from the right of the child to father and mother. Wrong is done to the child if it loses father or mother by divorce. The parents thereby deprive the child of something which is due to it by right, and the law in virtue of which it has that right is no human law but the law of the order of creation. On the contrary, it is the order of creation which prescribes to human law that it shall protect the right of the child, and where it does not do so, it is unjust. Nowhere can we see as clearly as here the influence of the Christian conception of justice on the framing of positive law. The protection of the right of the child in modern legislation is the fruit of Christianity.

"The century of the child," however, the emancipation of the child and the adolescent from the family union is not the fruit of Christianity but of individualism. For while Christian faith lays stress on the equal dignity of the child, it also teaches the differences in kind and function between the various members of the family and the community which is their necessary result. All members belong to each other—the father to the child, the child to the father, the mother to the child, the child to the mother, just as the husband belongs to the wife and the wife to the husband. But the manner of belonging is not the same. The child belongs to the father otherwise than the father to the child, and the child belongs to the father otherwise than to the mother. This "otherness" is determined by the divinely created order of nature. It establishes an unequivocal hierarchy of the family which, without prejudice to the equal human dignity of each member, is determined by the functions of the individual members. The father is the head of the family. If a father is incapacitated by weakness from taking his place at the head of the family, the mother must replace him, but if she is a real mother, she knows that it should not be so, that she is only taking another's place, that her position is not natural, not "normal." The hierarchy of the family, father, mother, child, which is the repeated and exclusive teaching of Scripture, responds to unspoilt natural feeling. Both uphold the authority of the father which is valid until the child comes of age. A just code of civil law gives legal expression to this order of creation without infringing the rights of the child as a person. On the contrary, the child has a right to a father's authority. It is deprived of something, it is injured, if it has a father whom it must not obey. A father who loves his child will not deprive it of the authority which demands obedience. It was only an individualism devoid of the sense of community which created the confusion of feeling by which all paternal authority became suspect, while all that was necessary was to stigmatize any capricious or unjust abuse of that authority.

A real family is the perfect example of the co-operation of love and justice, of the ethics of the person and the ethics of institutions. It is love which creates the equal relationship of all the members of the family to each other, but that love must take on a different form in father, mother and child, and that form is determined by justice. The father knows that he must exact obedience from the child, the child knows that it owes that obedience. Only a spoilt child imagines that the obedience due conflicts with love; only a loveless father imagines that his authority invalidates his love. It is the mother, however, who is the natural mediator between the justice of paternal authority and the love which springs freely, which is bound by no justice and no law. In her, love can develop most directly, with least hindrance, because she is not, like the father, immediately responsible for the order of justice, and for the authority which maintains that order. The wealth of relationships which issue in the family from these three facets of justice and love is absolutely inexhaustible and can only be alluded to here. At this point the theological teacher must make way for the Christian writer, a Pestalozzi or a Gotthelf.

. . . Chapter 18 . . .

JUSTICE IN THE ECONOMIC ORDER

THE LIFE OF LABOUR, THE DRAWING OF A SUB-
sistence from the earth, is an institution of the Creator. God has
created man with the duty and capacity of earning his livelihood
in that way. It is a false exegesis to deduce from the story of the
Fall that work is a consequence of sin. Even in the Scriptural
story of Creation, the command to dress and keep the garden
preceded sin.[1] It is only the special toilsomeness of work which
is regarded as the curse entailed by sin. In the Bible, too, economic activity is everywhere regarded, not as an individual
concern, but as the concern of larger or smaller groups, and in
especial, of the "house." The family is not merely the group of
parents and children; it is at the same time an economic unit,
a "family concern."[2] In the same way, the main source of production, the soil, is not an individual, but a communal concern.[3]
And finally, the proceeds of labour, in which wealth consists, is
never merely personal property, but is at the same time communal. It is necessary to consider the various factors in economic
life separately, and to discuss the specific problems they present
from the standpoint of justice.

1. THE JUSTICE OF PROPERTY

As we have already seen, there is no freedom without property;
hence property, private property(50) is a right established by
creation. That, however, implies neither that private property
is a purely individual concern in the sense of being absolutely

[1] Gen. 2: 15.
[2] Cf. Pedersen, *Israel, Its Life and Culture*, pp. 81 ff.
[3] Cf. e.g. Lev. 25.

private property, nor that only private property is just. Since this right, which is established by creation, belongs to everyone, that kind of property which excludes others equally entitled to it, namely the monopoly, is from the outset unjust. There are various kinds of property which are more or less far removed from the right conferred by creation. Hence we must first distinguish between natural and acquired property. In the strict sense of the term, only our own bodies and limbs are natural property, but in a wider sense, the term includes everything which is immediately associated with our person. The more closely property is associated with the person, the more necessary it is for the sake of freedom. Not only our clothes and household goods, but a house of our own has a positive significance for the freedom of personality. A house fosters the growth of the person; the huge block of flats checks it. Everyone knows what the free possession of land meant and still means for the development of a free, spiritually independent agricultural class. Every substitution of collective property for private property becomes a moral danger when it affects property which is closely bound up with the person. We may call this private property in the wider sense.

Strictly speaking, all ownership of things is "acquired." For nobody was born with it. The most natural kind of property is that earned by work, since it is most closely bound up with the person. What a man has earned belongs to him, he has a right to it. But from the standpoint of the order of creation, a further principle holds good: Even this property which belongs to him does not belong to him unconditionally, since it is held under God. With respect to other men, man is an owner, he has plenary control over what belongs to him. With respect to God he is always a steward, a man with an account to render. He is obliged, not by justice, but by compassion, to give to those in need out of what is entirely his property, but those in need have no right to it. It is, however, true that all property, from the standpoint of justice, is held subject to the reservation of fellowship. For all property is acquired under conditions which the acquirer has not himself created. He acquires property under the protection of the state, in a civilized world which he has not himself created. Hence the community has a right to what he has acquired, since it is a passive factor in the acquisition. This is clearly illustrated by the increase of value in land in the neighbourhood of a growing town. The owner of the land acquires wealth without doing anything for it. The community increases the value of his property without labour on his part. It would therefore have the right to appropriate the whole increase in value in the shape of taxes if it were also prepared to run the risk of a decrease in value. Since it is not prepared to do so, it can only appropriate a reasonable part of the increase in value if it is not going to commit an injustice. Yet on principle, all acquired property is in the same case. The acquisition is always to some extent affected by the community within which the individual works and earns. Hence the community always has a partial right to private property which it claims, for instance, in the form of taxes. Ownership, or, as it is usually called, property, raises a problem of justice(51) chiefly when it becomes "great possessions," firstly because, under the capitalist system, it entails economic power over other men, which will be dealt with later, further because, as landed property, it is held at the cost of others. While the possession of movables is on principle unlimited, and the wealth of one man does not exclude the possibility of wealth for another, landed property within a well-populated country always entails an exclusion of others from possession. Hence the demand for justice is nowhere so urgent as in respect of land(52). By the divine order of creation, every man has, on principle, the right to the land from which he can draw a subsistence. But since, in consequence of the division of labour and the whole development of urban settlement and industry, only part of mankind can really devote itself to primitive production, the claim for a just share of fertile land has been transformed into the claim for a just share in the proceeds of all labour, the problem of land remaining a special case.

This problem presents itself more exactly as the conflict between the historical and the real aspect of possession. Historically, landed proprietorship is founded on manifold titles of very diverse value—colonial settlement, conquest, robbery, distribution by the state, acquisition by purchase and inheritance, and so on. On the other hand, that legal title which is paramount for the proof of the justice of possession in other cases does not operate here, namely acquisition by personal labour, since the possession of land is the presupposition of personal labour on it. The claim of just possession, however, is most nearly fulfilled when it is based on future labour. The man who means to work the land is most justified in owning it. In the Christian view of justice, land "belongs" primarily to the man who tills it, and belongs, moreover, in proportion to his willingness and capacity to till it. It is unjust when a man owns land, but does not till it, and when the man who tills it does not own it. Hence a just system of property organized by the state must always be guided by the principle laid down in creation. That system is just insofar as it corresponds to that principle, unjust insofar as it does not. Measured by the standard of justice, all historical title-deeds must yield to this real principle. It is the business of the community to see that any man who is willing and able to till the soil shall have soil of his own to till, and that no historical title-deed should obstruct that primal justice. A free agricultural class is not only of the utmost value from the sociological point of view, but can be shown to be a primary postulate of the Christion conception of justice, while the Old Testament regards a free peasantry as the normal mode of existence once the nomad stage has been overcome.

The free peasant, however, means in concrete reality the peasant family. The union of economic life and the family—the *economica*—comes out nowhere so clearly as here. The peasant family is a natural unit of labour. And as the association between person and property is particularly close here, the continuity of property from generation to generation is also particularly evident. Not only does the peasant belong to his land, but the peasant family belong to their land. What the peasant does for his land he does, albeit unwittingly, for future generations. The work he does today, such as the planting of trees and the improvement of the soil, may never benefit himself, but only his grandchildren. Hence because the "house" as a whole is bound up with the land, we can see here the justice of a form of property for which it is not so easy to find an ethical justification—namely inherited property. The bond between the farmer and his land is not cut off by the death of one generation; the next is standing ready and has already grown into the bond. Hence it seems unquestionably just that agricultural land should pass by inheritance to the children, who will work it in their turn. The community has every reason to protect this natural continuity by its legal system and to keep it as free as possible of any factors which might affect it adversely.

One of these factors—the antithesis to the peasant right of ownership—is the individualistic conception of property.[4] It is precisely because the land does not belong to the individual farmer, but to the "house," to those who work it as a community, that the individual farmer should have no unqualified right to dispose of it in any way, for instance, by sale. Agricultural land is not marketable, it has a character of its own. It lies in the vital interests, not only of the family community of the farmer, but of the nation and the state, to see that agricultural land should not become an object of speculation and hence be arbitrarily alienated from its purpose(53). The bond between the individual right of ownership and the rights of the community is particularly close here.[5]

This, however, leads to the question of the justice of inherited property which is not agricultural land. It is at once evident that household goods and other family property are in exactly the same case as land. The principle that the personal factor in property—and here "personal" refers to the family—is the standard for just possession holds good in this case also. Whatever is associated with the family life would have a continuity outlasting death and hence is righteous inheritance. But the slighter the connection is, the weaker becomes the claim to just inheritance. The individualistic conception of property—

[4] Peasant inheritance is frequently mentioned in Scripture and is protected by the law. Cf. Deut. 21. ff.; Num. 36, etc.

[5] The Israelite law of inheritance is a beautiful blend of individual and communal elements.

in this case the conception of property embodied in Roman law —gives the owner unqualified right of disposition over his property even after death. We have had to reject this individualistic conception of property from the standpoint of the Christian conception of justice. We have already seen that a farmer should not have the right to alienate the land from his children at his own free will, by gift or by sale; in the same way, the ownership of money and "impersonal" property beyond death is not unlimited, whether in the sense of inheritance or in the sense of freedom of bequest. Here the reservation of the community enters into full force. There can be no question of an *unqualified* right of inheritance. Inherited property can neither be called unjust nor unconditionally just.

There is, however, justice in it. Inherited property is the concrete substratum of the family union, the bond of continuity through the generations. Where inheritance ceases, the family tie is apt to come to an end too. That is one of the reasons why family feeling is so terribly weak in the proletariat. Where the young family always has to make a fresh economic start, its sense of dependence on the previous generation is not sufficiently real. The abolition of inheritance by law, which has so often been mooted, would be a catastrophe for the family as a social institution. There is a second point. If a man's property were to pass at his death to the state and not to his family, we should soon have the communistic state. But, as we shall see later, the communistic state is the acme of injustice. On the other hand, it is obvious that the state has a partial right to property which does not accrue directly to the family but to more distant relatives, and it asserts that right, in the legal system of our day, in the form of graded death duties.

A central problem of the justice of property has, from time immemorial, been presented by the "just distribution of wealth." For equalitarian thought, just distribution means equal distribution. "Why should one have more than another?" While in the case of salary or wages, inequality of performance seems to justify an inequality of income, the inequality of distribution becomes less obvious to the sense of justice when possessions or ownership are concerned. The protagonist of inequality, at this particular point, incurs the suspicion of simply defending the *status quo*, if not of special pleading. From the standpoint of the Christian view of justice, this identification of equality and justice must be rejected. The principle of simple, arithmetical equality, as we saw, only corresponds to the order of creation where the dignity of the human being as such is concerned. On the contrary, wherever the question at issue is not the dignity of persons as such but their living together in the community, the ruling principle is difference requiring and capable of mutual completion. The aim of creation is not the equality of all, but most manifestly difference. Difference is the pre-condition of living intercourse, indeed of life itself, for it is the principle of organism. Equality in society creates mechanism, not organism. Our natural feeling tells us that nothing would be more intolerable than equality. Without the difference arising from inequality, there would be no social "incline," no current, no flow of intercourse. The Christian principle of justice does not mean equality but compensation. Inequality of possessions is the necessary result of difference in economic efficiency, in capacity for work, in energy, in thrift—that is, in the power to forego the immediate satisfaction of needs—and in enterprise. It is just that the man who does more should receive more than the man who does less. It is just that the thrifty man should keep the proceeds of his thrift, and should not be put on an equal footing with the man who spends what he earns, and it is just that the man who ventures should receive a larger share of the profits of the venture than the man who takes the safe road, risking nothing. It would be unjust if the industrious and capable worker were to receive no more than the lazy and inefficient one, if the savings of the thrifty man were taken for the benefit of the man who spends all he earns, and if the enterprising were deprived of the reward of their enterprise. Justice here tallies with what the economy of the state requires if it is to remain alive. All the conditions we have here called unjust would also paralyse economic life and result in general impoverishment—a fact which was demonstrated both in its positive and negative form by the

Russian experiment. The principle of equality is economically as ruinous as it is unjust.

That, however, is only one side of the matter. The actually existing inequality of possessions cannot only be attributed to and justified by the factors already enumerated. It is firstly due, in considerable measure, to chance—the one has "luck," the other none—but it is still more the result of an *exaggeration* of those motives which deserve a just reward, hence not merely of ability but of an unrestrained lust of gain, not merely of thrift but of avarice, not merely of enterprise, but of unscrupulousness and brutality in the pursuit of economic ends. The greater a man's possessions, the greater will be the suspicion that those possessions do not represent the just award we have spoken of, but are the result of energies devoid of public spirit. In our day we must consider the problem of property not only in timeless generalizations but also with respect to the peculiar character of contemporary economic life, which is marked by two features which are themselves merely two aspects of one and the same basic fact, firstly the development of the tool into machinery on the biggest scale in factories and large-scale industrial plant, and secondly the separation of the ownership of means of production from personal labour. A further factor connected with these two is the anonymity of property—share capital, etc. This form of economy is inherent in modern technology and is unalterable. But it lies in its very nature automatically to enhance the inequalities in possession and to foster motives which are inimical to community. Present-day industry cannot exist without large capital; the mechanization of economy creates a bias to the accumulation of capital and to the centralization of control. The result is that the possessing class grows automatically wealthier without any special effort of work or thrift and indeed without any special qualities of enterprise. It is in a sense quite alien to that of Scripture that we realize the truth of the Scripture saying: "To him that hath shall be given and from him that hath not shall be taken away even that which he hath." Hence it is absolutely right that very great possessions should be felt to be unjust, because even the plain man feels that there is in them no vestige of the just analogy between ability and wealth. This distrust of great wealth is in line with the Scriptural judgment of wealth(54), especially that of the New Testament, although the latter rests less on justice than on love and fellowship with God. The rich man is in danger of losing eternal salvation because he is tempted to become either avaricious and hard-hearted or godlessly sure of himself. The question at issue here, however, is merely that of justice or injustice. The present-day inequalities in wealth are unquestionably unjust because they are founded less on a greater achievement—whether in work, thrift or enterprise —than on the privilege conferred on the possessing class by the contemporary form of economy. That is the element of justification in the popular resentment against "capitalism" and the capitalist.

The tragic element in the development of the economy of our day, however, lies in the fact that the accumulation and centralization of capital, which runs counter to the economic order laid down in creation, seems to have taken on the character of an unescapable fate. We cannot go back to the handicrafts of the Middle Ages; the factory and the large-scale industrial concern are our destiny. Insofar as that may be accepted as the truth, we have only the choice between private capitalism and state capitalism, between the anonymity of wealth and joint stock enterprise and the bureaucratic machinery of the economic state. This question will be dealt with in detail later.

The Christian doctrine of justice demands, as we have seen, not equality but compensation. The economic law of the Old Testament aims, not at equality, but very definitely at compensation, at a mitigation of inequality. Very great possessions in the hands of the few always entail a danger to the community of the people; huge fortunes are as dangerous to the economy of a people as mammoth states to world politics. For immoderate possessions imply immoderate power, the abolition of equality before the law and a menace to the freedom of others. The mammoth trust is a state within the state, and can afford a course of conduct which would be permitted to no individual citizen. It is incumbent upon any economic order which aims at justice to combat this monstrosity. The modern state appears to be approximating the Scriptural idea of compensation by applying the sliding scale of taxes to excessive fortunes and profits. But however just it may be, and however much it may serve the common welfare that the burdens of the strong should be greater than those of the weak, the community will have to reckon with the fact that there is a limit to the process, and that to transgress that limit is in its turn unjust and disastrous to the vigour of economic life. It is killing the goose that lays the golden eggs. The accumulation of capital is necessary if the economic life of the community is to go on. But there is a degree of taxation which makes the accumulation of capital impossible and at the same time throttles the spirit of enterprise. We shall, however, see later that the apparent solution—the collectivism of wealth in state socialism, which must, of its nature, be state capitalism—is precisely the false solution.

2. JUST INTEREST

There is hardly an element of modern economics which has of late been so frequently, so vehemently and apparently so justifiably denoted as unjust as the interest on capital—"unearned income." That a rich man should have the right to become richer without labour for the simple reason that he is already rich, that he should pocket interest on his bank deposit, dividends on his shares, and yet more shares which bring in yet more interest, is in actual fact an outrage to our natural sense of justice and, in extreme cases, a cause of indignation. When the word "capitalist" is used as an insult it is mainly this aspect of capital which is meant. It must not, of course, be asserted, as it is often asserted, that this aspect of capitalism is typically modern and "capitalistic" and that it is to the glory of the mediaeval church that it did not acknowledge the institution of interest in its so-called canonical prohibition of interest. On the contrary, the Middle Ages were familiar with interest and the mediaeval church not only acknowledged, but profited largely by it. Indeed, a considerable part of its worldly possessions consisted of interest in the form corresponding to the economic system of the day, which was a natural economy, and to the contemporary form of capital, which mainly consisted in land. That form of interest was the rent-charge(55). Even the rent-charge was unearned income. The tenant farmer who worked the land paid the landowner, who did not work it, annual interest in the form of "tithes" on the harvest. The canonical prohibition of interest on money, however, which is held to be so important, was a result of the Aristotelian and scholastic theory of the "unfruitfulness of money," which, in its turn, corresponded to a certain extent to the real facts of that time. For the economy of that day was actually incapable of making money "bear fruit"; interest was, as a rule, not interest on productive loans but on so-called loans for consumption. The "usurer" exacted a (high) interest for a loan by which he helped some poor craftsman or peasant out of temporary distress. This state of things changed radically with the modern technique of traffic and production, when the factory and the large-scale industrial plant replaced the old workshop and the money and credit system gave the old business of loans a productive meaning. From that time on, however, money, transformed as "capital" into means of production, could "bear fruit" to an enormous extent. Indeed, by the technological revolution, the money capital lent for purposes of production became the determining factor in the economic order. Thereby interest and the problem of interest took on a completely new meaning and an unprecedented importance.

What the industrial worker of our day feels to be above all unjust, and what Karl Marx attempted to interpret scientifically in his theory of surplus value, is the fact that a very large part of the total income from labour in our day is deducted as interest on the loan of capital for production to become unearned income in the form of interest on bank deposits, debentures, shares, etc., and hence is not enjoyed by those who have done the work. "It is not those who have worked who become rich but those who have lent the money." So runs the judgment. The farmer is in exactly the same position with his heavily mortgaged land, for, at the end of the financial year he sees that, in spite of his fifteen-hour working day he has just got enough from his land to pay his ground rent, while the ground landlord, who receives the major part of his harvest, has not raised a finger to bring it in. That is why the worker and the farmer denounce unearned income as a crying injustice.

It would be useless to deny that interest on capital and ground rent are unearned income. Although most capitalists, in addition to being capitalists, are also *entrepreneurs* working full time for their firm, that has nothing to do with interest on capital as such. Not every capitalist is an *entrepreneur* and not every *entrepreneur* a capitalist. The capitalist is the man who pays money to others for work he does not do himself, but from which he draws the interest on his capital. Interest on capital has primarily nothing to do with the income of the *entrepreneur*; only the former is unearned income, not the latter. Hence it is incontestable that interest on capital is unearned income, and that is the point which renders it ethically dubious. To call income unearned does not necessarily mean that it is undeserved. It is not only work that counts for justice, but any service rendered. What service can the lender of capital claim to have rendered which would ethically justify interest on capital? His service is twofold. Firstly, any man lending ready money owns it in part as the proceeds of former work and as the result of saving. Saving, however, means the postponement of consumption. The whole of material culture rests on this foregoing of immediate consumption. A nation that neither will nor can save has no means available for cultural purposes, no reserves for material culture. Hence it is both unjustifiable and detrimental that of late years saving should have been held up to ethical suspicion or ridicule in various quarters. The great moral dangers doubtless involved in saving cannot alter the fact that it is a presupposition of all higher culture(56). In a dispassionate consideration of the problem of interest it is also of great importance to remember that a large part of interest on capital, especially that from the banks, accrues to the benefit of the small saver who year by year puts his hardly earned savings in the bank or the savings bank, or invests it in a debenture, and hence places his savings at the disposal of production.[6] It is not only the rich who draw their interest on capital and are hence capitalists, drawing unearned income, but also the majority of our certainly not rich, hard-working and thrifty fellow countrymen. Though this saving is carried on for personal reasons, it is, as a postponement of consumption, a merit which can by no means be morally taken for granted, and is, as a basis of the national economy, a very great achievement indeed. The fact that productive capital exists is due to saving. Even in a completely communistic economy there would have to be saving. Reserves would have to be built up for new means of production (factories, power stations, etc.) so that production could go on, only that this saving would take place automatically in the form of deductions from wages dictated by the authorities.

These individual savers would, of course, have the right to consume their savings themselves. When a man has collected a small sum by years of hard work and self-denial, he has a right to it. He might travel or buy something beautiful with it, and nobody could blame him. If he does not do so, but puts the money in the bank and hence makes its available for production, every year that he leaves his savings in the bank he renders a service to the national economy by his postponement of consumption, and he therefore has a right to claim an annual return for his self-denial and the service he renders. That return is his interest. Hence interest—we are dealing with its principle and not its rate—is unearned income but not undeserved income. It is, on the contrary, the income deserved by the postponement of the immediate consumption of money earned by labour. Interest, in the sense of this return for real service, is therefore just. The active saver has a right to a return since, unlike the man who immediately consumes his savings, he does not at once consume the remuneration for his work, but places it at the disposal of production in the form of capital.

There is a second point. The saver would also have the right

---

[6] In Switzerland there are about four million savings bank books representing a value of six milliard francs. A very considerable proportion of all interest goes to the small saver.

to hide his savings somewhere safe at home—to "keep it in a sock." Nobody could call such a proceeding unjust; the right is given him by his ownership. If he does not do so, however, but places his property at the disposal of the community for purposes of production, he takes a risk. He might think his money safer at home, in the sock, than in the bank, and the idea might well arise in the age of bank failures. If he accepts the risk of placing it at the disposal of the community for purposes of production by putting it in the bank, he has again a right to a certain return for that service which is useful to the community and cannot be demanded of him. Thus interest, besides being a return for self-denial, is also a return for risk incurred(57). Hence, as a matter of principle—always apart from the question of the rate of interest—there is justice in interest which consists of two components, a just return for postponement of consumption and a just return for the risk of lending.

Thus the matter is not, as many people imagine, that interest is unjust but inevitable, because otherwise people would not save and put their savings in the bank. The second statement is certainly true, the first untrue. Justice always means a correspondence between the service rendered and the return for that service. The service which a man renders by lending money to the community costs him something, namely the trouble of saving, of temporary self-denial and of overcoming the fear of loss. He can justly claim a return for this two-fold service. If the *Freigeld*⁷ theory claims that hoarding, the sock system, could be dealt with by other means than interest, there may be some truth in it, and the invention of "rubber money" does great credit to the ingenuity of its inventor. But even if the lending of savings could be enforced in this way, and even if we assume that thrift would not be paralysed, but fostered by it—a bold assumption—the just claim for a return for the double service would remain unfulfilled. Every thrifty man would feel himself a fool in comparison with the spendthrift, since he takes self-denial upon himself without getting any return for it.

⁷ There is no English equivalent for this word. It has been rendered as "money with a disappearing value." Tr.

It therefore bears witness to the Reformers' sense of justice that they regarded interest on capital as in itself just and stigmatized, not interest itself, but excessive extortionate interest, "usury," as unjust. That view goes to the root of the matter (58). It is not interest itself which is iniquitous but the disproportion between the share of capital (interest) and the share of labour (wages, salaries) in the total income, hence not interest in itself, but excessive interest. That is the germ of truth in Karl Marx's theory of surplus value, as seen from the standpoint of justice. But what is a just rate of interest? The Council of Geneva, under the influence of Calvin, laid down 5 per cent as the highest rate, and both Luther and Zwingli on occasion expressed similar views.[8] This calculation was clearly based on the simple consideration that a rate of 5 per cent corresponded roughly to what an owner of capital was entitled to by foregoing his right to consume his capital and lending it. If he were to spend that capital within one generation, there would be a yearly consumption of a certain percentage, to which must be added some small return for the risk run. Thus the 5 per cent is not a fancy figure. It cannot, however, serve as a standard for us. On the contrary, we must say that a "just" rate of this kind cannot be determined and that, moreover, in a free economy, a regulation by statute, even with the best will of all concerned could hardly be carried through without a dislocation of the whole economic apparatus.

The principle, however, is clear: *just* interest can only be that which corresponds to the service rendered by the lender to the community as compared with the service rendered by the workers. Hence it is clear that interest on capital which curtails the just wage of the labourer is unjust. The lender of capital has a just claim for a return, but it must yield to the claim of the worker for a just wage. The economic order, as divinely appointed, is not there to satisfy demands for high rates of interest, but to nourish the community and to provide it with the necessaries of life. The claim: I can demand a return for my savings is justified, but there is a claim which takes precedence of it: I

[8] For Calvin, see Wünsch, *op. cit.*, p. 335.

can expect a proper wage for my honest work. It is self-evident that the *entrepreneur* can claim a "wage" for his work, his personal stake in the whole and his enterprise, and again a "wage" which answers to his service to the community. From the standpoint of its justice, interest will always come second to the claim for wages in its various forms, while from the standpoint of economic necessity it will always acquire an undue ascendancy. For where there is no enticement of satisfactory interest, there is an end of saving and lending, and when that comes to an end, the economic system is paralysed. The only alternative is then the compulsory saving and compulsory lending of the communistic totalitarian system. Even where this alternative is rightly rejected as the greatest of all social evils and the most unjust of all conceivable systems, it is still within the power of the community to put a stop to the excesses of the system of interest— exorbitant rates, exorbitant dividends, and other excessive profits on shares—and to relieve certain classes of the population from oppressive and undeserved burdens of interest in a way which serves the welfare of the whole. But that it may be the Christian duty of the individual who is due to receive interest from another to forego, wholly or in part, the interest, legally due him, has no place in the doctrine of justice but only in the doctrine of love. It is, however, that very point which must be emphasized by Christian pastors in Christian teaching. Such was the admonition of Calvin: "It may happen that a man cannot make the smallest profit by interest without sin against God and wrong to his neighbour."[9] It is the duty of the community, on the other hand, so to organize the institution of interest within the limits of economic necessity that the primacy of the right of the workers over that of unearned (not undeserved) income may come most forcibly to expression.

But what if Scripture forbids the Christian to accept interest at all? It may seem surprising that we should turn to this question only at the end of our argument. Our justification will appear from a closer consideration of the prohibition. The view that a prohibition of interest is pronounced in the Bible is based on

[9] Quoted by Wünsch, *op. cit.*, p. 335.

Mosaic law, since the problem does not arise in the New Testament. The two passages usually, but erroneously, quoted in this connection[10] do not deal with the taking of interest but exhort men to lend to the needy for love even if they cannot count on repayment. On the other hand, there are various passages in the law of Moses which expressly forbid interest.[11]

The appeal to these Old Testament prohibitions of interest is a perfect example of that theological exploitation of Scripture which should simply be prevented by a true reverence for the word of revelation.[12] For what is meant by "interest" in these Old Testament texts has nothing to do with what we call interest today. Lending in the Old Testament is an act of compassion towards a needy neighbor. It is explicitly stated: "If thou lend money to any of my people that is poor by thee," and again: "If thy brother be waxen poor" . . . . No compensation is to be demanded for a work of compassion, charity is not to degenerate into business. There is no question here of productive loans, of a transaction to be regarded from the outset as a business proposition for the purpose of economic activity. The man to whom the loan is granted is not one who is going to build a factory or found a commercial firm, but a poor man who is to be saved from ruin. Thus the loan is not, as in our time, an integral element in a comprehensive economic system, but an exceptional case, an act of emergency. One of the integral elements of the economy of the day was slavery, which is not only not forbidden, but explicitly approved.[13] Anyone who attempts to make use of Scriptural law in the problem of interest must do so consistently; hence he must regard the institution of slavery as permitted.

Interest on capital in our sense of the word is not mentioned anywhere in the Old Testament because, like productive capital as a whole in our sense, it was unknown. On the other hand, in the parable of the talents it is certainly referred to. The lazy servant, who did not wish to work himself with his master's

[10] Matt. 5:42, Luke 6: 34.
[11] Exod. 22: 25, Lev. 25: 35ff., Num. 23: 20.
[12] Calvin also refuses to admit that the Old Testament prohibition is binding on us.
[13] Lev. 25: 44 ff.

money could have put the money to the exchangers, so that his master might have "received his own with usury."[14] This process, however, merely serves the purpose of an illustration in the parable; it raises no problem. The most that could be said is that it is presumed as self-evident and useful. It involves no condemnation of interest or the taking of interest. In short, a prohibition of interest can only be deduced directly from Scripture, even if the texts are used legitimately, by a monstrous confusion. It is utterly misleading to appeal to a Scriptural prohibition in the fight against interest on capital, however much the basic motives of Scripture, brotherly love and social justice, are dominant in this as in every other question of social ethics. But simply to speak of a "prohibition of interest"—whether in the Old Testament or the mediaeval church, is unwarrantable and misleading. Interest *is* ethically dubious; there is justice in it, but it is a subordinate justice which in no way is able to justify the enormous importance it actually has in the economy of our day. But how the community is to settle the problem in the sense of justice without ruining its economic system or plunging it into still greater injustice, remains for the present an open question.

3. THE JUST PRICE

It was not the Middle Ages, but Aristotle, who first raised the question of the *justum pretium* (59); we shall, however, see at once that there are difficulties in attempting to apply the notion of justice to this most complex of economic problems. The problem of prices does not arise in every form of economy. In primitive personal economy, where each produces for his own needs, it is unknown. Even the economic system organized entirely on communistic lines, in which vouchers are issued to all according to a definite system of distribution, has no prices because it has no market and no exchange. Prices only exist where there are free markets, i.e. in the non-communistic economy of division of labour. A price is what a man receives on the market as remuneration for what he offers. Abstractly formulated, a just

[14] Matt. 25: 14 ff.

price would be an equivalent remuneration. Thus the principle of justice as simple equality comes into force here; the just price, in this understanding of the term, was for Aristotle the perfect example of arithmetical justice.

What, however, is this "equivalent" for which the object of exchange is exchanged? Here we find, side by side, divergent principles by which this equivalent is to be determined. Firstly there is the subjective and the objective principle. An equivalent is what *has* the same value in the objective sense, in actual value for life, that is, what makes the same contribution to the structure of life. *Or* an equivalent is what *appears* equal to the individual in the subjective sense, i.e. what satisfies him as a remuneration. But since an objective vital necessity can at most be conceived for the maintenance of physical life, since all the more refined values only become necessities of life through the value attached to them or the enjoyment they provide—what can a Rembrandt etching mean to a savage?—and since on the other hand the subjective satisfaction cannot be a standard of justice, this objective valuation is superseded from another quarter by its labour value; the just price is determined by the expenditure of labour. The just price is the price corresponding to that labour. Yet even this principle proves unserviceable, for there is obviously worthless labour, and there are differences in the amount of labour to which there are no corresponding differences in value. None of these attempts to arrive at a just price by a direct determination of equivalent value leads to any satisfactory result. An objectively just price might possibly be discovered provided that the same commodity was equally necessary to everybody, and a subjectively just price provided that everybody attached an equal value to things. In the same way, a determination of the just price could be arrived at on the basis of the expenditure of labour provided that the time and energy spent on the labour corresponded to the value of the work. But since none of these assumptions can stand, none of these ways of determining the just price is practicable.

An indirect way may possibly lead us to the desired result. We may ask why there are unjust prices at all. How can a man accept, for something he offers, a lower value than it is worth? We are all familiar with the two diametrically opposite cases in which we can speak of an unjust price—namely when it is too high or when it is too low. The excessively high price arises when a scarcity is exploited by the seller. The excessively low price arises when an overstocked market is exploited by the buyer. But in both cases the "exploitation" means that the normal psychology of exchange is functioning—buy as cheap, sell as dear as possible. The not-unjust, i.e. the just, price would therefore arise when supply and demand were balanced, or when they were not balanced, but seller and buyer were prevented by the community from acting according to that "normal" psychology of exchange and compelled to exchange as if the balance existed. It would therefore be the duty of the community either to take charge of the balance of supply and demand, or by active intervention to regulate prices as if the balance existed. Something approximating the latter is familiar to us in the state regulation of prices. The former would require the complete control of trade and industry by the community, that is, something in the nature of the totalitarian state.

Quite apart, however, from the dangerous aspect of both these state mechanisms for the determination of the just price, two questions arise. Firstly, is there really such a thing as the balance of supply and demand? Is not demand always guided by supply? Who would not gladly buy all kinds of things if he could have them at a price within his means? The notion "balance of supply and demand" is obviously a fiction, without real value as a method of enquiry. Secondly, is the equivalent value with which the exchanger feels satisfied really the just price? Is not this satisfaction a mere acceptance of what is normally received rather than a *just* remuneration? Thus even this indirect way leads to no satisfactory result.

Yet there is in these two diametrically opposed "unjust" prices a hint, if not of the solution of the problem of the just price, at any rate of an important fact with which justice is concerned. A certain stability of supply and demand is actually in the urgent interests of the community, and not only that, but also, and above all, the freedom of the market from artificial control by monopolies. The freedom of exchange from all monopolies and from all monopolistic manipulation of prices is a great benefit, and a primary condition of a sound economic system.[15] This relative stability and relative freedom is a vital concern of the community. Further, it is to the interest of the community—and this is the element of truth in the notion of objective value —that vital commodities should be on the market in sufficient but not excessive quantities. When these conditions are fulfilled, something like a just price arises on the market of itself.

In this sense the somewhat slogan-like postulate of production for need in contrast to production for profit has a reasonable meaning, while used absolutely it is nonsense. For what is need? Where is the limit of need? What would have to be produced and supplied in order to cover a need? Let us put the matter more modestly: an economic system is sound when the main necessaries of life are produced or offered for sale in sufficient but not excessive quantities, whatever be the means by which this result is reached. That is a reasonable proposition, at any rate within the limits of a purchasing power assumed as stable. We can also say of such a state of the economic system that a seller, in virtue of this stability, would receive a relatively "equivalent" return for the goods he offers, and insofar a "just price." This idea, understood in very relative fashion and confined within definite limits, can serve as a guide for a just economic order. For the rest, we will admit that the problem of prices can only be brought within the scope of justice with great difficulty. That is not surprising, for it lies on the extreme circumference of ethics, and on the border line of pure technique.

4. JUST WAGES

Wages too can be brought under the heading of price as exchange value for labour. Labour will then be regarded as an object of exchange, and its justice will be as controversial as

[15] In the form in which it was then known, the monopoly was denounced by the prophets of the Old Testament as the supreme injustice.

that of price. Hence the first proposition of a doctrine of just wages must run: Labour must *not* be regarded as saleable goods. Only when this principle has been established is there any sense in enquiring what just wages are. Where wages become a market-able value, they are abandoned to the fluctuations of supply and demand, and when wages are made to depend on supply and demand, labour is shorn of its dignity as service. What was formerly called "the free contract of labour," on which the liberal theory of wages was based in the initial stages and heyday of capitalism, is now generally admitted to be a fiction. With reference to the individual worker, the large-scale employer has something like a monopoly; for the worker he is the owner of a monopoly of opportunity for work. On the worker's side there is no free exchange. While the employer is not obliged to take him and his work, the worker is obliged to take the work. As an individual he has no reserves which would permit him to reject the offer of wages. The association of workers in trade unions was primarily nothing but a compensation for this in-equality. Only the union, not the individual worker, is equal in power to the employer, and hence free.

The development of the trade union movement, however, has a deeper, more essential significance. It paved the way for a relationship of service in which labour is no longer regarded as a commodity. Hence it aims not only at a quantitative, but also at a qualitative change in the relationship of work or wages. This trade union movement is, more or less unconsciously, sustained by Christian motives, a thing which cannot be said of the socialist-communist movement.[16] From the standpoint of the Christian idea of justice, labour is a social, and not merely an individual matter.

Labour is not merely a commodity, an item in the costs of pro-duction. "The labourer is worthy of his hire."[17] Just as it is unjust according to the Christian principle of justice if the em-ployer simply dismisses the worker because he wants to or be-cause it is more profitable, it is also unjust if he pays him no

---

[16] For socialism, v. Note 62.
[17] Luke 10: 7; I Tim. 5: 18; Deut. 24: 14.

more than the wage which he must pay by the law of supply and demand, that is, the "cheapest" that he can bargain for. The trade union movement was primarily intended simply to force up this purchase price by an artificial scarcity of the "commodity," labour, to a higher rate than it would have reached in an individual contract. Gradually, however, it developed in another direction. Its aim is now to release the worker from this degrading dependence on the law of demand, to see that the worker gets "his wage," the wage that he and his work are worth. But what wage is he worth? Here we find two rival principles of wages— the wage according to need and the wage according to output. Which is just? It is just that the man who does more should receive more. It is just that the man who does his best, even though it be a poor best, should be treated as a full member of the working community, as a human being who should have the right to a human existence. Hence a combination of the two principles of wages must be arrived at. In accordance with what has been said above, "existence" must be taken to comprise the existence of the family. The resistance of certain labour circles to the recognition of the family wage arises from that atomistic, individualistic manner of thought which is the basis of Marxism. But it is only right if they resist the elimination of the wage for output. The lazy man should not receive the same wage as the hard worker, the incompetent as the competent, the unskilled as the skilled. A gradation is necessary not only as an incentive but in the interests of justice.

The most violent conflict in economic life rages round the standard of wages, which means in the first instance the workers' share in the total proceeds of labour. How much is the worker to receive and how much the capitalist? What underlies this question is simply the question of the relationship between work and interest, the remuneration which the employer receives for his work standing on the side of wages and not of interest. It is not felt to be unjust if the employer receives a substantially higher return for his initiative, enterprise and foresight than the ordinary worker. The stumbling-block is that the capitalist who, as such, does no work, should reap so rich a reward for his loan.

It is true that there is occasionally a personal union of capitalist and employer, so that it is difficult in practice to distinguish interest on capital from remuneration to the employer(60). Yet on principle the functions should be distinguished. Even the employer is "worthy of his hire," but the capitalist, regarded purely from the standpoint of justice, should receive no more than corresponds to the service rendered, which consists in abstention from consumption and acceptance of risk. The struggle of labour against the high dividend is always justified where high dividends exist side by side with low wages. But where high dividends go with high wages, the community must intervene to effect an adjustment in favour of the community, above all to stabilize wages as far as that can be done, for instance by the creation of reserves for times of depression. For the community has to reckon with a third possibility, low dividends and low wages. It must realize that it has the right and the duty to regard excessive fluctuations as a problem of justice. While in times of unemployment or trade depression its duty is to help the workman to maintain a decent standard of living, it has the right, in times of prosperity, to take its toll of excessive profits, not in order to swell the exchequer, but to obtain the means necessary for the fulfilment of its duty in time of need. This regulative intervention on the part of the community in no way entails Communism or state socialism. The community is not, and should not be, an industrial and trading concern. It is there to supervise and accommodate. That is its right and its duty.

The relation of economic labour to the community, however, gives rise to another postulate which is usually overlooked by those who demand a just wage. There is not only an exploitation of the worker by a profit-greedy capital; the reverse might happen—for instance as a result of economic exhaustion due to war—that the total revenue would shrink to such a point that it could no longer suffice to cover claims for wages which are in themselves justified. At that point the right of property becomes subject to the "social reservation." At such times the community has the right to limit the property rights of the wealthy and to take from the "substance," the existing wealth, what is necessary for the maintenance of a decent standard of wages for labour. Nobody has the right to live in ease and enjoyment in times of distress just because he is rich, while the majority of his fellow countrymen are starving. The right to adjust is an obligation, not of individual charity, but of social justice. The community is then as it were under military law, and laws come into force which would be operative in a state of siege. Capital is faced with the duty of service by adjustment.

For a man brought up in liberal ideas of economy, that may smack of "Communism" or "state socialism." But it has nothing to do with either. The principle of free economy is not called in question, private property in the means of production is not regarded as an evil, nor their socialization as a panacea. But the economic community is certainly regarded as a whole, and hence the right of the worker to a decent living wage regarded as a duty incumbent on the community. "Every labourer is worthy of his hire." A decent standard of living for the man who honestly does his duty is an obligation on society which it has to fulfil within the limits of possibility. But "possibility" does not mean what is possible while respecting all right of property. The right to property, from the Christian standpoint, is always subject to the social reservation. It is not an unconditional right. "Property" has to proceed to perform its duty of adjustment where this is the only way of providing the worker with a decent living wage. His wage must be made independent of economic fluctuations. That is the only way of respecting his dignity as a person. The person of the wealthy is not degraded if he is called upon to perform this duty of adjustment, and private property is not abolished thereby. To supervise and adjust does not mean to exercise unlimited control, but to participate, and this participation in property and in the distribution of national income belongs to society by the divine order of creation.

5. The Just Distribution of Economic Power

The discontent of the working class with the so-called "capitalist" system is not only, and, properly understood, not primarily, directed against an unjust wage, but against a degrading dependence of the worker's existence on the will of the "capitalist," whose sole ownership of the means of production has, till now, given him supreme power over all conditions of labour. The worker has no say in the distribution of the total revenue of labour or in the conditions of labour; he can be dismissed at the employer's will. The more anonymous, the more impersonal this dictatorial capitalistic owner becomes, the more degrading becomes their total dependence. The large shareholders of the joint stock enterprise, and even more the board of directors of the syndicate, are unknown to the workers, nor do they know the workers. They are bound to them by no interest of a personal, human kind. That is the very reason why there is a great temptation for them to act purely from the standpoint of the profit on capital, the share dividend. Thereby the worker is reduced to a mere factor in production, to an economic chattel. Quite rightly, he feels this situation to be an outrage upon his humanity; it robs him of his place as an organic element in the economic whole; his personal dignity is degraded.

Like the dependence of wages on supply and demand which has just been discussed, this disparity results from the individualistic conception of property. It is the standpoint which has been called the "master in the house" view of property, and is shared by many, though fortunately no longer by the majority, of employers in our country. The working class does right to revolt against it; but not right when it condemns and attacks every employer and capitalist as *ipso facto* one who shares that view. Employers and capitalists are right in defending themselves against such an assumption; they are not right in inferring an unqualified right of disposition of their property in the means of production. For this "master in the house" standpoint infringes the order of economic life as an organic whole, which is the order laid down in creation. It is first and foremost the employer who should realize that he, the master, is the servant. Luther's dictum of the *servus servorum* holds good here. It is true that industry needs competent and responsible leadership. It is true that economic democracy in any formal sense would be the ruin of industry; it is true that the organic union of all in the economic community does not mean "equal rights of self-determination" for all, but, like the family, implies a certain hierarchy of competence and responsibility. But that hierarchy does not abolish a co-responsibility on the part of the worker proportional to his capacity and output. By paying the workers their contractual wage, the employer has not fulfilled his duty to them, for work is not a commodity that can be bought, but a service whereby a communal relationship is established.

The idea of a community of labour and organization is a necessary inference from the Christian view of the relationship established by labour. Where there is a just order of labour, employer and worker do not confront each other as exploiter and exploited, but as members of a labour community in which the welfare of the one is the welfare of the other. Properly understood, the welfare of the "firm" is the welfare of the workers, and vice versa. The "welfare" of the workers must be understood not only in the physical sense, but in the general human sense; the consciousness of forming part of things, of sharing the responsibility belongs to it. The employer must listen to what the workers have to say and the workers to what the employers have to say. This listening to each other is the concrete expression of mutual recognition as members of a community.

It is desirable that the employers should themselves, of their own free will and in free agreement with the workers, make this community an effective reality, as happens partially by the free contract of labour. It is, however, necessary that where the employers themselves cannot acquire this insight, the community should compel them to abandon their "master in the house" attitude. What can be achieved by the law of the state is here, as everywhere, only a substitute for something that would be better done voluntarily. But, here as everywhere, the law is an indispensable instrument for enforcing a minimum of justice. The ownership of capital confers no right to override this organic responsibility. Hence the employer with a sense of responsibility will not dismiss his workmen when it is no longer profitable to keep them; he will not dictate where there would be a possibility of discussion and agreement; he will, as far as lies in the circumstances, give his workers their share of responsibility and allow them their corresponding share in the profits to the extent and in the way in which the business risk is also a common one. If he does so, he is acting in accordance with the idea of economic justice as it is founded in the creative order of economic life; where he does not do so, the state must compel him.

6. CAPITALISM AND COMMUNISM

Applied to the economic order, the antithesis between individualism and collectivism appears as the antithesis between capitalism and Communism. Capitalism(61) is, in the strict sense of the term, unchecked and unlimited individualism. On the positive side it asserts that the best economic order comes into being through the absolutely free play of economic forces which unfolds when ownership is private and economy completely free. The negative corollary to this positive assertion is that any intervention by the community, and especially by the state, is detrimental, and checks the normal flow of industry. This consistent individualism was a feature of the early stage of the modern industrial epoch, that is, the epoch of the machine and the credit system. Since then it has been modified in many directions by state and other interventions by the community, by opposition from labour itself and not least by the sense of responsibility of many employers and capitalists, so that the present economic order, even apart from the totalitarian revolution and war conditions, can only be called capitalist in a very restricted sense.

Early capitalism provoked its own reaction in the socialist-communist(62) labour movement, the leaders of which believed that the evils of capitalism could be overcome by the socialization of productive capital. This communism has its theoretic basis in the Marxist theory of surplus value, which, as we have seen, is in its turn based on a conception of justice which influenced the mass of labour much more deeply than the economic theory. That theory states that the increase of value created by the work of the industrial labourer, owing to the capitalist's right of disposition over the income from labour, unjustly benefits the capitalist instead of the worker. If the productive capital belonged to the labouring community instead of to the private owner, this surplus value would benefit those to whom it belongs by right, namely the workers. From this premise, communistic socialism deduces its claim for the socialization of the means of production, that is, the abolition of private property in productive capital.

Thus while in capitalism private ownership is regarded as the primary condition of all economic justice(63), in communistic socialism collective ownership is conversely regarded as the remedy by which alone economic justice can be established. From the Christian standpoint, the standpoint of the order of creation, both theories must be rejected as equally fallacious and one-sided. The individualistic conception of property, which necessarily results in the "master in the house" attitude, has already been demonstrated as a fallacy arising from the disregard of the "social reservation." In the Christian view there is no absolutely private property within the limits set by the welfare of the community, by responsibility towards the community. And this "social reservation" is the more effective, the less property is associated with the personal life and being of the owner. The capital placed at the disposal of purposes of production represents a maximum of alienation. The capitalist, insofar as he is not identical with the employer, does not himself work with his capital, but places it at the disposal of others in the form of machinery, industrial plant etc. Hence his right of disposition over the work done with that capital and its revenue is quite peculiarly subject to the social reservation. The more anonymous and impersonal capitalistic ownership becomes, the less question there can be of sole rights and dictatorial rights. Hence *pure* capitalism is a highly unjust economic order.

Socialistic Communism, however, is open to no less weighty objections. It is true that Marxism, unlike certain more primitive forms of Communism and socialism, does not aim at abolishing private property altogether, but only private property in the means of production. What that means, however, is not merely that economic life becomes a communal concern—which would be the right thing—but a *collective* one. Under this system there would be no individual but only a collective economy, no individual, but only a collective right of disposition, no individual but only collective responsibility. Every single economic transaction would be subjected to the dictatorship of the collective will in which everyone—whether every worker or every citizen is a moot point among Marxists—has an equal voice. Every individual is an official, a dependent earner, an employee of the collective. The collective is the sole employer, every individual is delivered over to it for good or ill. It is true that every individual has a share in the collective will, but so fractional a share creates no freedom. In case of disagreement, the individual has no alternative but complete submission to the collective will. The dictatorship of the collective over the individual is absolute. The collective, as sole employer and bread-giver, has the individual absolutely in its hands; the individual is an absolute serf, a slave of the collective. He may have private property, but only what the collective allows him in the form of wages, or, more properly speaking, of the right of consumption. This private property, however, has not the qualities of an area of freedom. If the free labour contract of capitalism was a fiction, the alleged freedom of the individual in the collective economy is a still greater one. What has once become the will of the collective—that will in the creation of which he has only an infinitesimal share—absolutely coerces him. Every space in his existence is occupied and determined by the collective will.

It took the Russian experiment to reveal to the world these consequences of Communism. Before then, people always allowed themselves to be misled by the example of communal or state concerns which they saw functioning within a capitalist economy, without reflecting that because they were working side by side with free, individualistic forms of enterprise, they were quite unable to develop their ultimate consequences, and hence looked far more harmless than they would if the whole economic system were working on collective lines. The abolition of private property means, if not in intention, at any rate in effect, the abolition of freedom, even though the harmless private property in goods for consumption remains in existence. For the latter is not capable of protecting the individual from the tyranny of the collective. Just as in Rousseau's Social Contract, there is a total alienation of individual rights to freedom to the general will, here there is a total alienation of all economic freedom to the collective will.

The evil, however, is not collective economy in itself, but the exclusiveness of collective economy, such as is aimed at by communistic socialism. That ensues from our reflection on the relation of property to the person. There is hardly one of us who would be ready to abandon social services which have long since proved their value in transport and in the supply of water, gas, electricity, and so on, for these are economic fields in which there is no necessary connection between object and owner, owing to their stability on the one hand and their impersonality on the other. They offer little scope to the spirit of enterprise to conquer new fields and to adjust production to the fluctuations of the market. The same holds true, in due proportion, for branches of industry still organized on a private basis, such as mining. Whether the changeover from private to public ownership is justified, is primarily a question of expediency.

Neither private nor public ownership is in itself just. We must not forget that the demand of the working classes for public ownership is not, in the last resort, based on a special predilection for public ownership, but arises solely from the opinion that public ownership would create more just conditions of life for the workers. If private ownership had fulfilled the requirements of justice, the demand for public ownership would hardly have arisen. The bias of the working classes to Communism springs from no preference for Communism but from the capitalist *bourgeoisie's* neglect of its duties of justice. It is only the fact that so many capitalists misinterpreted their rights of ownership in the sense of irresponsible rights of disposition which fostered the view, quite unjustified in itself, that public ownership would guarantee improved conditions of life for the working classes. The solution must not be sought in the alteration of conditions of ownership. The community must compel owners to fulfil their duties of justice. It was a comprehensible but disastrous fallacy to believe that the irresponsibility of private ownership could only be brought to an end, and hence better conditions of life guaranteed to the working classes, by the socialization of productive capital. While even in the political sphere it is false optimism to believe that the community takes best care of the common welfare, it is far more false in the economic sphere. This collectivistic assumption is as erroneous as the individualistic assumption that unlimited right of disposition over property is necessary to freedom. The truth of the matter is that individualism no more creates true freedom—as we have been made to realize in all conscience by the Manchester school of economics—than Communism creates true communal freedom—as we can see just as clearly in Russian Communism. The individualism of unlimited right of disposition over private property results in economic anarchy, but Communism results just as inevitably in totalitarian tyranny. The guarantee of a just economic order does not reside in the abolition of the freedom which is inseparable from private property, but in the community's limitation of the right of disposition by the requirements of justice. This is the way Switzerland took, with her exemplary factory legislation, and it proved to be the way of salvation in both wars, since it provided for the supervision of private enterprise by the community. Public enterprise is highly dangerous, not only from the economic standpoint, but also from the standpoint of justice. Indeed it is a devastatingly fallacious solution of the problem, except in the special cases mentioned, where public enterprise is the obvious thing. Totalitarian tyranny, which is, not by chance but by necessity inseparable from Communism, is no whit better than the anarchic tyranny of capitalism. It is not the capitalist himself who is the enemy of economic justice, but the irresponsible capitalist. Humanity, however, suffering under economic injustice, cannot wait until all capitalists deal justly of their own free will. It must use state legislation to compel those to deal justly who do not do so of their own free will. The changeover from private to public ownership remains only as the *ultima ratio* in special cases.

7. The Just Economic Order—The Problem of Economic Planning

Having proved both individualistic capitalism on the one hand and Communism on the other to be unjust forms of the economic order, the question of economic planning still awaits our attention. The demand for a planned economy must in no case be identified with Communism, nor must the demand for the freedom of the economic market be identified with the rejection of economic planning. What we have established as unjust is, on the one hand the irresponsible, unrestrained use of private ownership of productive capital in the sense of profit economy, on the other the tyranny of collective Communism. Between these two extremes however, there is plenty of room both for the economy of the free market and for economic planning.

The economy of the free market seems at first to be a purely technical question of political economy and hence without interest in a doctrine of Christian justice. In actual fact it has an absolutely direct bearing on the Christian idea of justice. For exchange is what corresponds to the Christian idea of the community as the natural form of economic community. The principle of exchange, properly understood, stands in contradiction to both extremes, on the one hand to the individualistic notion of the independence of the self-sufficient individual, on the other to the communistic notion of the authoritarian regulation of all economic life by the collective will. Exchange is a natural form of the principle—community in freedom, freedom in community. Exchange presupposes mutual interdependence; free exchange presupposes that men, in this interdependence, deal with each other as independent persons who recognize each other as independent persons. Hence when the principle of the free exchange market is held responsible for the evils of unchecked capitalism, people have rightly protested. What is called capitalism by its opponents consists largely in the absence of free exchange, since monopolies exist which permit prices to be artificially raised by an artificial scarcity of goods. The free market, where everyone, according to his judgment, exchanges his goods for what seems to him an equivalent in the goods of another, is one of the most important forms both of freedom and of community.

State intervention is, however, necessary, if only to safeguard the freedom of the market. For exchange, if left to itself, generates phenomena which destroy free exchange, among others economic monopolies and powerful organizations of the nature of monopolies(64). The modern trust, the syndicate etc., did not grow out of the old feudal property nor out of state privilege, but out of the economy of the free market left to its own devices. The community, therefore, must exercise some supervision. It is a liberalistic prejudice to believe that general economic welfare will naturally ensue from the freedom of exchange. Economic planning is necessary both in the interests of the genuine supply of necessities and in the interests of freedom. State or communal supervision and regulation by corporations which are themselves rooted in economic life is necessary if there is to be an end of the anarchy of the free market, which becomes visible primarily in great trade depressions and mass unemployment. If demand is to be satisfied, not only must production be directed, but consumption also, since the desire to consume does not by any means correspond to real need. People do not always buy what they need; they buy what they think they need. The prices they pay do not by any means correspond to what the goods are worth, but to what they seem worth. The economy of the absolutely free market will always be the prey of frivolous purchasing and of profit-greedy production with its caprice and changes of fashion, with its artificial stimulus of purchasing by advertising and its speculative ventures in production. The production based on the *immediate* desire to purchase is, from the standpoint of the general welfare of the community, always anarchic, capricious and chaotic. The community cannot afford to leave its economic strength at the mercy of the purchasing public, that is, to make its apparatus of production solely dependent on the law of demand. But production determined solely by the motive of profit, by the return on capital, is just as arbitrary. For the sake of profit it creates artificial needs, squanders a large part of its revenue, i.e., of the national revenue —on advertisement, which simply means an artificial increase of the volume of production of one producer at the cost of another; it plunges into risky, ill-calculated productive ventures, and is distributed quite haphazardly, by adventitious calculations of profit, over the country. It cares nothing for the damage done thereby to its natural scenery, to the workers' conditions of living, nor for the exhaustion of the natural resources of the soil. The desire to purchase and the motive of profit alone are bad guides for national production. An economy based only on them —and that is planless economy—is a huge extravagance which the community cannot afford for long and which is of necessity committed at the expense of the necessary wages of labour.

The conclusion from the Christian view of a just order of the community is planning in the service of freedom and in the service of the welfare of the community. War economy has shown that such planning is possible even without collectivism. In Switzerland especially, a perfectly new type of state intervention has evolved which does not operate at the cost of freedom and does not reinforce the bureaucracy of the state. This is co-ordinated planning. The state does not intervene in order to do things itself, nor even in order to regulate them, but in order to co-ordinate productive forces and bring them to a reasonable self-regulation.

The great danger in the immediate future is twofold. On the one hand there is a tendency to exploit the evils of capitalism in order to discredit free competition altogether and to belaud and propagate state socialism or totalitarian Communism as the sole alternative. On the other hand there is the opposite tendency to exploit the grim phantom of communism and the troublesome experiences of war-time conditions to reopen the door to *irre-*

sponsible capitalism under the banner of "free competition" and to stigmatize any reasonable economic planning as totalitarian Communism.

The Christian principle of justice contains both components, the freedom of the individual and responsibility to the community. In collectivistic economy, freedom is submerged; in individualist economy, responsibility to the community is submerged. There is a temptation to infer the principles of Communism from the Christian idea of the community, but that is as mistaken and as detrimental as to infer the principle of individualistic liberalism from the Christian idea of freedom. The Christian communism of the primitive community did not abolish freedom, as state socialism must of necessity do, yet even so, as the pure communism of love, its end was poverty and the other communities had to be called in to support that at Jerusalem. Christian community has as little in common with Communism or state socialism as Christian freedom with capitalistic liberalism. The principle of love cannot serve as a principle of order in the community; only the principle of justice can do that, but the *motive* of love can, properly understood, serve justice. A small Christian community, living apart from the great economic process and without state compulsion might very well take as an example the community at Jerusalem; even then it is questionable whether it would not soon have the same unhappy experience. But as a public, general regulation of the national economy, equipped by the state with compulsive law, Communism is a totally different thing. It is a travesty of the Christian community, just as capitalistic individualism is a travesty of Christian freedom. From the point of view of the Christian conception of justice there is another law of economic justice which combines freedom of property and initiative with responsibility to the community. That alone is able to steer the national economy between the two extremes.

... Chapter 19 ...

THE MASS MAN AND THE JUST
SOCIAL ORDER

ONE OF THE MOST FUNDAMENTAL PROBLEMS OF
our time is that presented by the creation of "the masses."
For the totalitarian state could neither have been conceived nor
put into action had it not been for the fact of the mass man.
That fact must be faced by anyone who attempts, seriously and
realistically, to grapple with the problems of the social order.
It must above all be faced by the church, which is finding its
work of creating true fellowship hampered by unprecedented
difficulties due to the existence of the mass man. Neither the
fact itself nor its far-reaching significance is denied(65). But
it is a sociological problem. What has it to do with the question
of justice? The connection between the two groups of problems
will not become apparent as long as we regard mass as a quantitative fact and imagine that the mass man is a product of
modern industrial technique, which concentrates large numbers
of people at one place. In actual fact the congregation of large
numbers of human beings in economically favourable areas is
merely a *predisposing* cause for the emergence of the mass man;
it is never its *effective* cause. That cause lies far deeper, in
spiritual circumstances. The essential nature of the mass is not
large number, a quantitative thing. It is qualitative, it is the
absence of structure. Mass is amorphous; it has no articulation;
it is the mere juxtaposition of identical particles. This amor-
phousness, however, is identical with spiritual homelessness.
The *deepest* cause of mass is religious homelessness; its immediate cause, the consequence of that homelessness, is the mod-

ern dogma of equality. Religious homelessness tears man out of the *metaphysical* structure of his existence; he is no longer rooted in an eternal order of things. The dogma of the equality of all tears him out of the *social* fabric; it destroys organic structure.[1] Millions of men may live crowded in one place without turning into mass men—there are no mass men in the Chinese metropolis, nor were there in the swarming humanity of the large mediaeval city—while a small village may be invaded by the mass man. Think of the difference between a small village in the Emmental and an American suburban village. Not number but structure alone is the determining factor. But structure is only created by difference based on inequality. Since both equality and inequality function here, the question concerns justice also.

Pre-Christian humanity did not know the mass man. It knew only the man in his place, fitted into a whole, with his established niche in the social and metaphysical world. That structure, however, was on the whole unfree. It was a stratification of classes; it was more or less a caste system. To the idea of the natural stratification of society, Christianity added that of the equal personal dignity of all men. In the eyes of God there is "neither bond nor free, neither man nor woman." Modern rationalism, however, tore out of this synthesis the element of inequality, which is just as integral a part of the Christian idea of creation as equality, and thus, in the name of "freedom and equality," destroyed the structure of society. What rationalism had conceived as an idea was put into action by the French Revolution.

The individualism based on the rationalistic conception of man did not, however, create the mass man himself, but only the conditions in which he could emerge. For as long as the idea of the equal dignity of persons and of freedom was rooted in metaphysics and religion, as long as freedom and equality were a source of genuine, deep emotion, the mass man had not

---

[1] That is why the Israelitic community of the Old Testament knew nothing of the problem of the masses. Its members were at home, in the religious and social sense. They had roots.

yet come into being. Not until positivism had blended with this rationalistic individualism, and had brought about the complete secularization of the individual, was he created. The idea of freedom and equality was reduced to an empty husk and man was torn up from his religious and social roots.

This process was mainly consummated in the industrial proletariat, though not primarily because it was a proletariat but because it knew itself to be a proletariat. The coal miner of the canton of Valais, filled with living Christian faith and firmly rooted in the family, is no mass man. Not until his proletarian manner of thought alienates him from the community of the church and the family, not until he stands there alone with his hollow theory of freedom and equality, bound to his fellow men by no other bond but that hollow theory, is he a mass man, and even then the process is not complete until that idea has been so emptied of its religious content that it can no longer inspire him with enthusiasm and move him to fight for justice. The religious feeling born of the proletarian idea of equality(66) checked the development of the mass man as effectively as Marxist materialism produced him.

The Marxist doctrine of the class war is a product of Rousseau's rationalistic ideology of revolution. In the rationalistic ideology of equality there is no room for a social order resembling that of the family. Every such order is stigmatized in advance as unjust, since it conflicts with the idea of equality. In the name of equality, and with the whole emotional force of an idea of equality primarily conceived on a metaphysical and religious basis, war is declared on the class principle. If we bear in mind the degenerate form which the class principle has assumed in the reality of that time, nothing is more comprehensible. From the very outset, the Christian social order—an order of service in which inequality had been co-ordinated on the basis of the equal dignity of persons—had been intimately associated with the feudal system. But for centuries the Christian spirit of responsibility had left its impress on the feudal system of power and authority. In the course of time, however, especially when the class structure of society was combined with monarchic absolutism, it took on increasingly diseased forms—for instance in the degeneration of the guild system after the Reformation —and could no longer be tolerated by a middle-class bred on the rationalistic idea of equality. The first great breach in the class structure was the revolution of 1789, the second its aftermath in 1848.

Meanwhile, however, a new pseudo-structure, emerging from individualism itself, entered into the heritage of the feudal hierarchy, and in part, for instance in England, derived its sub-stance directly from feudal inheritance. That pseudo-structure was capitalism. When Karl Marx, as the spiritual heir of the rationalistic prophets of equality of the Enlightenment, iden-tified the hierarchic principle with the "class" principle, it was undoubtedly the English capitalism of his time which provided the actual basis for the identification. *Unrestrained* capitalism, which regards private property in the means of production from the master-in-the-house standpoint does, indeed, create "class" and not "station." The social stratum which thinks and acts in this fashion can only be understood by the proletarian worker as an "exploiting class," on which the exploited are to declare war with the avowed object of "expropriating the expropria-tors." The class war is the necessary outcome of the pseudo-structure of capitalism and the rationalistic battle cry of equality.

What, however, is a genuine social structure? The answer to this question lies to hand in the Christian conception of man, in the combination of the equal dignity of persons conferred by creation and the unlikeness of kind and function established by creation. A true social order of "stations"' is that community of men in which every single member of the community has his own place, his "station," to which he has a just claim in virtue of his equality of value and unlikeness of kind. Hence it is identical with the truly just social order. The prototype of this genuine structure is the family. Here every individual member of the community occupies the place due to him by the order of creation, in virtue of his equality of value and unlikeness of kind. Here there is—and this is the decisive factor—genuine, original, non-delegated authority, the corollary of which is concrete responsibility. The father has authority over the child, true, original power of command. He is at the same time responsible for the child. He is not, however, responsible *to* the child. He need not give an account of himself to the child; that is the very reason why his authority is original and undelegated. He is answerable to God for the child. It is precisely on that genuine, original authority that the confidence of the child rests; it knows that that responsibility is the guarantee of its security. In the family the equality of personal dignity is embodied in this relationship of confidence which is based on the responsibility conferred by God. The unlikeness of kind and function appears as concrete, original authority and obedience. The structure of the family is the product of the equality of its members as persons and their difference of kind and function. The father has only a functional authority over the child. The child is not his property, but it belongs to him. Both belong to God equally, but the equal belonging to God creates, by reason of the difference established by creation, different "statuses." The "status" of the father is not the same thing as the "status" of the child. Every member of the family—father, mother, children —is a full member of the community, but each has his particular "status," and with that status his particular rights and duties. The meaning of all these rights and duties, and with them of the whole social structure, is service. The family is a structure of service, a community of completion, but this structure of service, this social organism, is not its ultimate purpose. As a whole it serves the higher purpose, the life of the person himself. It is true that the authority of the father is genuine, undelegated, primary, but it is not unqualified. On the contrary it is entirely conditioned by the personal purpose of the child. The father must exercise his authority in order that the child may become a person, may develop in personality. Hence the principle of the co-responsibility of the child is included in it. In proportion as the child grows to maturity the father's authority declines. He makes proper use of his authority only when he reduces it by stages corresponding to the growth of the child in personality. The family is a genuine corporation. What is called a corporation in the legal terminology of our day is a totally different thing. It is an association, a contractual organization on the basis of formal equality. Hence the only authority it includes is delegated authority. The family is not an association; it is not created by contract, it is not based on formal equality, it contains genuine, undelegated authority. Hence in contradistinction to the formally democratic, modern "corporation," it is the genuine, original corporation. This might serve as an illustration of the essential elements of true social structure.

We are, it is true, still faced with the question whether it is feasible to take the family as the prototype of a just social order, whether, that is, a genuine social order must be "patriarchal." Modern rationalism has, since Locke (67), objected that the family is a special case owing to the natural inequality of adults and children, of those, that is, who have already reached "years of discretion" and those who have not. In the social order, on the other hand, everyone must be regarded as having attained years of discretion and hence as equal; thus the family cannot be taken as the prototype of the social order. Every patriarchal system implies the reduction of part of human society to a state of minority, which means to deprive it of dignity.

One thing is true in this objection—the family is in fact a special case and hence the order of the family, which is based on the inequality of its major and minor members cannot be forthwith transferred *in toto* to society as a whole. But the idea that, because every member of society is to be regarded as having attained years of discretion, the principle of inequality no longer functions, is wrong and detrimental. The inequality of men even outside of the family is no trifle; even there equality is an empty word unless it means the equal dignity of the person, which is the basis of the family also. It is the difference of kind and function which characterizes men as created beings. This difference, however, does not consist, as the rationalists imagine, in a greater or less share of reason, hence in a quantitative element to be judged as a deviation from the ideal of rationality. On the contrary, difference is a qualitative thing and, as we have seen, it is in difference that the possibility of a concrete community of completion lies. By difference, human life becomes rich in mutual give and take, in mutual aid and dependence. It is owing to difference that we are able to conceive the social order as an organism of service. A true social structure has nothing to do with either political privileges or economic advantages. The higher "station" is rather the expression of the fact that human beings, equal in dignity as persons, but differentiated by the service which corresponds to their difference of kind, stand in a community based on mutual completion.

The only really hierarchical organism which survived the French Revolution is the army. We Swiss, who have had a militia from time immemorial, are privileged in that our army has always been present in our minds as a community of service. For us, "service" means military service. Our army is an organism of service, where one exists for the other according to their difference in rank. The general[2] "serves" just like the private. But it will occur to no reasonable man to imagine that the general should be elected by councils of soldiers, should give an account of himself to them and have his appointment ratified by them or not, according to that account. Everyone knows that such a proceeding would mean the end of the army. An army constituted on a basis of formal democracy is unimaginable. But no Swiss doubts that the hierarchically constituted army is a legitimate institution of the Swiss democracy.

In the army there is real power of command, undelegated authority. The general is responsible *for* his men, not *to* them. This power of command is necessary to the purpose of the army. Only an army under a command of this kind is an active fighting force. From the purpose of this service, there follows the gradation of "commissions," competences and responsibilities. But that gradation is rendered possible by the difference of capacity. At the head of the army there must be the man who has the capacity, who *can*. The elective machinery by which the various grades of this hierarchical order are filled has not the pur-

---

[2] In time of war, a general commander-in-chief is appointed to the Swiss army, and is familiarly known as "the General." In time of peace the highest rank is that of colonel.

pose of making the elected dependent on the electors and hence answerable to them. That would mean delegated authority, which would be the end of the army. On the contrary, its sole purpose is to discover the man who is capable, who can be entrusted with the power of command. This mechanism may be more or less efficient, it may function more or less well in the sense of the institution, but in any case its purpose is this: to find the man upon whom power of command may be conferred and to confer it upon him. In the army every man has his place, with it his responsibility, greater or less, for the whole, and the competence corresponding to it. None is without responsibility, without competence, not even the private—and woe to the army in which even the individual soldier is not esteemed as a full member of the community! But in the army there is a strictly ordered gradation of competence necessary to its purpose, a graded, but always genuine, undelegated power of command which is firmly organized not only downwards but upwards. The major or the colonel has no more right than the private to interfere in matters which are within the captain's competence. It is a bad officer who cannot respect the full competence of his subordinates. Thus the army too exhibits the principle of graded co-responsibility combined with genuine authority. That is the very reason why it is a living organism of service, a structure of mutual responsibility and complementary service. No reasonable private feels degraded because the officer has to give him orders without accounting to him for those orders. But the officer can only gain the confidence of his men if they can feel that his orders are well-founded and that they express a sense of responsibility to the whole of the service. Thus the true army is, with the family, a genuine example of patriarchal social structure.

The army itself, however, is only *one* example of genuine order. Owing to its special purpose it has its special structure, its special kind of graded power of command. Hence there is no suggestion here of militarizing the social order. The military hierarchy is only an illustration of genuine social order, not its principle. The mistaken idea that an analogous—not an identical—organization can have no place in economic life is a prod-

uct of individualistic capitalism, the master-in-the-house standpoint on the one hand, on the other of the rationalistic equalitarian theory which is the reaction against it(68). Both have
ceased to regard the economic life as a community of service,
both misunderstand the common bond and responsibility established by creation. The capitalist or employer who regards his
workers merely as "factors in production," as "hands" whom he
can dismiss whenever he finds it more profitable, who feels no
common bond with them but his immediate interest in profit,
repudiates the bond of common service with them. He regards
his workers in the same way as a bad general regards his men
as cannon fodder. The Marxist worker, on the other hand, for
whom even the employer whose attitude is totally different,
and who has a full sense of responsibility, is only the exploiter,
denies the community of labour and rends asunder what belongs
together by the order of creation. The primary wrong has to be
laid to the charge of that kind of capitalist, but the secondary
wrong, arising as its result and hence more pardonable, is not
less disastrous. On both sides the class war is the mutual destruction of the community of labour. And yet economic life is precisely the field in which the mutual bond, the mutual dependence of the responsible chief with the authority vested in him
by the matter in hand, and the worker submitting in confidence
of his own free will, exhibits most clearly the difference of kind
and function and the equality of personal dignity established in
creation. It is a very reassuring sign that a generation of master-
in-the-house capitalism and communistic socialism aiming at
class war, where employers and employed faced each other as
enemies, seems to be coming to an end, that people seem to be
beginning to realize on the one hand the responsibility of the
chief for the worker, on the other the responsibility of the
worker for the "firm," and that those who had long since
grasped these things can at last feel that their view is becoming general.

Both employer and employed are becoming increasingly
aware that each needs the other, that the independent, responsible employer and leader of industry cannot be dispensed with

and that the wage-earner cannot be regarded as a purchasable means of production. Yet the way to full insight into the necessity of a real "community of labour" is blocked by the individualistic ideal of freedom on the one hand, and on the other by a collectivistic ideal of equality, which, however, rests on the same rationalistic basis of the idea of equality. There are still a large number of employers or owners of large-scale means of production who will not realize that they are part of a community of service, that independence of leadership does not mean to do as one likes. They have still not realized that property in the means of production does not give them *carte blanche* to exploit the chances of profit at the cost of those participating in production. And there are still many workers who cannot realize that formal democracy in industry would be as futile and as ruinous as formal democracy in the army. They still believe in the nationalization of ownership as the universal panacea and cannot see that a collectivistic system offers just as little guarantee against exploitation and tyranny as an individualistic one, that the forms of exploitation might change, but not the thing itself. Above all, a large number of them do not see that there must be, even in industry, genuine, undelegated authority, a hierarchic order of responsible competence of decision, since industry, like the army, must be a fighting force, though the object of the fight is not men but economic and technological problems.

A true, just, hierarchic and patriarchal structure of industry is not far off wherever employers and employed both understand their work as a community of service or labour. The responsible leader of industry with genuine, undelegated power of command is as aware that he is necessary as reasonable workers are. Any band of schoolboys playing pirates first chooses a leader. Why should they realize the necessity of leadership and not workers? But the leader of industry with a sense of responsibility knows too that this power of command is not personal to him but serves the purpose of the whole, that he is not responsible *to* his workers, but *for* his workers, that he, who has the ultimate right of decision in full, unshared responsibility, must give his subordinates co-responsibility according to the measure of their real capacity, that he must admit all the workers, step by step, to their share of responsibility for the conduct of business, that whatever else happens, he must regard and treat them as full members of the community of labour. The solution cannot be that the workers should be employees at fixed wages of the sole employer, the state, nor that economic community should be replaced by a political scheme of formal democracy, nor that workers' syndicates(69) should become in their turn the sole owners of the means of production, and hence monopolists of production, which would inevitably result in the exploitation of the consumer. The solution lies in industry's retaining its freedom but learning to realize that it is one whole of mutual service, and, where it does not learn, being compelled by the state to learn. The economic order which is patriarchal in the true sense of the word, which combines responsible freedom of action on the part of the chiefs with graded responsibility towards the common interest on the part of the workers, is a just social order in the economic sphere.

It is disastrous fatalism to believe that the mass man is the necessary product of industry and technology. Technology is never the enemy of humanity; where it appears in that light, it is only the sign that human society has already entered upon a process of disintegration which the machine merely precipitates. Large numbers create problems, it is true, but not insuperable ones. Man is created and fitted to deal with large numbers. The true problem is always the relation to the other man, the knowledge and intention of justice. Even a large-scale industrial concern can be organized in the sense of a "community of labour," provided it is built up on a federal principle, on concrete communities of the workshop. The master-in-the-house standpoint on the one hand, the class war on the other, are abolished, the way lies open for a genuine economic order, with each in his "station," in which each receives his due because each, in his own place, has his rights and his honour.

Honour stands in the closest relationship to a true social structure. It is threatened by the same disintegration. In the family, each member, father, mother and child, has his or her particular honour. This specific honour of each depends on the specific function and place of each within the whole. The pure example of honour is again the army; it is in the army that the idea of honour has remained relatively intact. The honour of the officer is different from that of the private, because he has a different responsibility, a different status in the community of service. But in the Christian view (70) "honour where honour is due." Honour is the subjective reflection of the hierarchic structure of order. The most appalling feature of the economic anarchy created by irresponsible capitalism is not bad wages, nor even insecurity and unemployment. When the work of the wage earner is regarded as goods, as purchasable means of production, when he is made to feel that he has "no say in the matter," he has been robbed of his honour. Man has become a chattel. The truly patriarchal order—the family order—restores his honour; indeed that is the only order that can give it to him. For that honour is identical with the fact that, as a person, he is a member of a community of service.

... Chapter 20 ...

JUSTICE IN THE POLITICAL ORDER

THE ESSENCE OF THE STATE IS NOT JUSTICE BUT power. Even the unjust state is still a state, but the impotent state ceases to be a state. Wherever, in a contiguous territory, the will of the individual human being is subjected to a unified will transcending and commanding him, wherever that will can impose itself unconditionally upon him, the state exists, whether the will that commands with unqualified power is just or unjust. The state is the unified will binding on all individuals; it is the sovereign power. We may call the state that is characterized by power and not by justice an evil, unlawful, tyrannical state, nevertheless it is a state. We can refuse to apply the name of state to an organization of power of such a kind, but in that case we shall have to devise a new term to denote this unconditionally sovereign unity of power, and shall realize in doing so that we have denoted a reality which is manifested to us in political history. We simply have to admit that there exists in the history of mankind this absolutely real phenomenon of power and unjust sovereignty.

There is, nevertheless, a true observation of fact underlying the refusal to bestow the name of state on such a monstrosity of power, namely that an entity of power of such a kind cannot maintain itself in the long run unless it takes thought for the requirements of justice. There is a secret affinity between injustice and anarchy on the one hand and between justice and power on the other. A band of robbers can, for a time, exercise a kind of state sovereignty over a territory, but it will soon perish by reason of its own wantonness. And vice versa, the justice of a political system is always a considerable factor in its stability and power. The first point to be considered is this relationship between political power and justice.

1. The Four Stages of Political Justice

Although there has never been, and never could be, a stateless condition of human society, we must take that abstract possibility as our starting-point if we are going to understand the connection between justice and the law of the state. Anyone who believes that man is by nature good will regard a state of anarchy as desirable and possible, and will therefore contest the necessity of the state. But for anyone who admits that evil, the instinct to the unjust appropriation of what belongs to others, is part of human nature as we know it, for anyone who reckons with the ambition, greed, brutality and selfishness of man, anarchy calls up a picture of appalling and intolerable chaos, of discord and conflict in which no higher social and intellectual life can develop. He will come to the conclusion that this condition of anarchy must be checked at all costs, that anarchy must yield to ἀρχή, that is, a sovereignty which will put an end to the *bellum omnium contra omnes*. The more weight is attached to the element of evil in the estimation of human nature, the more weight will be attached to the necessity of ἀρχή in place of anarchy. This is the basis of the pronouncement that the state is an ordinance of God.[1] It is, therefore, obvious that the Christian faith, which, in its doctrine of the depravation of human nature by sin, accords a decisive importance to the element of evil in human nature as an object of experience, has quite a special understanding for the necessity of the state.

Let us take the reality of the state as our starting-point. We shall realize that its mere existence as a unified and sovereign power of compulsion transcending the individual is a matter of cardinal importance. Even if that power is exercised by a despot devoid of any intention of justice, the mere fact that this central

---

[1] That is the reason why, in the New Testament, the divine institution of the state is primarily based on criminal law. In the Old Testament, law is mainly developed as criminal law.

will exists, and effectively claims for itself the monopoly of coercive power, that above all, by claiming for itself the power over life and death, it removes that most dangerous element from the hands of the individual, has a beneficent influence. The state of anarchy ceases, the most extreme menace to everything humane and spiritual is abolished, a certain order of peace, however brutal, is established. That is the first stage of political justice. The monopolization of power by the one will transcending all individual wills has, though unintentionally, this peaceable effect. We might call it a first stage of justice because it is the primary condition of all justice. In a state of anarchy, no justice is possible, since "the devoutest of men cannot live in peace if his wicked neighbour does not so desire." But under a unified coercive power, however little it may trouble about justice, justice is at any rate possible since the mutual use of force by individuals is eliminated by the state monopolization of power. Even without wishing to, the unified coercive power safeguards the life of individuals against each other by reserving to itself the right to kill. Every higher kind of justice is only a higher kind of justice insofar as it can presuppose this primary, absolutely fundamental order of peace. (71)

Even the despot cannot rule in the long run without transforming the capricious dictates of his personal will into a generally valid law. By proclaiming *law*, henceforth binding on all, he creates the second stage of order. Even though this law springs from no intention of justice, but merely from the lust of power, it is, quite involuntarily, effective in the sense of justice. From then on, everyone is subject to this one law. The law cannot but create a certain equality, and equality is a determining element of justice. Even the mere constancy of legal rule is a victory of mind over the mindlessness of wantonness and caprice. Something now "stands." There is something to be relied on, and all are bound in the same way by this one law. One thing is valid for all—the law. Even the despotic legislator cannot but set limits to his own arbitrariness by the law he proclaims, for even his law cannot but be a permanent and general rule. He has now relinquished at any rate part of his arbitrariness, he has abdicated his will to the law. Hence it is not, as Pascal thought, stupidity, but right feeling if the plain man has a certain sense of satisfaction at being treated according to the law, even though that law is in substance extremely unjust. The mere form of the law, of the generalized and durable will, is a boon in comparison to the haphazard improvisations of power. The law has, it is true, by its very generality, a hindering, hampering effect. "Law becomes nonsense and beneficence a torment." Every law is a limit to spontaneous spiritual utterance, to creative improvisation. But as the law of the state rarely penetrates to the innermost sphere, but only regulates outward things, this hindrance hardly counts in comparison with the beneficent effect of stabilization and equality.

There is, however, the difference between "just" and "unjust" law. Just law is the third stage of political justice. Just law, as distinguished from unjust law, is that which embodies the human rights of the individual and the community as established by creation. No juristic formalism and no historical arguments against the law of nature can do away with the fact that there are requirements of justice which it is the task of the just legislator to embody in laws. A great deal of political history is the history of how just laws were wrested from the state as a mere entity of power, how, by long struggles, the claims of justice were given real expression in the law of the state. We have not yet to deal with the question of the distribution of political power. The justice of the laws obtaining in a state is in the first instance independent of who promulgates those laws and is responsible for their execution. Even an absolute monarch can promulgate just laws and rule in the sense of justice. And vice versa, even in a republic or a democracy, unjust law can be created by the will of the majority, while the just law that was necessary is not created. The question of the justice of the law is primarily independent of the distribution of power in the state. On the contrary, it is a fatal prejudice of modern times that the republican or democratic constitution of itself guarantees the justice of law. The classical example in disproof of that belief is the Athenian democracy in the post-Periclean age. The decisive factor is not who wields the power in the state, but whether the actually existing sovereign power is guided by the knowledge and intention of justice.

Not until this point does a requirement of justice arise in the actual exercise of power, and the question arise of the distribution of power in the state. This is the fourth stage of justice. A glance at the history of modern times shows a truly disastrous reversal of the order of these stages, a devastating over-estimation of this last, fourth stage of justice(72). Both reversal and over-estimation spring in their turn from rationalistic optimism, from the notion that the "people," once it has acquired power, will of itself put true justice into action.

To forestall any misunderstanding, it must be said at once that democracy, given the necessary conditions, is doubtless the most just of all polities, because it gives every citizen a share in the responsibility for the exercise of political power. That statement, however, of itself implies that democracy is not *in all circumstances* the best political order, the one which provides the best guarantee of justice. It does so only in definite circumstances which we Swiss particularly, having lived under democratic institutions longer than any nation on earth, are only too inclined to take for granted. There are circumstances in which democracy can be the worst of all political orders, namely when the people is not ripe for it, or when social conditions are so disorganized that only a strong central will, a "strong hand," is capable of curbing the anarchy latent or manifest in the body social.

This consideration is a necessary inference from our analysis of the four stages of justice. The basic requirement of political justice is the ἀρχή which stands opposed to anarchy, the power of the state to create any order and peace in the country at all. If that is possible in the democratic form, so much the better; if it is not possible in that form, then any other form in which it is possible is preferable, even if it were the dictatorship of an individual.

We can by no means simply assume that democracy is capable of this primary achievement of creating order. Democracy is the supreme limitation of the state's coercive power by the will of the people. In democracy the power of the state is as a rule so strictly limited that it hardly appears as power. Hence democracy is always threatened by anarchy; it is at all times in danger of losing its power over the divergent and conflicting forces in the people(73). Only a long and firmly founded tradition, centuries of training in the sense of political freedom, renders democracy immune against the danger of anarchy. Democracy presupposes a living insight into political necessities on the part of the individual citizen. Where this insight cannot be taken for granted, at any rate of the majority, democracy is always on the verge of anarchy. It is only where the power of the state is so firmly articulated from within as not to permit any disruption of the separate groups of the people that its superiority to every other form of state stands beyond doubt. The maxim *corruptio optimi pessima* holds good here. That is the reservation which has to be made in the first stage of justice. Those which are necessary in the second and third stages are no less important.

In any case, the question of just or unjust laws and government is more important than the question of democracy or not democracy(74). It is a modern axiom of very dubious value that laws and government will become just of themselves if only the majority of the people can direct the decision. Even in so sound a democracy as Switzerland, it has happened again and again that the majority of the people has rejected the just law and chosen the unjust law. That cannot shake our confidence in our democracy because, by and large, our people's "political instinct" and intention of justice have, thanks to centuries of training, stood the test. But it makes us realize that democratic liberties, the "sovereignty of the people," do not, as Rousseau imagined, stand to the justice of laws in the relationship of a pre-established harmony(75). Not only Aristotle but Calvin also pointed out the danger that democracy easily degenerates into mob rule. Aristotle was speaking from his terrible experience of the mob rule in which the Athenian state foundered, and Calvin was far too good a judge of human nature to believe that it was only necessary to press a ballot paper into every citizen's hand in order to guarantee the health and justice of the state. Firstly, the will of the majority can become an appalling tyranny for the defeated minority, secondly it can, just like the individual, prefer the immediately agreeable to the truly just and necessary. An unconditional confidence in the guarantee of justice implied in a democratic constitution can flourish only where men believe, with Rousseau, in the goodness of human nature. Anyone who realizes what demonic powers it harbours will certainly not expect justice in action to issue forthwith from the will of the majority.

It is, of course, possible, like Rousseau, to speculate on the hope that the just will issue as the product of the egoisms of the separate groups, as the necessary compromise between the self-seeking aims of individuals, hence that the injustice of some will of itself act as a corrective to the injustice of the others. The danger of such a speculation is obvious. Just laws will never come about in such a fashion. They will come about only where it can be assumed that the people is imbued with an adequate sense of justice, that there are enough citizens able and ready to place the welfare of the community before their private interest. But that means that democracy will produce a state of justice only where a considerable degree of moral and political justice can be assumed as already existing. Where the people has become a mob, there are poor prospects for justice in a democracy. Hence it is disastrous that the struggle against the totalitarian state, which is *the* struggle of our time, should be carried on in the name of democracy, while the problem of the totalitarian state has practically nothing to do with the problem of democracy. It is not democracy that is at stake today, but social justice and the real freedom of citizens, which are threatened by monopolistic capitalism on the one hand, on the other by communistic syndicalism and the totalitarian state.

2. THE INJUSTICE OF THE TOTALITARIAN STATE

History has seen many examples of just despots. For the people of Israel, the reign of the dictator David was the ideal of just government. But the totalitarian state is inherently unjust. Not because it is brutal or greedy of power; brutality and the lust of power have often been the characteristics of non-totalitarian states, while we can, on the other hand, well imagine the totalitarian state without brutality and imperialistic lusts. The fundamental injustice of the totalitarian state is, like that state itself, unprecedented in history. For it is the omni-competent state. The totalitarian state turns men into tools of the state, instead of the state being the instrument of men. The politicization of all life, of human beings themselves, that is the iniquity of the totalitarian state, and that is what is new. The totalitarian state makes itself into the absolute master of men. It takes upon itself to form men as it will. It lays total claim to them, body, soul and spirit. There have been dictatorships at all epochs. The totalitarian state came into existence in 1917(76). It is characterized by complete control of the lives of all its citizens, inward and outward, religious, cultural and economic.

Since the state of yesterday did not possess the means of exercising that control, it could not be totalitarian. In earlier history there are approximations to the totalitarian state, especially where the state sought to rule the inner life of its citizens in the name of some orthodoxy. But in these cases the citizens always retained a large area of life which was free of state control, especially in the domains of economics and culture. The state first became capable of totalitarian government through the modern technique of rule over large territories, of organization and mass suggestion. The superiority of mechanical arms, the production and use of which it monopolizes, permit it to carry this totalitarianism over all inner resistance. But what is far more important is the monopoly in the creation of public opinion, that is, in education and the press, in all methods of propaganda, combined with the organization of an absolutely effective censorship of news and propaganda. Hence its conflict with the churches is not accidental, but inevitable(77), at least as long as a church exists which is aware of the absolute necessity of its spiritual independence. It is precisely the spiritual, far more than the material, independence of the church which it cannot tolerate,

because it wants men's souls. That is what it wants to dominate
and to form in its own image. But the totalitarian state is only
consummated when it has taken to itself the monopoly of industry by abolishing, through state Communism, private property
in the means of production and the private leadership of industry. That is a point which all who regard the nationalization
of the means of production as a desirable consummation would
do well to realize quite clearly. They are the pioneers of the
totalitarian state, though they neither know nor wish it. In the
totalitarian state, men are sold totally to the state, they are slaves
of the state.

We shall perhaps understand the nature of the totalitarian
state best if we take as our starting-point its extreme opposite,
the individualistic liberal state. Here the opposite principle prevails; the scope of the state is reduced to a minimum, so that the
scope of freedom of the individual may reach a maximum. While
in the one case, the community organized as the state is paramount, in the other the individual *qua* individual is paramount.
The functions of the state are reduced to what is absolutely
indispensable—the army, the police, the law courts. As far as
possible, human life is not regulated by state laws and state
interventions. The state interferes as little as possible. Economic
life proceeds, without state intervention, according to its own
law of supply and demand. Life is built up on the principle of
laisser-faire, *laisser-aller*. The state budget is reduced to what
is for us an incomprehensible minimum. The state is mentioned
as rarely as possible. It is a necessary evil; the less it does, the
less it requires, the better. The experience of last century, and
especially that of the last ten years, with their gradual approach
to the totalitarian state, make it easy for this antithesis of the
totalitarian state to appear as an ideal(78). But we must not
forget that this principle of state abstinence works out greatly to
the disadvantage of the economically weak and of the community
as a whole. The weak individual becomes the prey of asocial
economic forces. Social life and social interests completely lack
state support. The freedom of the individual results in a state of
things which, in economic life at any rate, is not far removed

from anarchy. The powers accorded to the state are so restricted that it can inadequately fulfil only its most primary function, the checking of ever-latent anarchy and the care for public justice and welfare.

Once again we can see that the justice of the political order, as the Christian faith must understand it, points neither to individualistic freedom nor to collectivistic state totalitarianism. While in the totalitarian state the rights of the individual atrophy, in the individualistically conceived state the rights of the community atrophy. While the totalitarian state regulates everything by its law and directs everything by its own hand, the individualistic state neglects its duty of creating justice by its law, where justice is not done spontaneously by the moral force of individuals. That is why the individualistic, liberal state must be the ideal of a replete *bourgeoisie*, just as the communistic totalitarian state must be the great temptation for hungry masses of workers.

Where the mean of the true state lies between these extremes cannot be pronounced once for all. On the contrary, it depends entirely on the moral force of individuals and free social groups. The more forcefully state-free justice, the social *ethos*, has developed, and the more thoroughly it shapes society according to the law of justice by its own strength without state compulsion, the more state help can be dispensed with. The fundamental Christian realization is that the state has only to intervene where individuals, families, free social groups, the churches, the municipalities, cannot perform their tasks. Any justice created by the state is a makeshift, a substitute for the justice which human society should create of itself. The more closely society approximates to this conception, the more "liberal" the state can be and the greater the space left free of state intervention. And vice versa, the greater the decline in the moral vigour of society, the more tasks the state must take upon itself, and the greater the expansion of the element of compulsion in justice, the nearer the approach to the totalitarian state.

Hence the rise of the totalitarian state is in the first instance quite simply a judgment on the wretched moral condition of modern society. We must not fear to add—a judgment too on the Christian church and its powerlessness to direct the moral forces of society in the sense of the justice of creation. Let us take as an example the welfare work of the state, which has already assumed monstrous proportions. This would not have been necessary if the family in the narrower and wider sense of the word, the social community, the Christian community and the economic community of labour had not so conspicuously broken down. If, for instance, industry in its heyday had not, on the basis of an erroneous conception of property, diverted the proceeds of industry, in the form of high dividends and employers' profits, one-sidedly to the owners of capital but, after deduction of the necessary reserves and capital for investment, had transformed it into just wages and welfare institutions for their workers, the state would never have had to take over these crushing burdens. If the Christian church, at a time when its standing and authority were still intact, had more effectively reminded its wealthy members of their social duties in the sense of the requirements of justice, not of charity, and had used church discipline to give effect to its admonitions, a proletariat would probably never have come into existence. The social budget of the state, which has swelled to its present huge dimensions in all countries, is the consequence of a moral deficiency which we rarely have the courage to face squarely. The undesigned bias towards the totalitarian state, which seems like fate, and is present, not in some, but in all countries, not excluding those with democratic ideals, records like a barometer a moral depression. This is to be seen most clearly in the fact that far and wide the proletarized working class prefers to take upon itself the bondage of the communistic totalitarian state rather than continue to bear the deprivations laid upon it by the lack of social justice in the liberal state.

What is disastrous is the blindness which becomes manifest in the mistaken idea that the most effective antidote against the totalitarian state is democracy. Formal political democracy offers not the least guarantee of the justice that is the crying need of the day both in the social and economic spheres. On the contrary, by its origin, the formally democratic state has a markedly individualistic trend, a tendency to economic *laisser-faire*. But if social justice cannot be obtained by democracy, the social class suffering most from injustice will unhesitatingly prefer the dictatorship of the proletariat in the totalitarian state to formal democracy. That is the bitter truth which the liberal *bourgeoisie* must face or be killed by. The worker loves freedom too, but we cannot blame him if he feels social justice to be still more important. If it is not put into effect within the framework of a democratic constitution, whether by social or political methods, the proletariat will turn its back on the democratic state and hail rejoicing the unfreedom of the communistic totalitarian state, which, however deceptively, at least promises him social security.

3. JUST LAW

Between the thought of most jurists and that of other people there has long been a deep gulf. The plain man is of the opinion that there is right even where there is no law of the state, right prior to and beyond the state. He says: I have a right to this or that, even where no state law grants him that right. He expects the legislation of the state to endeavour to embody in laws this right which is prior to law, to abide in its jurisdiction not only by the law of the state but also by this "natural" right insofar as it is not explicitly excluded by the law of the state. The majority of jurists of our day, however, unlike those of almost all previous centuries, are of the opinion that there is no law but the law of the state, that it is impossible, confusing and fallacious to speak of a right prior to and beyond the state(79). This dispute may be in part, but is not entirely, a verbal quibble(80). There are few jurists who would deny that there are requirements of justice which have not yet become the law of the state, hence that justice covers a much wider field than the law of the state. And even the layman who speaks of rights that have not yet become the law of the state knows that the element of legal compulsion in the law of the state is quite a different thing from that of the right prior to the state. Although in this dispute we stand rather on the side of the plain man than on that of current juristic doctrine, we can grant to the jurists that it is necessary for the sake of the clarity and security of state legal procedure to draw a clear distinction between state law and the requirements of justice which do not fall within its sphere. The opposition to "the law of nature," that is, to rights prior to and beyond the state, was primarily set up in order to prevent any encroachments by the law of nature on the sphere of state law, since any such encroachment would actually mean a grave danger to the legal procedure of the state. We might settle the dispute in this way; there is, in fact, only state *law*, but there are requirements of justice prior to and beyond the state.

The purpose of the legal system of the state, however, is not only, indeed not primarily, justice. There is a great deal in state law which has practically nothing to do with justice. The relationship of the whole legal and administrative apparatus to the idea of justice is very indirect and often hardly recognizable. The law actually obtaining in any state has its origin just as much in the fortuitous circumstances of history, in reasons of convenience, and above all in constellations of political power, as in the endeavour to embody justice in law. State law is the sum of all the regulations in force in a state, no matter whether they agree with the requirements of justice or not. We must not forget that all state law is also above all the product of the struggle for power between the various groups in the state.

Yet it is not by chance that law and justice are allied terms. The most important ordinances of the state, whether in constitutional law, civil law or criminal law, regulate those mutual relationships of human beings in which claims to certain "rights," to something which is "due," are concerned, and where therefore, the question of justice necessarily arises. Their deepest source and most living force is, after all, the "sense of right," the conviction that what they establish is just, that it is established "rightfully." Law would perish if the views of certain formalistic schools of jurisprudence were to get the upper hand in the legal thought of the people, views in which law has nothing whatever to do with justice, but is a mere matter of expediency, of frictionless procedure or formal logic, if, that is, legal thought were to lose the deep emotional force it has derived from justice from time immemorial, which gave law its share in the secret of the holy (81). The sense of law, however, is still more gravely menaced by those who see in it nothing but the product of struggles for power, nothing but the actually valid order imposed by the class or group which happens to be supreme in the state(82). In actual fact no ordered legal system is possible unless there is in the mind of the people a close connection between state law and the requirements of justice, which lives in the plain man's sense of right. That is why great legislators have at all times had and proclaimed their intention to give expression to the requirements of justice in their legal code. Even when, as in the totalitarian revolutionary legal systems of our day, traditional ideas of law have been cast overboard and replaced by new ones, it is claimed that the new legal system embodies a valid standard of justice, whether in the abstract equalitarianism of communism or in the anti-equalitarian racial state and *Herrenvolk*.

That conception of law as power, according to which the law of the state obtaining at any given time is simply and solely the product of the elements of power present in the state, is to a large extent right as a description of fact. Looking at the history of law, we cannot fail to recognize that great part played by the factor of power in any actual system of law. It is true not only of the struggles between states, but also of struggles between rival groups within the state, that the victor imposes his will on the vanquished in the form of law. "That now stands. It is my will." *Sic volo, sic, jubeo, sit pro ratione voluntas*. We can find no cause for idealistic palliation of that bitter saying in the actual history of law, whether in ancient or in modern times. Yet one thing must not be forgotten; in that very struggle for power, it was justice that was objectively at stake. That holds good in particular of all the struggles in which the outcast and unprivileged, those who were in the first instance the weak, fought for and won their "good fight" by joining forces. The consciousness of fighting in a just cause is an element of power of paramount importance. And vice versa, as we can see from very recent examples in the international sphere, the consciousness of wrong can weaken even a physically superior adversary. A good conscience and a bad conscience are potentials which should not be underrated in the struggle for power. Hence the assertion that a given legal system was the product of a struggle for power is far from implying that justice was not the moving impulse and determining factor in that struggle. Power can help just law to assert itself. For power is not in itself antagonistic or contrary to justice. The diffamation of power is as fallacious as its glorification. The question is always whether power is based on justice or on the egoistic will to self-assertion and lust for dominion in which there is no room for justice.

What is just law? After what has been said there can be neither doubt nor confusion in the answer. That law is just which allows the rights of man and the claims of the community established by creation to assert themselves. But, as has already been pointed out in the discussion on static and dynamic justice, allowance must be made for the variability of the historic situation. There are certainly immutable *principles* of justice established by creation, but there is no timeless system of just law on the basis of the law of nature. True justice lies equally far removed from the relativism which sees law as conditioned only by the contingent and the ceaseless flux of circumstance, and from the rationalistic *system* of natural law. Justice is the precept of the order of creation accommodated to concrete historical circumstance. And we, as Christians, know that concrete historical circumstances contain a constant factor of deviation from the order of creation, namely evil. The allowance for the evil which is in man is even a characteristic feature of every good system of law, that is, of every system which endeavours to extract a maximum of justice from the given situation.

Let us take marriage as an example. We, as Christians, can only recognize as a just legal institution that which protects marriage as a lifelong and exclusive sexual union. Hence we reject as unjust a legal institution which, as in the initial stage of Communism, regards the difference between marriage and any other sexual union as immaterial, where even marriage itself is held up to contempt as a vestige of the hated "bourgeois" manner of thought and abandoned defenceless to the anarchy of sexual caprice, or which, as in advanced National Socialism, turns marriage into the barrack order of the state. But as Protestant Christians, making full allowance for the "sinful depravation of man" we also reject the postulate of the Catholic church, according to which the law of the state should not in any circumstances permit divorce. "For the hardness of your hearts" the law of the state must provide for a possibility which is absolutely excluded by the original law of God in creation—divorce. Once again just law must make allowance for the evil in human hearts, in this case the frivolity and capriciousness of sexual desire and the social irresponsibility of many, while not turning that possibility into a wide-open door, but so hedging it round with stipulations that it becomes a rare exception. In contrast to much legal *practice* of our day, Swiss civil law has set up legal provisions exactly answering to the Christian requirements of justice. In what it admits and what it excludes, it is a perfect example of just civil legislation.

Just law, however, will, in the future, have to solve grave problems in the sphere of economic adjustments, the state, especially in the emergency regulations of war-time, having already played a considerable part in the framing of this section of law. For the legal system of a country can become unjust not only through what it regulates, but also through what it fails to regulate. Even the gaps in the legal system must be taken into account when we come to speak of the justice of law. Indeed today, in the non-totalitarian state, the injustice of law is rather to be sought in its omissions than in its positive provisions. But the injustice of law can also consist in the regulation by the state of what it has no right to regulate. It is an essential element in the totalitarian state that it regulates and orders everything and everybody by state law, and that is its cardinal iniquity. Still worse, whether in the form of communistic Russian or of National Socialist totalitarianism, it sets in the place of the principle of justice laid down in creation others which flout the divine order of creation, and that not accidentally, but as the necessary consequence of its basic conception of man, which is hostile to that of creation.

4. JUST POWER

The word power has an enormous range of meaning and hence very diverse associations. It is a long road from Jakob Burckhardt's dictum that power is in itself evil to the praise of the almighty power of God. Burckhardt, however, is not speaking of evil *qua* evil, but of power *qua* power, and means political power which is not limited by law. In this sense his saying is absolutely true. On the other hand, the powerless state is no whit better, for it means anarchy. The state requires power for the sake of law, in order to fulfil its task of establishing peace, order and justice among men, who would not be willing or able to be peaceful and just without it. Law unsupported by power is impotent. Thus power does not belong only to the state as a reality, but to the state as a creative ordinance of God. That is why Scripture briefly denotes the state, the administrator of that order, as "the powers."[2]

In order to be able to perform its task, the state must possess *supreme* power, power absolutely superior to every individual and every group. For that reason it has the monopoly of physical force, the power over life and death. The existence of the state is based on this monopoly of power over life and death; without it, it does not exist. This fact does not forthwith provide a basis for capital punishment, but it does entail the right and the power to suppress any resistance, if necessary by death. A state abrogating that right would abdicate; it would become the plaything of those who by no means abrogate their desire to kill, and there are such in every nation. Without the certainty that the state is willing and able to suppress all resistance, there is no security in law, indeed anarchy, latent or manifest, exists. The more supreme the power of the state, the less it needs to exhibit that power. The more that certainty can be taken for granted, the

[2] Rom. 13:1; John 19:11.

less power is felt to be force. The justice of the state, however, increases its power, for as a rule that power is a moral rather than a physical fact. People do not normally obey the state because disobedience would be punished, but because they feel it right to do so, quite apart, of course, from mere force of habit. But where doubts of the justice of the state arise, its power is already undermined. *Oderint dum metuant* is not good political wisdom. The state lives far more on its moral credit than is generally believed, and that means on the conviction of its lawfulness and legality.

This unqualified power over every individual and every group in the state is, however, its dangerous aspect. To possess power is a constant temptation to abuse power. This abuse of power can be twofold; it can be spiritual and appear in the form of arrogance—*superbia*—or it can be material and appear as the use of power in a way contrary to justice. The state must know its limits. Hence, as has already been pointed out, its realization of its subordination to a higher power is no mere political ornament but the foundation of all political wisdom. The atheistic or positivistic state cannot but degenerate; it has no alternative but to set itself up as absolute by means of the conception of the sovereignty of the state. There is only one limit to the sovereignty of the state; it is the knowledge of the sovereignty of God. The first commandment: "I am the Lord thy God . . . thou shalt have no other gods before me" is the one safeguard against the power of the state setting itself up as absolute. Thus the old doctrine that the state needs religion is no crafty device of princes who imagine that religion gives them a better hold over their subjects, but the basis of all true statesmanship. Where it is lacking there is no limit to the *superbia* of the state, for there is only one remedy for *superbia*—the fear of God. How else shall the power which claims for itself the title of "supreme" realize its limits save in that most supreme power? By the will of the people? As if the will of the people could not itself fall victim to that *superbia*! The unlimited sovereignty of the people and the unlimited sovereignty of the state are simply two forms of *superbia*, the one individualistic, the other totalitarian.

The power of the state can, however, be unjust by being made use of for unjust, and not for just, purposes. The power of the state exists in order to put justice into action wherever justice would not be done and injustice done without the intervention of its power. When the state acts in this way, its power is just, it is a just state. That justice must be understood equally as the right to freedom of the individual and the rights of the community the common welfare. Thus the state has primarily not to do what the people wants but what is just. Now it is an element in the specific nature of the state to do so by its sovereignty. Who bestows that sovereignty upon it, how the share of individuals in the creation of that sovereignty is regulated, is a subordinate, if not unimportant question. What is disastrous is the fallacy that in a democracy with universal and equal franchise there could be no sovereignty. The state, even the democratic state which is equivalent to the people, can only perform its task by its sovereignty. The sovereignty of the state is created by two means—legislation and government. Both limit the freedom of individuals, who are under orders. The law commands, the government commands. However law or government come into being, their meaning is command. And their command is a just use of power if the substance of that command, the laws and acts of the government, are just.

These commonplaces must be re-expressed today, in this age of fine phrases about democracy. The doctrine of the sovereignty of the people has obscured the essential authority of the state and fostered the delusion that there is no sovereign in a democratic state, but only administration. Even in a democracy there must be effective command. Hence it is of vital importance to the just state that the power of command should be *effective* in it, that it should not be hedged about by democratic forms. There is not only a positive abuse of power, which will be discussed immediately, but also a negative abuse, a non-use, and that in a double sense: either the state is entirely impotent or it does not make use of its power where it should. The experiences of very recent times show that it is precisely the democratic state which is in danger of being hindered in its just exercise of power, or even totally paralysed, by capitalistic or syndicalistic, communist associations.

Here we encounter a fundamental fact which is to be inferred from the foregoing argument and is often overlooked. Two things must be avoided, firstly that the power of the state should be misused for unjust purposes, secondly that it should be altogether checkmated. The democratic movement, however, from Magna Carta onward, arose with the object of checking the misuse of power, and the various components of the Constitution, the separation of powers, the Constitution, the representative system (parliament) and the franchise were created for that purpose. They exist in order to curb the power of the state, state sovereignty, and to force it with bit and bridle to do justice. Their achievements in this sense are unquestionably great. But two things must be borne in mind: that these components bear in themselves no guarantee of just government, and that they can be so exaggerated that the power of the state is not curbed, but paralysed, so that it cannot perform its task.

As regards the first, we have already seen in another connection that the constitutional components of the state afford in themselves no guarantee of the justice of the state, of the just use of power. What, then, is their relationship to justice? Let us take as an example the most far-reaching of them, the equal franchise of all citizens in the democratic state. Is it not a requirement of justice that this right should exist? Certainly not primarily. It is no requirement of justice that everyone should have an equal say in the state, for that would mean equal treatment of unequals in a connection in which inequality is of great actual importance. Men are neither equally capable of recognizing the just, nor equally able and willing to put it into action. The choice of the men who make the laws and the choice of the men who are to govern cannot have the sense of "representation." The "representatives of the people" are not *merely* representatives of the electorate, making laws in the people's stead; they are also the *elected* of the people, whom the people trust to have more expert knowledge than themselves. The tied mandate is a degradation of democracy. The so-called representatives of the people should not decide what their electors want, but what is right. And that is precisely what the truly democratic citizen expects of them. The same is true of the government. It has not to do what the people want but what is right. In actual fact it ought not even to do what the legislative body wants; it has to do justice, to do the right thing. In a genuine democracy with a responsible government, the government does not first consider the will of the people, but the weal of the people, justice. Where the government considers from the outset, not what is just but the will of the people, the justice of the state is in a sorry plight. The government is not of its very nature really "government." The people elects a government which is to govern according to justice, not an executive to do the people's will.

That is primary and must remain primary. But now comes a secondary factor which is constantly confused with the primary one—the control necessary to prevent the abuse of power. There are very good reasons why the constitution subjects the government to the law and the legislature, and even perhaps to the popular vote. That is a precautionary measure. In case of doubt whether a proposal of the government is just, the will of the legislature and eventually the will of the people must decide directly. The *discovery* of what is just is handed over to the government or to the legislative body; the test or judgment of what has been discovered is left to the people. That does not imply a degradation of government into mere administration; it is merely a precaution, the creation of a channel of control. If it then happens—as quite frequently does happen—that the people rejects the just and decides for the unjust, it should not be said that "the government has been defeated." On the contrary, it is the people that has been defeated, but owing to the abuse of power the decision of the people stands. The government must "submit." But now, if it knows what true government is, it will not conclude that it must make better enquiry next time into what the people wants. It will strive with the people for insight into what is truly just. Still less ought it—as happens in false parliamentarianism—to conclude that it must resign as a result of its defeat. Where the government has to resign because it has not met the will of the people or Parliament, it is a sign that the power of the state is disintegrating, and that democracy is already tending towards mob rule. This sense of original, non-Rousseauesque democracy is maintained in our Swiss constitution by the fact that the Federal Council can be defeated without having to resign. That is the only way in which it can continue to govern in spite of the finality of the popular decision.

This brings us to the second point. The constitutional precautionary measures of the state may take on such dimensions that government becomes impossible. If, for instance, an attempt were made to put the extremely democratic institutions of Switzerland into action in a country of the size of the United States, government would soon come to an end. Only a small country, well trained in democracy, can afford the luxury of extreme formal democracy. It is, however, less the institutions themselves which endanger the intactness of the power of the state, than a mistaken idea of them. Where the people imagines that democracy means doing the people's will, things are in a bad way, but where the government itself falls victim to that fallacy, it is at an end. To take the Swiss example once more, we can afford the referendum and initiative because we have the necessary counterbalance in the—practical—irremovability of the Federal Councillors, and above all in our people's sound understanding of the sense of those institutions. But in other circumstances, the excessive development of constitutional factors can so weaken the power of the state that a condition of anarchy ensues which will in all probability be superseded sooner or later by a dictatorial reaction.

The justice of the state's exercise of power can, however, be rendered insecure by quite other factors, and of these problems, probably the most burning is the anonymous, illegitimate power of groups. The "lobbying" by the secretaries of unions in the corridors of Parliament is as familiar a phenomenon at Berne as it is at Washington and elsewhere, and its dangers have hardly been fully recognized. But it is only a symptom of a much more deep-seated malady. The neglected factor of economic power takes this anonymous and illegitimate way in order to assert itself in our democracies. It is the business of the state to care not only for formal freedom but also for material welfare. The real struggles for power in our day, however, take place in the economic sphere. Hence the state must defend the real or material freedom of the worker against an unjust economic power, but it must also protect the citizen, and maybe even the leader of industry, against the group egoism of a working class which is unjust in its demands. It must therefore exercise its supreme right of supervision precisely at the point at which the liberal, individualistic state pronounced its parole of *laisser-faire*; it must compel the economic powers to submit to the law of the common welfare, and not only those on the right, but also those on the left. To do that it requires great power, for the monsters to be domesticated are very great. Above all, it must have an incorruptible insight into what is just. If it allows itself to be guided by the will of the people in this matter instead of by justice, it will of necessity fall into vacillation, opportunism and bargaining, a bit here, a bit there, to keep both sides quiet and myself in my seat.

The components of the Constitution—law, the separation of powers and the appeal to the people—are those factors of control which are rendered necessary by the abuse of power. That they can cause the power of the state to be dangerously weakened can be seen in the rise of dictatorial reactions in our time. In the dictatorships, however, we can see the other side of the problem —the abuse of power which has become an institution, the demonic force of despotism, of tyranny. The tyrant has no regard for the will of the people, but he has no regard for justice either. His sole regard is himself. That is the "power in itself" which is "evil." It was on account of that power that the democratic movement came into being and the components of the Constitution were created. Power is worst when it is disguised as the executive of the will of the people, when it is able to persuade the people that its only aim is to carry out the people's will. It then combines mass suggestion with the demonic force of power. We have seen with our own eyes how that power has dragged whole nations into the abyss. But we should not now forget whence it sprang: it is partly the result of an anterior weakening of power, but above all of a universal alienation from justice. Its most appalling feature, however, is always revealed by the necessity of expansion, by imperialism.

This brings us to a final problem—the question of the size of power, of the external bounds of power. Like the great wealth of individuals, great power in a state involves an almost irresistible temptation to an unjust use of power. The great state is quite peculiarly exposed to the temptation of *superbia*. The awareness of its greatness easily degenerates into criminal arrogance. But even from the standpoint of justice the great state is dangerous: it can afford to neglect justice towards other states and to carry on a ruthlessly imperialistic policy. The powerful man can allow himself more than the small one—who is to set limits to him? He has to fear no man, and hence tends to fear nothing. And there is a third point. The bigger the state, the more abstract and schematic is the community it creates. Community is only possible in a restricted space, where to a certain extent people know each other. The almost inevitable standardization and stereotyping of human circumstances by the great state is a danger both to individuals and to groups. The great state is compelled to centralize its organization and hence enters on the path which leads to the totalitarian state. It is true that the great state is faced with tasks which the small state cannot perform; it will have to face them as long as there is no compulsive political medium above the states. It is possible, however, or even certain, as the next chapter will show, that the great state is the main obstacle in the way of union. Yet the small state too has its dangers, though one of the greatest of constitutional historians, an incomparable interpreter of the nature of the state, wrote this splendid passage:

The small state exists so that there may be a spot on earth where the largest possible proportion of the inhabitants are citizens in the fullest sense of the word. This small state possesses nothing but real, actual freedom, an ideal possession which fully balances the huge advantages of the great state, even its power. Any degeneration into despotism cuts the ground from under its feet.[3]

The very size of the great state forces imperialism on it; a non-imperialistic great state is a miracle which has not yet happened. But in the age of total warfare, imperialism means that every form of culture, and with it all justice, is imperilled.

5. JUST PUNISHMENT

It is not by accident that the only passage in the New Testament which deals at all in detail with the problem of justice in the state, Romans 13, takes criminal law as the *pars pro toto*, as the paradigm of the legal system of the state as a whole. It corresponds to the origins of state law which was in its beginnings mainly criminal law and was embodied in the court of criminal justice. This preferential position of criminal law answers to the view that the state and its coercive power are only rendered necessary by the existence of evil. If men did of their own free will what justice demands, there would be no need of a legal system in the state. The state would then be necessary at most as a supreme centre of co-ordination, as a "traffic control" in the broadest sense of the term. If everywhere and in every case the unqualified intention of justice and the clear knowledge of the just could be presumed, coercive power, that element of the state which is its most essential characteristic, would vanish. The existence of this coercive power, which is symbolized by the sword, is bound up with the fact of evil. Hence the primordial function of the state is criminal justice(83).

For that reason the relationship between justice and jurisdiction is peculiarly close in all languages. Legal procedure, the judge's sentence, is the most primary and concrete form in which the principle of justice is embodied. It is only where a disturbance arises in the course of the just order of life, hence where, by a special intervention, that order must be restored and the insecurity arising from the disturbance eliminated, that the idea of justice becomes conscious, just as we first become aware of

[3] Jakob Burckhardt, *Reflections on History.*

health in the presence of sickness. The court of justice is the expression of social disease, and in ancient times the judge and the physician were often one and the same person. If we consider the matter deeply enough, we shall realize that the tribunals of the state belong to the pathology of human society.

It is true that the court of arbitration can compete in point of real and historical priority with the criminal court. Before being he who inflicts penalties, the judge is he who distinguishes between right and wrong, who decides what belongs and what does not belong to the one party or the other. Hence he is detachment personified. He stands above the parties. It is expected of him that the disturbance in the just order brought about by subjective and arbitrary claims, by desire and passion, should have no effect on him. He is in his person the embodiment of just order itself, and his sentence is therefore the primeval form of all state legislation. This is the more conceivable since in most ancient times the judge was usually the king himself or his direct plenipotentiary. Both historically and really the judge's sentence precedes written law.

It is only from this standpoint that we can truly appreciate the nature of criminal justice. By his verdict, the arbitrator restores a just order which has become unstable; in the same way the criminal judge also restores a just order. The man who has been robbed has his property returned to him, he who has lost his good name receives it again, he is restored to honour. A sentence is essentially a process of *restoration*. From this point of view we can see that the most ancient rule of criminal law, the *jus talionis*, an eye for an eye and a tooth for a tooth, has a profound meaning. In a general way the sense of a judgment is restoration, the return to its right place; the injured party receives back what was taken from him. There are, however, cases in which this direct restoration is not possible. The lost eye cannot be restored to its socket. Therefore instead of actual restoration, of the restitution which is not possible, there is a representative, symbolic restoration. The injurer is made equal to the injured by the infliction of an equivalent injury, and thus the social equilibrium, the order, is restored. This symbolic restora-

tion is the *talio*, the eye for an eye, the tooth for a tooth(84).
The wrongdoer who cannot make the actual injury good now receives his due in the form of a just penalty, or symbolic atonement, that is, a penalty corresponding to the injury. Thus the
primary concept of justice in punishment is seen to be equivalence, the balance of guilt or injury with symbolic restitution
or punishment. Punishment is just retribution for the disturbance
of the social order.[4] That is the meaning of the falsely decried
terms "retribution" and "atonement."

Hence it is entirely fallacious to attempt to discredit retributive punishment by connecting—still more by identifying—it
with the motive of revenge(85). We can only admit the connection if we also recognize in vengeance an impulse to restore a
disturbed order, an impulse which may be obscured by passion,
but which has an objective basis. By punishment, things are replaced in their right order; the advantage which the wrongdoer
has unlawfully acquired is taken away from him; the injury
suffered by the community is repaired, if not actually, at any rate
symbolically. Hence retributive punishment is not in any way
subjective in character, but purely objective. Strictly speaking,
we should have to speak here of a subjective act on an objective
basis. Symbolic retribution can only take effect on the subject, for
only the subject can understand the symbol as such. The criminal
has to be made to realize by punishment that he has injured the
community, and by the punishment of the wrongdoer, the community is to be given the "satisfaction" of seeing that the restoration of the disturbed order is a matter of importance, hence that
that order, in spite of the disturbance, still prevails. In punishment, the order which has been disturbed asserts itself as still in
force in spite of the disturbance. What is at stake here is the order
of the community, not private claims. By the *jus talionis* retribution is taken out of the hands of the individual injured party,
whose feelings cannot be relied on, and carried out in strictest
detachment, as it were with the precision of a mathematical
instrument, in favour of the community. In this way the much

---

[4] Aristotle: Punishment is the ἀντιπεπονθός the corresponding punishment.
Nic. Ethics, pp. 5, 8.

discussed transition from blood vengeance to retributive punishment inflicted by the state becomes comprehensible and leaves in retributive punishment no taint of the satisfaction of subjective, arbitrary emotion.

It is this sense of retribution which also underlies the religious conception of punishment. Or we might say that it finds its clearest expression in the Scriptural idea of the judgment of God. For here God is not only a judge, but the personal incorporation of objective, sacred order. The order which has been disturbed is His Order, the crime has been committed on His creation, the damage done to His property. The wrong, the sin, is rebellion against Himself. If God were to let the wrong go unpunished, it would mean that His order had no force, that He did not take His own commandments seriously. The just judgment of God, by which a man reaps what he has sown, is unshakeably founded on the idea of the divine holiness.[5] This, the unparadoxical, comprehensible justice of God, which Scripture proclaims side by side with His paradoxical justice and in indissoluble relationship with it, is the prototype of all earthly criminal justice.

It has been maintained that the term "a judgment of God" is a mere transference of the principle of human criminal justice to God. That is putting the cart before the horse. It is exactly the converse which is true. All earthly criminal justice is based on the presumption of a divine, holy order which must not be infringed, and the infringement of which requires restitution, atonement, punishment. Properly understood, the human judge is merely a representative of God. He acts in the name of the divinely established order of the community. That is why "the powers" wield the sword as λειτουργός, as holy servants of God,[6] whether they know this God or not. What they do in the name of the state, they do, albeit unwittingly, by God's command. It is precisely the sword, the punishment of death, which should be the expression of God's holy wrath at the infringement of

---

[5] Both in the Old Testament and the New. Cf. e.g. Matt. 25 or Matt. 21, 40 ff; Matt. 22: 13.

[6] Rom. 13: 9.

the divine order. Hence it is absolutely in accordance with Scriptural doctrine if criminal jurisdiction, the judgment over life and death, was regarded and practised as a holy office.

Christian personalism, however, made it impossible for men to maintain the objective idea of atonement. The measure of guilt is not only to be seen in the objective injury; it is also determined by the measure of insight and evil intention. Pure objectivism leads to the monstrous conclusion that he who kills a man by pure accident is as guilty as the man who commits a fully premeditated murder. To make allowance for the subjective element, the motive and the whole circumstances of the transgression by no means mitigates the original sense of the *talio*, of the equivalence of punishment. It only refines it. It is because the punishment is only a symbol, i.e. a subjectively determined restitution or restoration of balance, that it is quite in line with the rule of retribution if the person of the transgressor is taken into account. Proportional equality takes the place of simple, arithmetical equality. The same crime meets with the same punishment, account being taken of personal inequality where the outward circumstances are equal, or of personal equality where outward circumstances are not equal. The intention to injure and the injury are considered together, since not only the actual damage, but the intention to injure endangers the order of the community. The proportional measure, however, which is of the essence of retributive justice, is preserved. To abandon proportional punishment would be to interfere with justice itself. By its very nature, justice is proportion, like for like. Here again the principle of equality is manifested, refined by the principle of inequality, as the essence of justice. Justice admits any refinement of the equation, but not its abolition. How far the reformative significance of punishment can find room in it cannot be discussed here. In any case, one thing is clear; reform or improvement can never be the determining principle of punishment. The sole and exclusive principle of punishment is and remains atonement, that is, the restoration of order by symbolic restitution.

... Chapter 21 ...

JUSTICE IN THE INTERNATIONAL ORDER

OF LATE YEARS, JUSTICE HAS MAINLY BEEN DIS-
cussed in view of the problems of international politics and questions of international law. It is quite easy to understand why; the brutal lust of power, which respects no precepts of justice, but cynically overrides all the limitations of law as a matter of course, can work itself out with least restraint in the field of international relations, and because, on the other hand, it has become clear that all orders of justice within the state, all endeavours for social and economic justice, are frustrated by war as it now is. The cry for a just order among the nations is therefore particularly urgent. This urgency, however, is confronted by the equally undeniable fact that it is particularly difficult even to form concrete ideas of a just order in this sphere, not to speak of the actual, apparently insuperable difficulties which lie in the way of its realization.

Nor does the teaching of Scripture give us any direct guidance. The subject finds no place in the New Testament. It is true that we have there the one unity embracing all peoples and abolishing all differences between peoples and races, the *corpus mysticum Christi*, the church of Jesus, in which loyalty to one Master takes precedence of all other loyalties, and the "patriotism" of those who have their *patria*, country, conversation, "household"[1] in heaven supersedes all national patriotisms. The *regnum Christi* has no national or racial frontiers. It alone is the unconditional, unlimited community of all men all over the world. But this unity exists as an actual fact only where Christ is recognized as Lord. Only the submission in faith to this one Master, who is

[1] Eph. 2: 19; Phil. 3: 20.

225

the Lord of Lords, creates it, because the sundering power of earthly dominion is only overcome by the recognition of that Lordship(86). But since, in the New Testament, the community of Christ is assumed to be a "little flock," a minority scattered all over the earth but nowhere dominant, and that not only in the contemporary but in the historical future, we are given no picture of peace on earth among the nations. On the contrary, prophecies abound of the most terrible tyrannies and wars among the peoples as the end of future history before the final consummation, which transcends history, the resurrection of the dead and the Last Judgment.[2] The hope of peace among the peoples is alien to the New Testament. The hope of "an earth in which dwelleth righteousness" is bound up with the expectation of "new heavens and a new earth,"[3] that is, with the expectation that the conditions of life in the reality of earthly history will entirely pass away. The reign of peace belongs to metahistory, to the realm of eternal life. The last ages of earthly history, however, are not in any way looked to as times of perfect peace, but as times of an unprecedented world tumult.

The attitude of the Old Testament seems different. Everyone is familiar with the moving picture of the reign of peace,[4] when swords shall be beaten into ploughshares, when not only men, but the animals which are man's grim enemies shall lie down in peace side by side and the lion eat straw like the ox. But Isaiah's lovely picture of the future is not contained in history; it is the end of history. He too sees that future which is not bound by the conditions of earthly life, a future in which, for that very reason, even the sub-human creatures obey other laws than those familiar to us in the ages of earthly history. Even if the prophetic pictures of this ultimate future are painted in earthly colours with earthly figures, what is meant is a state of things which is no longer of this earth, which transcends time. We cannot therefore draw any conclusions for the possibilities of international relations in earthly history from these apocalyptic visions. But if, in Scriptural

[2] Mark, 13: Rev. 15 ff.
[3] II Pet. 3: 13.
[4] Isa. 2: 4; Isa. 11: 6 ff.

zeal, anyone were to attempt to find standards of international law for the international relations in the Old Testament, he would only show that he had no feeling for the special and unique character of the history of Israel. The relations of the chosen people to the other nations were regulated by the peculiar law of the Old Covenant, in which Israel was not only a nation but also a religious community. The religious intention, the expansion of the community of Jehovah, was also a political intention; the dominion of Israel over other nations, that is, political imperialism, was not yet clearly distinguished from a universal religious mission. That distinction was first drawn in the New Testament. Hence the Old Testament can only be regarded as the source of standards for international law insofar as such use is admissible from the standpoint of the New Testament. But then, just as in the New Testament, nothing tangible emerges, nothing, that is, but the principles which have guided our investigation from the outset—justice conceived as the rights of the individual and the rights of the community; freedom of individuals and the common welfare. Scripture gives us no hint of what that would mean in the sphere of international law. Hence, as far as lies in our power, we must try to ascertain it ourselves.

A preliminary question, however, must first be cleared up. The church is charged with the duty of proclaiming the Gospel of repentance and reconciliation to the nations. Hence it has to call upon them to turn away from their godlessness, injustice and egoism. Its duty is to show how the catastrophe which has befallen the international order of our day is attributable to that godlessness, injustice and self-seeking. Hence it has the right to say that only a spiritual conversion of the nations would render a just and peaceful ordering of international relations possible. That has also been recognized by leading statesmen who now have a voice in the future of international relations. A number of them are convinced that nothing would promote a better international order than a sincere return of the nations to the Christian faith.

On the other hand, when the time for making peace comes,

statesmen must act whether that conversion has taken place or not. They cannot postpone the new order until the conversion of the nations is fulfilled, for they fully realize that the church of Christ will hardly achieve in the immediate future what it has failed to achieve in two thousand years. Insofar as they are Christians, they also know that Scripture contains no promise that a general conversion will take place within historical time; they know that the community of the disciples of Jesus will always remain a minority, and thus that they, as statesmen, have to reckon with a world much of which cannot be called Christian at all, and a large part only in a very vague sense.

In the present work, the problem is considered not from the standpoint of the preaching church, but from that of the Christian statesmen. We ask, with him, what could be the meaning of the expression "a just international order" in the present situation. Hence we do not ask what kind of international order would be possible if all men were good Christians, but what is possible on the assumption that a small minority of men are good Christians, the only assumption that a statesman can go upon. Hence we shall not follow the usual—and perhaps admissible—course taken by the Christian proclamations[5] of today, embark on our investigation with a sermon and mingle exhortations to greater justice in thought and intention—which are good and necessary in their place—with the critical consideration of the fundamental problem of practical politics in the international sphere, namely what is the meaning of a just international order here and now.

But if the statesman should ask us, who are not statesmen, by what right we take it upon ourselves to speak at all in this matter, our answer will be that the Christian faith implies two things which are of importance for the practical statesman too, and which Christian faith alone combines. The first is an incorruptible realism which, without falling into cynicism, allows nothing to be glossed over by optimistic idealism, the second is an absolute justice of intention arising from the clear knowledge of the principles of justice and obscured by no doctrinaire disregard

---

[5] In particular, the peace proclamations of the Pope. v. Note 91.

of practical possibilities. We shall, however, have to be on our guard against overstepping the limits of principle and entering upon questions of practice, which are really beyond our competence.

1. THE ORDER OF PEACE

The mere fact that it has not yet been possible to establish an order of peace among the nations shows that we have to reckon with the fact of evil in the sphere of international relations more than anywhere else. Within its own territory, the individual state has again and again succeeded in overcoming anarchy by its monopoly of force, and in establishing a peaceful order in which every individual can feel relatively secure. The *bellum omnium contra omnes* has been eliminated. Except for individual crimes, the citizen can count on going about his business in peace and safety without being put to the necessity of self-defense. The individual state has achieved this peaceful order—its most primary and essential function—by monopolizing for itself and its central organ all power and the right to kill. The more unequivocally, the more absolutely it does so, the more secure is the foundation of the order of peace, and the less that sinister background of political power, the right to kill, becomes manifest.

But it is as if evil, repressed by the lawful force of the police and armed power of the state, must of necessity burst forth in more appalling form in the relations between the states. The very power of the state, which was the means of establishing peace within its frontiers, becomes, in the international sphere, the most potent factor of anarchy. Evil, suppressed but not overcome in the state, having found no outlet inwards, erupts outwards all the more violently. The state, beneficently powerful internally, becomes a brutal oppressor and robber with respect to the outside world. It is the Christian's duty to face these facts with all the realism of his insight into sin and to relinquish all idealism. The conduct of the nations among themselves is not very different from the conduct of individuals in a completely anarchic society. There may be some who are more concerned for justice and peaceful concord than others, but the total picture of the world of nations forces one to the conclusion that every state, according to the measure of its power, is out to take as much of the good things of this earth as it can and to leave to others only as much as they force it to leave or as seems necessary in its own interests. The distinction between peaceful and warlike states is illusory. If we ask whether there are nations or states which are prepared, of their own free will, to forego advantages which their power would permit them to secure, or whether they are not at all times prepared to take by force whatever seems advantageous to them, the answer can hardly be in doubt. The sphere of international relations is dominated, apart from rare exceptions, by a purely egoistic principle of power, veiled more or less by diplomatic courtesy, but mitigated only by the calculation that wars are expensive and their issue often or generally uncertain. Up to the present, in any case, national egoism, the intention of every state to take as much as possible and to give only what cannot be withheld has been, practically speaking, the dominating motive in the relations of states to each other. Whether this national egoism achieves its aims rather by indirect and diplomatic, or by direct and warlike methods, is a subsidiary question and determined less by the warlike character of a nation or a ruling class than by outward circumstance. A relatively unassailable state can give weight and effect to its self-seeking in a less warlike fashion than one less favoured by its situation. A satisfied, self-sufficient state which has all the economic necessities and is, purely by reason of its size and "potential," an opponent to be feared, can better camouflage its lust of power by peaceable gestures than another which would first like to have what the others have got. The wealthy nation, or the nation which has acquired wealth, whose ambitions of power are more or less satisfied, can afford a display of peaceableness, since it has as great an interest in preserving the *status quo* as the poor one in changing it, while the poor state, being out for change, must take upon itself the odium of disturbing the peace(87). Judged from the standpoint of justice, the conservative egoism which aims at peace is no better than the egoism which aims at war. Those who claim their national monopolies as their self-evident right must be prepared for others simply not to recognize that monopoly and therefore to become aggressive. This is said merely in order to demonstrate the egoism of power in its two forms—the conservative and unwarlike and the aggressive and warlike—as the dominant principle of international relations, in comparison with which the difference between warlike and unwarlike is of minor importance. In this twofold form, evil dominates the picture of political reality. Even the difference between the egoism of power on a small and on a large scale is merely relative. Minor states participate in the egoism of power no less than great ones, although here, as in the individual sphere, the egoism of the smaller is, so to speak, more pardonable than that of the great. Their peaceableness is often mere resignation and the shrewdness which realizes that their comparative powerlessness simply rules out any active and aggressive policy of power. It would be foolish to imagine that we can see in their attitude any special national virtue, a natural modesty or self-effacingness.

In view of the incontestable fact that evil—namely national or imperial egoism—dominates the nations, what can be the substance of the first postulate of justice—an order of peace? The first point to be emphasized is the extreme urgency of this postulate. It takes unqualified precedence of all other social problems. For until the international anarchy, manifested in the constant round of preparation for war, threat of war, and war, is overcome, all that social justice can achieve will become more and more illusory, since war has developed in such a way as to call all civilization and all culture in question.

It is no longer admissible to speak of war as people used to do. For what is war today is no longer what war used to be. There are two points to be borne in mind here, which have given the problem of war, and with it the problem of the order of peace, a quite unprecedented turn in our day. The first is the fact of world war, the fact that in most recent times the mutual involvements of nations have become so general and so close that war can, and almost must, become a world conflagration. The age of local wars is over; the age when all war means world war has come. The second new fact is total war. In former times there were wars carried on by armies of mercenaries which certainly caused great regional devastations and disturbances of peaceful life. On the other hand, they did not greatly affect the peaceful activity of the population as a whole. Since national armies have been created, and all national goods and forces pressed into service, and quite especially since war has been mechanized, it has taken on so devastating an effect, and makes such inroads in the national reserves, that it is threatening mankind with utter ruin. World war, and total war have created an absolutely new situation, have given an absolutely new urgency to the postulate of an order of peace. That this anarchy, which bears the name of total world war, should be overcome is the presupposition of all future civilization and of all other endeavours to establish justice. If we do not succeed in doing so, all culture, and with it all just order, is called in question. Such are the dimensions to which evil has grown. Anarchy, which the individual state has mastered to a certain extent, now threatens the continuance of human life in the form of international anarchy. But what possibilities are there for an order of peace?

Theoretically, there are three possibilities, and only three:

> peace by means of a superior, uniformly coercive force
> peace by law
> peace by law combined with force.

The first of the possibilities is the Pax Romana, the elimination of war by a power imposing uniformity. The Roman Empire was, at any rate for a few generations, an order of peace for the Mediterranean peoples. The Pax Romana was no fiction, no mere propagandist catchword of imperial orators, but a political reality. In a general way it was an order in which the nations could live side by side not only in peace, but even in a certain degree of comfort, though with an almost total sacrifice of their national independence. Quite apart from the injustice involved, it is precisely this question of national feeling which puts any attempt at this order of peace out of court today. The national sense of independence is too strong to submit to any imperium, even if it were able to offer the nations a peaceful, and, in the Roman sense, comfortable life. Even if such an *imperium* were established, the national sense of independence would be a cause of ceaseless revolts and wars of liberation. But this solution of the problem is above all impracticable because a number of great powers of relatively equal strength exist, none of which would be prepared to accept the other as a "world empire." On the other hand, a triumvirate of great powers, or a similar combination of powers, even if the establishment of a durable and uniform government could be expected of it, would never offer the same guarantee of peace as an *imperium* with an absolutely unified basis of power. On the other hand, another variant of this solution does not lie beyond the range of practical possibility, namely the creation of a universal state on an ideological basis, for instance the extension of the communistic dictatorship of the proletariat over the whole world. The proletariat as a whole is not particularly interested in national units, but is in part extremely interested in the universal expansion of the communistic state. Hence it is not entirely beyond the bounds of possibility that an order of peace of this kind, imposed by force on all nationally minded peoples, might one day become a reality. The Christian, of course, could see in an order of peace of this kind nothing but the realization of the apocalyptic vision of "The beast coming up out of the earth,"[6] since it would imply the annihilation of all those claims to justice which are contained in the Christian conception of personal freedom and the organic structure of society. It would be a peace to which the present dangers of anarchy would be preferable.

The second possibility of peace is that established by law, that is, the treaty of peace on a basis of international law. This was, more or less, the "solution" of the problem during the whole of the middle ages and modern times. The solution of the problem of anarchy was very relative. War followed war, but peace always returned and the localization of wars prevented the disturbance of peaceful life from reaching the intolerable dimen-

[6] Rev. 13.

sions which we see in the total world war of today. Apart, however, from the restriction of wars in scope and intensity, there were in former times bases for this solution of the problem which hardly exist today(88). There was at that time in western humanity a certain spiritual unity born of the universality of Christendom. There existed the *Corpus Christianum*(89) which provided a basis for a certain loyalty to treaties. The principles and agreements of international law represented a relationship and obligation which was certainly relative, but yet not ineffective, and which set effective limits to "Machiavellian" politics. That awareness of international law only remained in force as long as a certain degree of common Christian convictions really united mankind and its rulers. Machiavellianism, the theory of which was not by accident a product of the Renaissance, was certainly in practice long before Machiavelli, yet until last century it always encountered a determined, and politically not ineffective, resistance. The basic principle of all international law, *pacta sunt servanda*, was something with which even coolly calculating statesmen had to reckon; it was a moral reality. This principle, and the feeling among the nations that they were "Christendom," a spiritual unity, formed a powerful counterbalance to the egoism of power in the individual states, which even then existed.[7]

In proportion, however, as this common Christian substance was exhausted, as positivism became the prevailing philosophy and the ethic of solidarity lost its basis in reality, the moral scruples militating against the breach of treaties vanished, and finally, as the era of the totalitarian revolution approached, there was little left in the international sphere but the selfish calculations of power politics and reasons of state. Above the national states and great powers there no longer existed any spiritual power to form a bond of union. Only then was anarchy in the international sphere consummated. When solemnly concluded treaties could be called "scraps of paper," the last vestige of supra-state union was gone. The Kellogg Pact to ban war was not only powerless to check the process; it actually accelerated

[7] Cf. Max Huber, Note 88.

it, since, when the parties to the pact signed it, none of them took it seriously. The upshot was that the treaty of peace, as a guarantee of peace was more than ever discredited. It was only after the totalitarian revolutions, however, that the impotence of treaties to guarantee peace became fully manifest. From then on, it was clear that no moral scruples were to be allowed to stand in the way of the self-seeking politics of power. The moral capital which makes treaties possible had been fully spent. The sacredness of treaties has become an empty phrase—what else was to be expected of statesmen, members of Parliament and nations that have abolished the holy? The treaty no longer counts as a guarantee of peace. It must, however, be pointed out that the international treaty, even when there is a prospect that it will be kept, is always a very imperfect instrument. It is morally justified, its binding force rests on that moral justification, only if it can be assumed that circumstances will remain what they are. To insist on the fulfilment of the terms of a treaty when circumstances have completely changed can be a supreme wrong. Here the *summum jus* becomes the *summa injuria.* Furthermore, many treaties are not concluded by free consent, but are forced upon one of the parties, in which case their legality is a fiction. In any case, the peace treaty can no longer be taken into serious account as a guarantee of peace, as a solution of the problem of anarchy.

The third possibility is the establishment of a supra-state power on a federalistic, co-operative basis which will guarantee peace by enforcing obedience, after the common consent of the members, upon the disturber of the peace, that is, upon the member which does not submit to the decision of the union of nations. What this idea means is that the solution of the problem of anarchy in the individual state is applied to the world of nations. In the democratic state, the individual relinquishes his right of self-defense to the unified state power standing above all, which represents the "will of the people" and holds the monopoly of force; in the same way, it would be expected of the individual nations that they would surrender their right of self-defense to a supra-state organization and submit to the superior will of the "family of nations." The first attempt at a solution of this kind, Wilson's League of Nations, came to grief. There were many reasons for its failure, but two made that failure inevitable. The solution could only succeed if the analogy with the solution of the problem of anarchy in the individual state held good even in a relative sense. But it did not hold good, firstly because the individual nations did not, in actual fact, disarm, and hence the supra-state power had no monopoly of force; secondly because the primary condition of a central power which is to be absolutely superior to every single member is, and must be, a fiction as long as there are great powers(90).

Hence, in a new plan, even if the first condition were fulfilled, and all the individual nations disarmed, the second condition would remain not only unfulfilled, but unfulfillable as long as great powers exist which, as a result of their pure potential of armament, whether latent in the present or realizable in the future, could not be forced to submit to the will of a central power. The solution of the problem of anarchy in the individual state was rendered possible by the fact that the individual citizen is powerless against the state as a whole. The many are so superior in power to the one that he cannot but yield. If the world of nations consisted of a large number of roughly equal "individuals," something like an analogy would exist. But it actually consists of a few dozen small or medium-sized states and a small number of great powers which have shared out the major part of the globe between them. It is fantastic to assume that a central power could be created on a federal basis, that it would be capable of compelling one of those great powers to do or leave undone what it does not want to do or leave undone, but what has been decided by the council of nations or agreed on by treaty. The superiority of the many to the one which establishes and secures the order of peace in the individual democratic state does not exist owing to the enormous inequality between the individual members and their power in relation to the whole. Hence the analogy with the solution of the problem of anarchy in the individual state breaks down.

Yet another difficulty must be pointed out. It is not only in the enforcement of the common will that obstacles arise; even the creation of a unified will is extremely difficult in a democratically organized federation of states or nations. Democracy is not the easiest but the most difficult form of political will to manipulate. We have already seen in considering the problem of the individual state how difficult it is for democracy to ward off anarchistic and divergent trends. It must be far more difficult where the individuals are not human beings, but states and nations with totally different histories and traditions, with different outlooks and ideologies and quite different constitutions. Can we expect states which do not shape their own lives on democratic principles suddenly to have the power of participating fruitfully in a democratic supra-state organization? True democracy is only possible where not only the state, but the very cells of which the state is composed are permeated with the democratic principle. It would be superfluous to show that this assumption cannot be taken for granted today.

All these considerations lead to the distressing conclusion that an institutional solution of the problem of anarchy is not possible. Neither the *Pax Romana*, nor the treaty, nor the supra-state organization on a federative basis opens up the possibility of a solution. That is the fact that must be faced by every man who has to do responsible work in connection with the problem of international peace, and cannot be satisfied with utopian dreams.

Then must anarchy remain? Must humanity go through recurrent world wars, steadily increasing in scope and intensity until it at last perishes of exhaustion? Our feeling rebels against such a conclusion, and not only our feeling, but our conscience too. There must be some way to establish an order of peace. And there is one, only we must have no illusions about its cost. No institution can in itself guarantee peace: that is the incontrovertible result of our consideration. The way to peace, therefore, must be sought elsewhere, namely in the intention of peace.

If nations were willing to place what is just before their own advantage, it would be an easy matter to establish an order of peace. But if we were ready or obliged to wait until that intention of justice existed, the world could perish a thousand times in the meantime. It would, however, be possible to establish an order of peace all the same if the nations and states were ready to abandon their self-seeking politics of power, not so much for the sake of justice as for the sake of peace, and to fulfil a minimum of the requirements of international justice and peaceableness, even at the cost of sacrifice, in the interests of peace. It would be fantastic and utopian to reckon with the possibility that nations and states which have, for thousands of years, been mainly guided in their international relations by the selfish principle of power, should suddenly become convinced adherents of the principle of justice. But it is not fantastic to believe in the possibility that, in view of the horrors of total world war, the nations and states should be ready to make sacrifices in order to preserve peace, that they should not simply assume the selfish standpoint of power, but that, in the distribution of land, of economic interests and benefits, of political influence, they should make allowance for the needs and rights of others. Anyone who condemns that possibility as utopian must realize that he is declaring the next world war to be inevitable. The intention of peace of nations and states, which in itself must also be the readiness to make national sacrifices for the just claims of others, is the only possible guarantee of peace for the future. The farther that intention goes, the stronger it is, the sooner a lasting order of peace can be established. The less it exists, the more inevitable is the next total world war.

This intention of peace and justice will of itself produce certain institutions of supra-state co-operation, though these will, as we saw, of themselves offer no guarantee of peace. They can, however, be both necessary and useful as instruments to implement an existing intention of peace. Since we cannot for the time being reckon with a reduction in the size of the colossal great states, nor with a surrender of the national sense of independence in the medium-sized and small states, this co-operation of the nations for the establishment of an order of peace, that is, for the establishment of a relatively just order, will only be able to proceed if the great states again and again forego the use of their power to enforce their self-seeking intentions and negotiate with the others as if they were not the powerful ones, and if even the minor states no longer aim simply at carrying through their individual interests at all costs, but are prepared to make sacrifices for the sake of a just order. An order of peace can only be rendered possible by a limitation of sovereignty, not in a formal, legal sense, but in a moral and practical sense, unless supra-state institutions can be created by this common and general intention of peace which will guarantee effective legal protection even to the small states against the great ones. But since, as we saw, these institutions cannot of themselves give that guarantee, the formal legal limitation of sovereignty will only be possible when the intention of peace and justice in the leading political powers, the great powers, is unequivocally manifest, and not merely proclaimed in high-sounding phrases.

2. LAW: INTERNATIONAL LAW

The second stage of justice is law. All international law rests on the sacredness of treaties. Without that, there are agreements, such, namely, in which each party reckons from the outset that the other will break them when he deems it to his advantage. But there is no international law. Law only exists where agreements remain in force, where they remain valid, even when the parties would prefer to break them. In view of the monstrous atrophy of the respect for and loyalty to treaties, we are justified in enquiring whether treaties of international law are possible at all in the legal sense. At any rate, the present crisis in the respect for international treaties makes it incumbent on all those concerned with religious education, or any other kind of education, to work for the restoration of that respect and of the conviction of the sacredness of treaties.

There are, however, even in the present precarious state of feeling about treaties, doubtless many problems which can be solved by international treaties, namely such as do not touch the—real or imagined—vital interests of a state. By the restoration and expansion of the Court of Arbitration at The Hague, which had too little scope for development between the two wars, a good deal might be done for a regulation of interstate disputes on the basis of legal treaties, even though it cannot be seriously reckoned with as an instrument of peace in the narrower sense of the word. Even the League of Nations, at the very time of its failure to safeguard international peace, achieved fruitful and lasting results in the sphere of international hygiene and in other departments.

Above all, however, the development of the procedure of international negotiation and co-operation opens up a wide and promising field. These formal possibilities should neither be over- nor underrated. Forms of collaboration for the solution of problems which interest many or all states are possible, necessary and hopeful even when, in themselves, they offer no guarantee of peace. The international courts of arbitration had hardly come into existence when they were overtaken by two world wars and prevented from developing any useful activity. But as an institution, they contain great possibilities of development, and nobody can judge what sources of conflict might be eliminated by these courts once they had been able to function for any length of time. The intention of peace and justice in the states and nations must take practical effect in the composition of such bodies, which must be guided, not by the national self-interest of the members, but by the intention of creating an order of peace. The more this happens, the more such bodies are established as impartial authorities, and the less national egoism is allowed to criticize or check their impartial judgment, the more they will be able to do for peace as well as for justice. An equally necessary and beneficent method would be the development of obligatory processes of negotiation for the settlement of international disputes, of a "justice of the peace" procedure which would be interposed between the appearance of the difference and drastic action, and would, above all, secure the open discussion of the controversial facts and views in the press. In all these things, however, which represent an endeavour to overcome the principle of power by legal forms, absolute equality before the law must prevail. If things are to proceed by right and not by might, the great state must claim no rights but those it is ready to concede to minor states.

Yet however valuable all these legal instruments may be, their effectiveness for the establishment of a peaceful and just order must not be overrated. Here again the great powers will be the difficult parties. There is considerable guarantee that a minor state will submit to the verdict. Unfortunately that is not equally the case with the great power simply because it can afford to refuse. Hence even here the legal form in itself cannot guarantee justice and peace, but only that form of law which is firmly founded on the intention of peace and justice. No court of arbitration can prevent a great power from doing as it likes; it can only be prevented from so doing by the realization that a course of conduct dictated by the egoism of power contains in itself the germ of the next world war. Hence it is also important that the present dread of world war, the existing maximum will to peace, should be utilized for the creation of a maximum and optimum of such legal forms, which then, when the impression of the world war has somewhat faded, will be already in full working order and will have stood the test.

3. JUST INTERNATIONAL LAW

The third stage of justice is "just law," that is, an ordering of international relations which shall render to every nation its due, its rights to freedom and its duties to the community. This requirement must be stated and its importance realized even in this vague and generalized form. Every nation must have its rightful due. International law is only just when it renders "to each its due." This proposition must be accepted before we go on to consider the difficulties presented by its more precise interpretation(91). Those difficulties are certainly very great. The first concerns "every" state or "every" nation. What is here the *quisque* to which the *suum* is to be rendered? Since Wilson's day, "the right of self-determination of the peoples" has been a current phrase. It has recently been proclaimed anew in very prominent quarters. Primarily it means the right of the nations to self-constitution, i.e. wherever a sufficient number of human beings inhabiting a contiguous territory unites to become a state, there that right must be granted to it. Every man must be able to decide for himself which state he is to belong to, and every people must be able to decide how it is to be bounded off from other nations or combine with other nations to form a state. If it has once so constituted itself, its right to existence as an independent state must be recognized. That is the first sense of Wilson's postulate. The postulate itself stands in urgent need of examination.

What we have here is the problem of the "individual and the community," only that here the individual is the nation, the community the family of nations. But while in the first case the individual is the tangible, physical person, in the case of the "nation" it is a unit which is difficult to grasp. What is the "nation" which has as well-founded a right as an individual human being to the recognition of its existence as a state? If we think in terms of creation, in what sense can we say that a people is created by God? Is the determining factor here the present intention to belong, or not to belong, together? It is not by accident that it was an American who endeavoured to establish the right of self-determination of nations as the principle of international justice, for in the Constitution of the American federation, the covenant of self-determination played a decisive part. The majority of the other states did not come into being in this way. They are not the product of the declaration of an intention, but of a historical process. There is even a catch in Renan's definition of the nation as *un plébiscite de tous les jours*. What does *tous les jours* mean? Who is to guarantee that those who wish to live together today will wish to tomorrow, that those who part today will not repent the parting tomorrow? Should not the nation be regarded as similar to a marriage or a family rather than to a contractual organization? Is not the union born of history more important than the momentary intention of union?

If we turn to history, fresh difficulties arise. What point of historical development is to be the starting-point? The *status quo ante bellum*? As if we did not all know the strain under which the sense of justice in political matters was then labouring! How far back should we have to go to discover what really belongs together? But there are still further difficulties. The intention of union as well as a former community of fate would bring together populations now geographically separated that could only be reunited by vast re-settlements, which in their turn would involve great injustice. Further, geographic and military, and above all economic factors would have to be taken into account in the creation of a state with any prospect of survival. The claims of "justice" vary according to which factors stand in the foreground. Here the Balkans present the most striking illustration.

On the other hand, we should not, as the nationals of large territories are prone to do, take these difficulties as necessarily invalidating the principle of nationality altogether, and hence assume that the small state is obsolete for economic or military reasons(92). From the standpoint of community, of culture, of spiritual values, the small state is superior to the great state. It is not the small states which are abnormal, but the great states. It is not the small states which have to produce ethical justification for their existence, but great states. Just as the individual is more than the state, the small state is in itself more than the great state. That is a point which must be clearly expressed in the age of the worship of pure size. The monsters of great states present in very truth no ideal of national community. Seen from a wider historical perspective, their justification lies in their being provisional makeshifts for the not yet extant supra-state unity. If we had that supra-state unity, the small state would be all the more able to claim its rights and to exercise a function of community which is beyond the power of the great state. It is, however, the great state which is the most insuperable obstacle to the formation of that supra-state unity, as we have just seen.

It is not size which determines whether a nation has a right to exist, but its capacity to create a political form which can really stand on its own feet. When it is said that small states are defenseless against military attack by the great state, that is first of all only partially true, and secondly, it is to the discredit, not of the small but of the great state. The great state must simply be held in check by a legal system in such a way that the small one can live beside it without fear. Every nation which has proved its capacity to form an independent state, and has the lasting intention to do so, has also the right to that independence. Only an international organization which can guarantee that right can lay claim to be relatively just.

Whether this right of the individual nation to independence and self-determination is unlimited is quite another question. This question must be answered as definitely in the negative as the first one in the affirmative. But again this negative applies not only to small states but also and equally to great states. Here, however, we already have reached the second question. What is that which each has a right? What is its "due"? The primary political reality is territory. To what territory has a nation a right? To that territory which its nationals now inhabit, to more or to less? This question can hardly be answered on general principles, because just rights intersect at this point, namely the power of survival of a nation, that is the territory it needs if it is really going to live; its natural frontiers, which are of importance as long as a nation stands in need of self-defense, that is, as long as there is no supra-state organization of power; its historical tradition, i.e. its historical right. Many thorny problems, the colonial problem, for instance, could be solved if only economic life could be detached from its close connection with national political states. Above all, one thing holds good of nations as of individuals—the wealth of the rich is unjust when it entails the poverty of others. Rich nations must realize that they are always an effective cause of future wars if they persist in regarding their economic monopolies and the advantages accruing from them as their "due," if they are not prepared to let others have a share of what is theirs in virture of their power. The economic imperialism of great powers, that is, the harnessing of superior political power for the preservation or acquisition of economic advantages, is incompatible with a peaceful international order. The most far-reaching detachment of world economy from power politics is one of the most urgent postulates of international justice.

Not only the imperialism of the great states, however, but the nationalistic imperialism of the minor states is a great obstacle in the way of a just order. Here there would be a rich field of activity for impartial arbitration. If the leading great powers were to back an impartial court of this kind with their power and prestige, and if they were really concerned, for the sake of peace, to keep that court free of imperialistic influences, much might be expected for the establishment of a just order. No just international order can come into being until the states, primarily the great states, and secondarily the small states, begin to realize that the just settlement of international disputes can alone provide even a relative guarantee of lasting peace, until, from their own interest in world peace, they become interested in justice, and support the impartial settlement of disputes instead of sabotaging it in advance by the egoism of power.

According to the interpretation current hitherto, the right of self-determination of the nations means not only the recognition of their national independence, but also the recognition of their right to adopt the form of government they consider right. Even here, however, the principle of the right of self-determination requires limitation. That right of the nations to live in the form best suited to them is subject to the condition that the security of the other nations is not jeopardized thereby. Not every form of constitution provides that guarantee. Dictatorships are admittedly more prone to warlike action and aggressive policies than democracies. Totalitarian states, however, must simply be handled as political epidemics which have to be dealt with by an international "sanitary corps." Further, it belongs to a policy of consideration for the common welfare of the nations that the rights to freedom of individual states should not include the right of unlimited armament. Any state organized on a military basis is a danger to its neighbours and hence to international peace. The world has recently had proof of how dangerous the liberal principle of *laisser-faire* becomes at this point. The restriction of armament in the individual nations, which is in itself in the interest of every single state, is, however, only just when it is enforced, not by the hegemonistic aims of individual great powers, but by planning in the service of the family of peoples.

The subordination of the rights and duties of each individual nation or each individual state to a just order of the whole presupposes, as we have seen, at any rate a moral limitation of the sovereignty of individual states. It is part of the tragedy of the modern political development that while a world economy was breaking down all national frontiers and making the world smaller, a newly awakened nationalism was provoking a contrary movement of mutual exclusion which culminated in the idea of national autarchy. The idea of the nation, and of national unity and independence, took on a significance which it had had neither in the classical world nor in the Middle Ages.[8] While modern technology, world traffic and world economics required the greatest possible elimination of frontiers, nationalism postulated exactly the converse, namely, mutual exclusion. Napoleonic imperialism was the first product of these two factors. The other imperialisms followed suit, while at the same time the rise of new nations on a basis of national independence created new centres of conflict. Paradoxical as it may sound, the two world wars were the first clear expression of the solidarity of the nations, of the inescapable community of their destiny. But at the same time they were the expression of an exacerbated national egoism. Is there a solution of this problem of elemental crosscurrents?

The fact that the nations are actually united by fate renders unlimited national sovereignty impossible. *Laisser-faire* has proved as unserviceable a principle of order in the international sphere as Manchester liberalism in economics. The limitation of national sovereignty in favour of supra-national planning of justice is indispensable. But as long as great powers exist, a formal limitation by international law could only mean a veiled

[8] Cf. Werner Kaegi, *Historische Meditationen, Die Entstehung der Nation.*

vassalage of the small to the great states. Hence the limitation can, for the present, only be moral in kind. Nations and governments must come to the realization that peace, which all desire, can only be guaranteed by mutual consideration, by a policy of neighbourliness. This policy of consideration, and the voluntary limitation of sovereignty by the recognition of an obligation to a community transcending them all, must be required from all. In particular, it must be required from the great powers, since they, purely by reason of their size, always represent the greatest danger to a just international order. If a new order is to be created, the great must first and most obviously relinquish the assertion of their superior power. Otherwise it must be regarded from the outset as an unjust, egoistic order of power and the starting-point of further world war. The great powers have no right to force self-denial on the small states which they are not ready to take upon themselves.

For a certain type of thought, with a bias to unity determined purely by economic motives and infected with the spirit of size and standardization, the existence of the small state is altogether a nuisance. They are regarded, so to speak, as traffic obstructions in international economy, and their sense of independence criticized as an obsolete manner of thought corresponding to no real need or value. In actual fact the reverse holds good. The national differentiation of Europe is its greatest treasure. Totalitarianism would involve a monstrous impoverishment. There are, it is true, a large number of activities which could be standardized without danger to intellectual life. On the model of the world postal union, an international currency, an international transport system and many other things which belong to the outward frame of human life could be internationally standardized and centralized without danger. With respect to the industry of a country, however, that only holds good to the point at which its vital nerve would be struck by international centralization. We shall, therefore, need both: supra-state economic planning *and* preservation of national forms of culture even in the economic sphere. Otherwise it might well happen that the life of Europe might be saved but its soul lost. From the standpoint of a federalistic idea of justice, such as is set forth in this book as implied in the Christian faith, a determined stop must be put to all rash and radical attempts at union and centralization.

We must not fall victim to the illusion that even the wisest and best-intentioned statesmen will ever be able to create "the" just order, or even to imagine it. There are so many just, yet conflicting claims that even Solomon's wisdom would not suffice to settle them so that all parties would be convinced of the justice of the solution. And as to what is just in individual cases, even the most impartial arbitrators will often fail to agree. A great deal will have been achieved if even an order of this kind can be established; for the individual parties it will be in any case preferable to a new war. In the attainment of this goal, the most important factor will be the statesmen who take a leading part in framing the international order. It is true that even the best intentioned and wisest statesmen can only put a small measure of justice into action if the people behind him are not with him: it is the tragic lot of really good statesmen that they are often forced by their people to act otherwise than their own insight dictates. Fortunately, however, it can also happen that a nation's sense of justice is stronger than that of its statesmen at a particular time, and demands from them a policy of justice to which they are personally disinclined. The intention of justice of the Christian people has to work from both ends—that of the statesmen and that of the people. Through both, the intention of justice can become effective. The effort in the cause of justice, even on the part of the humblest citizen, is not quite vain, and none, even that of the most powerful of statesmen, can ever quite attain the goal it aims at.

The requirements of justice and those of an order of peace are connected in the first instance by mutual implication. Only what is just creates lasting peace. For the very sake of peace, justice must become a reality, because injustice, when it is too great, provokes indignation and hence leads to war. Since the intention of peace must in future be the dominating factor in all international politics—since the alternative to peace is total world war, and peace is only possible on the basis of justice—there is fresh hope for justice in the sphere of practical politics. Unfortunately, however, this is not the only aspect of the relationship between the two factors, peace and justice. There are also short-term guarantees of peace by brutal but superior power which takes no heed of justice. The psychology of victorious peoples after a war tends towards a short-term solution of the problem of peace. It will be the task of all far-seeing men to work for an order of peace of the first kind. Christianity can have no doubt as to which side it should stand on. It knows that "justice alone exalts a people," that the supreme measure of justice gives the supreme guarantee of peace. It will, it must demand that power should not be used selfishly in its owners' interests, but that the requirements of justice shall be fulfilled first. That is the only justification of power before the tribunal of conscience. Justice without power is impotent; power without justice is brutal, devilish.

Power in the service of justice—that is the watchword which issues unequivocally from Christian insight.

4. THE DISTRIBUTION OF POWER

The fourth stage of justice is the just sharing of the power which establishes international order. Even within the individual state, it is the last requirement in the series, the postulate of democracy. It is still more so in the international sphere. It is not the most urgent need of the nations of our day that as many nations as possible should have as equal a share as possible in the determination of an international order. On the contrary, there is only one really urgent interest now—that some order should be established, by whomever it may be, in which the nations can live in peace and in which every nation shall possess its independence and freedom in the ordered framework of the whole. Who establishes this order, whether a few great powers or all the nations, is a subordinate question. An order of the peoples on a democratic basis is, as we have seen, a utopia as long as giant states and dwarf states exist side by side.

The only question now is whether the great powers which

actually have the fate of the nations in their hands have insight and sense of justice enough to create a relatively just order in the interests of peace, or whether, interested as they are in concluding peace as soon as possible, they override the just claims of the individual nations and create an order which serves their monopolies rather than a lasting peace. For that reason, and for that reason alone, it will be necessary for the great powers to listen to the minor powers when peace is being made, if they are not to create an order of peace which will soon stand revealed as an illusion, as the cause of further wars. On the other hand, to put forward the demand, at the present moment, for the most democratic order of peace possible is utterly to misunderstand the facts. It may well be that every great power will put forward that demand, but their object will only be to camouflage their power politics as democracy. The great powers are—we can indeed say unfortunately—once for all the determining factors in the framing of an international order. No democratic League of Nations programs, no matter how well intentioned, can alter that fact. It is not democratic institutions of that kind which guarantee justice, but the great powers' intention of peace combined with the realization that, if understanding is to be real, the voice of all the peoples must be heard. The justice, and hence the permanence of the order of peace, depends on whether the great powers pay attention to the statement of the just claims of all. But it is part of the justice that men hope for and demand that the small nations also get their rights, that they too shall not be treated as the objects of an imperative of power, but as subjects of a community.

Here one circumstance which might in itself militate against the future peace may possibly work for future justice, namely that there are a number of powers with a leading say in the matter. The conflict of interests between the great powers has always been the opportunity of the small ones. A world empire can afford to override the claims of the individual nations; a number of more or less rival great powers cannot. They will have to court the favour of the smaller nations, and that gives the latter an opportunity to voice their claims. But as to what form this play of political forces will or should take, no principles can be laid down.

5. EXTRA AND SUPRA-STATE POSSIBILITIES

The present face of the world of nations and states, which, it is to be assumed, will be changed in many points of detail by the post-war order, though not in its main outlines, is characterized by the existence, side by side, of a number of national states and a few great empires. As long as this order of national states and empires is taken for granted as a kind of political axiom, world peace and justice will always be insecure. The actually existing link which unites the destinies of the nations, and the actual living unity of individual human beings all over the world, finds only a very imperfect and uneasy expression in this picture of national states and empires. The present national and imperial frontiers are far from coinciding with the present conditions of human life. They cannot be the final term in the political ordering of the world of nations. From more than one quarter there is an urge to the development of a more universal order.

Firstly, there is the economic order to be considered. It has long ceased to be a self-sufficing national economic order. World traffic is no longer, as in Columbus' time, confined to the exchange of articles of luxury and occasional adventures by enterprising individuals. Even the most remote mountain village in the Alps has its branch of the co-operative society through which it obtains its goods from all over the world, and the purchasing power of the franc earned by the day labourer there is partially determined by what goes on on the money markets of New York or Tokio. In the immediate future a still greater intensification of the economic interdependence of all regional and national economies is certainly to be expected. An accommodation to world economy is hence indispensable to the economy of every single country, whether it seems desirable to that country or not. But that accommodation has its political premises and consequences. The longer the national policy of the individual state is carried on, the more it will be felt as an obstruction, as a garment which has grown too small, and the need of a more universal, spacious order will make itself increasingly felt. It is true, as we have seen, that this process involves grave dangers to the inviolable values of separate national existence, but an economic system has something of the irresistible power of natural processes. It is useless to kick against the pricks. The only help here is wise and far-sighted planning. It is just because of those dangers that the bond between economics and politics must be loosed. It is just because the world-wide economic network contains causes of recurrent conflict that economics must be detached from the statute of political national states far more radically than has ever been the case, and organized on a supra-state basis insofar as is compatible with the specific cultural task and nature of the national units.

A supra-state planning and supervision of this kind will become the more urgent because otherwise world economy is bound to become the prey of profit-greedy international capitalism. It must in justice be admitted that the world economy has done vast pioneer work. Without the enterprise and farsightedness of the great, free *entrepreneurs* we should not have a well-stocked world market at our disposal, by which we are spared the recurrent famines of former times. But this pioneer body of *entrepreneurs* has increasingly developed into a monopolistic group of world magnates which exploits the nations on both sides of the globe in the interests of their profit. It is this very development which national politics is simply unable to cope with.

The new phase upon which the colonial problem has entered points in the same direction. In the last few centuries the colonies were, in the main, objects of national exploitation. This state of things is felt to be intolerable on both sides—by the colonial nations themselves and by the home countries possessing colonies. A supra-state co-operative administration of colonial territories which are not yet mature enough for self-administration is becoming an urgent necessity and this new problem can only be solved if the imperialistic policy pursued hitherto is abandoned. A great deal of the substance of international conflict would vanish if only the phase in which this or that part of Africa or Asia "belonged" to this or that European country were relegated to the past. Here, above all, it will be possible to see the sacrifices which wealthy nations or states are ready to take upon themselves in the interests of peace as well as of justice. The combination of world traffic and colonial empires is one of the prime causes of the two world wars.

The second factor in human life which rises above international frontiers is culture. Culture, it is true, tends far more than economics to take on individual forms, is far more directed by individual peculiarities and is far more deeply connected with the root forces of personal communities. On the other hand, it is the ground on which the universality of the spirit is made manifest, and that knows no national frontiers. We of our day who have experienced the paroxysm of political nationalism are more in a position to recognize the value of that humane citizenship of the world which the last century, in its unhistorical and unnatural rationalism, strove to deride. In any case we see ourselves compelled by the political events of recent times to reflect seriously whether there is not, above the nations, a European cultural heritage to preserve. We wish to be good Europeans again, and not only Swiss, French or Dutch. Beyond that, however, science in particular is forming international links of increasing strength, and future world traffic will bring not only those engaged in economic life, but those active in the sphere of culture, much closer together than has been the case hitherto. The national isolation and alienation which politics imposed on the nations by force had for long past ceased to answer to the thought and feeling of their intellectual leaders. The time will come when the community of culture will refuse to regard the members of other nations as "enemies" for the sake of politics.

In this connection, however, one element will be of decisive importance. From the outset, one body, the Christian church, was the supreme bond of union of the nations, and it has remained so throughout the centuries in spite of the many dark times it has passed through. The pronouncement: "Here is neither Greek nor Jew, neither Scythian nor barbarian"[9] has always remained a living force in the consciousness of the Christian church, in spite of all church nationalism, and has taken practical effect especially in missions and the connection with mission churches, though not perhaps always with the clarity, force and responsible solidarity which were enjoined upon the church at its foundation. We may, however, say that a new awareness of the universality of the church has, within the last generation, arisen within the various ecclesiastical groups and is felt as an obligation. The Roman church is particularly well equipped for this task by its unity and its organization. Protestantism and the non-Roman groups, however, have at any rate recognized the obligation in the world-wide "œcumenical" movement, and have taken important steps towards its conscious fulfilment. It is only just to acknowledge that the church—and not only, nor even primarily, the Roman church—has stood the test of interstate solidarity, if not perfectly, at any rate better than any other kind of international union in this second world war, although, in view of the enormous national preoccupations of its members, that solidarity was not only not to be expected, but was almost beyond human powers. In spite of all deviations on the part of ecclesiastical leaders and bodies—not excepting the Papal Chair—this time an awareness of a solidarity transcending all political and military conflicts has held, and there is not the slightest doubt that once the war is over, these personal and indirect relations will not only be fully re-established, but will be reinforced and promoted in a quite unprecedented fashion. It is therefore no matter for surprise if, even today, and far beyond church circles, the interest and the hopes of many are turning towards the church as that factor which will be most capable of establishing the bond of union between the nationally isolated peoples and of creating a solidarity in the spiritual and social sphere which will not only symbolize the idea of a *family* of nations, but will turn it into a personal and practical reality.

Economic life in itself runs too close to the egoistic aims of man to create a solidarity which could stand the test of sacrifice.

[9] Col. 3: 11.

Culture has not enough inherent energy to give the unity of men, which it sees and feels, an expression in reality which would be of any significance in the political field of force. But the church, provided it is alive and spiritually awake, can create a supra-national community which may yet set effective limits to purely national and imperialistic calculations, as it did in former times. It is, however, to be expected that all three factors, though in widely different fashion, will necessarily create in the future a new political order which will not allow itself to be forced into the national political schemes of the political thought of our day, a development which we may predict the more confidently as the probable future in that the sheer instinct of political self-preservation of the nations, in view of the standing threat to world peace by national and imperialistic thought and intention, points in the same direction. As regards the form this supra-national political future will take, however, no definite prediction can be made at present, nor any concrete requirements put forward. But there is one demand which the church must never cease to proclaim, in spite of its vagueness, namely God's will that the nations, whose Father he is, should be as a family living with each other by that law of peace and justice which is even now to a certain extent a visible reality in the life of a truly Christian family.

The church cannot surrender that demand if it is to remain true to itself. But how to secure its *fulfilment* within earthly, historical time in view of that fundamental evil which was the prevailing force precisely in international politics, is a different matter. In that point, the Christian church, which reckons, and is obliged to reckon, more seriously than any other religion and any philosophy, with the fact of evil, has neither the right nor the duty to speak(93).

Even if we count on fundamental transformations which would permit a fresh solution of the problem of a just international order, however, we must be on our guard against exaggerated hopes. The optimistic view of the future as eternal world peace among the nations is, insofar as this historical, mundane world is concerned, not the view of Scripture. The reign of peace of which Scripture speaks does not enter into the world of historical time. It belongs to that future whose beginning is called "the resurrection of the dead" and whose substance is called "eternal life." The confusion of this Scriptural vision of the final consummation with that conjured up by the belief in human progress can only lead to the greatest bewilderment and to repeated disappointments. The Kingdom of God, which is proclaimed in the New Testament, lies beyond the bounds of earthly history, in which sinful men and self-seeking nations are the agents of events. It is dangerous and fantastic to imagine that sinful men are capable of making the reign of justice and eternal peace a reality. In this respect the prudence of Scripture does not contradict historical experience, which shows us that human evil is particularly active in the sphere of international life, where it bursts forth in huge and concentrated eruptions.

That is not to say that humanity will not one day put an end to the appalling scourge of war, which can from now on only appear in the guise of total world war. It may yet be that the realization of the incomparable horror of modern war will compel the nations and states to devise forms of political organization which will exclude this suicidal way of settling disputes. If the idea of eternal peace within historical time is a utopia, it would be false pessimism to deny the possibility of overcoming what is called war today. If, under the influence of the Christian conception of the dignity of man, it was possible to put an end to the primeval and universal social evil of slavery, the hope of overcoming war is not a utopia. We must only bear in mind that even if we succeeded in eliminating the war of weapons, we should not have the slightest guarantee of the realization of the earthly paradise. Just as there are worse things than death, while not to die is yet the condition of everything else, there are worse things than the war of weapons, even though life can have a meaning only if that war ceases. Whatever its prospects of success, the task of framing a just international order, an order in which the present anarchy as well as the present inequalities of wealth and poverty among the nations will be no more, still remains. A dispassionate consideration of reality and the testimony of Scripture which coincides with it may, however, put us on our guard against setting up practical proposals in a spirit of exaggerated optimism, which would only have a sense if men and nations were not what they are, but which, given the world as it is, would promote injustice rather than justice. That is quite unequivocally true of a certain kind of pacifism which imagines that war can be abolished by the cry: "Lay down your arms," while the recent past has shown us how a heedless pacifism can render the very people defenseless who would be most capable of creating a peaceful order in the world if they had the necessary means of power at their disposal. The protection of right by might will never be unnecessary as long as there are men who do not submit of their own free will to the judgment of right, that means, as long as there is evil in the world.

Conclusion—Limits

To know what justice is, to recognize the just in the various spheres of social life, is a great thing, but it is not everything. For a time which despairs even of knowing what justice is because it has lost all solid ground under its feet and its wandering in the slough of relativism, the first task is knowledge. Before we can take the right way we must know what it is. Before we can mobilize our forces to put justice into action we must know what we ought to want. The specific malady of our age, as compared with earlier ages, is groping in the dark and confusion of thought. At the very time when men have means of realizing their aims such as they never had before, they are utterly at a loss as to what those aims should be. In their preoccupation with discovering and devising those means they have even forgotten how to enquire into their aims. The way in which the gigantic forces of technology, formerly unknown, have been harnessed to the purpose of destruction in war is the perfect expression of the gulf between the means and the end of intention. The condition of the world at the end of this war will provide the dreadful proof that all this technological power cannot protect humanity from impotence if knowledge of the ends has not advanced abreast of knowledge of means. It is the proof of the primacy of ends over means. To know what is just is by no means to put the just into action, but if we no longer even know what is just, the very possibility of putting justice into action is cut off. Hence our first task is to regain a clear, convincing knowledge of justice and the just. That means to obtain an equally clear insight into all that passes itself off as justice, into the false doctrines of justice, on whose winds our contemporaries are tossed about. The susceptibility to infection by totalitarian ideologies—Communist as well as National Socialist—is proportional to the lack of true knowledge. What is worse than both, however, is the relativism which declares that there is no real justice. Scepticism, another word for relativism, is the deepest malady that can attack the human soul. It means the complete blinding of the soul.

If ignorance of what is just is the specific and acute malady of our time, the absence of the intention of justice is the chronic disease of humanity. To know the just is by no means to possess the intention of justice, to possess it in such a way as to fight for it and make sacrifices for it. It is part of every man's natural disposition that he wishes to be *justly dealt with,* but it is by no means part of every man's nature to *deal justly with others,* and to intend justice even when it runs counter to his own advantage. It is a sophism to say that justice is identical with our own interests. In any case, justice often enough stands in the sharpest contrast to that which is naturally regarded as our own interest. That is why it is such a long road from the knowledge of justice to putting the just into action. For the most part, the just must be wrested from those with whose interests it conflicts by those with whose interests it coincides. If justice in action were dependent solely on the selfless intention of justice, much less of the just would be put into action than is actually the case. It is, if we may put it in this way, a good thing that the satisfaction of a just claim nearly always coincides with somebody's advantage.

Justice, however, would be in a sorry plight if it could count on no partisans but those it benefits. We must therefore complete the foregoing statement as follows: it is a bad thing for justice that it can hardly ever be put into action if it cannot find at least a minority of adherents who serve it selflessly because they possess the selfless intention of justice. It would be a misunderstanding of the Christian doctrine of the sinfulness of all men to infer from it that there are no human beings with a sincere intention of justice, with the capacity to make sacrifices for its realization. The confusion may arise from the failure to distinguish the Scriptural conception of "righteousness" from what we call justice today. There is in actual fact no human being who is "just in the sight of God," who can say of himself that he is without sin. But fortunately there is at all times, in all nations and civilizations the distinction between those whose sense of justice can be depended on, who will work for the just even to their own disadvantage, and those who are predominantly or always guided by self-seeking motives. It is the first who matter when it comes to putting justice into action. The dynamics of justice are in them.

To a certain extent, men can be educated in the sense of justice. Anyone who has studied the matter knows what can be achieved for "fair play" by early training in public spirit. We must therefore not be too pessimistic in our estimate of the possibility of adult education, although, where the training of the will is concerned, its scope is restricted. In respect of the just, family education is certainly more important, and together with it, the influence of custom and tradition, the real exponent of which is the community. If we enquire, however, into the deepest sources of a good, just, selfless will, if above all, we enquire into the forces which can transform an unjust will into a just one, a self-seeking man into a man of public spirit, the answer of history is unequivocal. That transformation only takes place when revolutionary, regenerative forces burst in from a region outside the human will, which lies beyond the reach of human effort or educational endeavours. The experience of "rebirth," of becoming new and other, takes place only when the very spirit of God touches the human heart, when the creative God creates a turning-point, a "conversion" in the inmost soul of man by His word of salvation. No doctrine, no education, no co-operation, no organization, can create a just will where it is not already latent. It can only be created by an awakening through the spirit of the Gospel. That that should happen is more important than any theory of justice, be it ever so necessary and right.

One of the fallacies of the modern mind is a vast overrating of knowledge. Knowledge is necessary and precious, but what good is knowledge which does not lead to action? Yet anyone with the slightest insight into the workshop of the soul knows that mere recognition of the good by no means creates the intention of good. Action for good is not only hampered by ignorance, but by selfishness, inertia, cowardice, laziness, the love of pleasure. The best of theories is powerless to remove such obstacles. They can only be removed by upheavals of the soul which cannot be brought about by knowledge, but only by "repentance and faith." That is the most important limitation which anyone who endeavours to obtain knowledge of the just must bear in mind.

There is, however, another limitation. Even should it be possible to create a just order in every realm of life, what would be gained by it? It lies in the very nature of justice that it cannot touch the deepest depths in man. It is concerned with the person in the institution, not with the person *qua* person. Hence it comes that the most perfect organization, the best of orders, in the last resort provides no guarantee of a truly humane life. The evil in the human heart is so deep-seated that it can transform the most just of institutions into injustice. And personal freedom belongs so profoundly to the God-created nature of man that not the best of institutions can satisfy him. That should not prevent us from doing our utmost to create a just order, but it should safeguard us from the illusion that the problem of human life will be solved by it. The living force of the soul is stronger than all institutions, both for good and for evil. Therefore both things can happen—the most just of orders can be ruined and turned into evil from within, and the most unjust of orders

can be used from within for good. Hence, measured by the ultimate standard, all justice is only relatively important. Let us
recall the slave Onesimus and his Christian master, that complete transformation of an unjust relationship from within without any change in the actual institution. That must be said here,
at the end of our enquiry, to forestall the objection that justice
has not been taken quite seriously. It will only be taken seriously
if we know something higher—namely, love.

Love is greater than justice—that love which is God himself.
Justice can be taught and learned, but not love. Love can only
be given by Him who is Himself the source of all love. Where
that happens, the supreme service has also been rendered to
justice, for where love is, there too springs the fountain of the
just will. Love is always a mile ahead of justice. Where the
divine love becomes an event, the claims of justice are fulfilled
of themselves. For "love is the fulfilment of the law." Justice
is nothing but that form of love which has currency in the
world of institutions, that materialization of love which is necessary as long as men live in institutions. That is why love is always just too, but justice is not always love. Whoever can open
up the fountain of love has rendered the greatest service to
justice.

The Gospel of Jesus Christ is the Gospel of this justice which
is identical with love. Hence it is the message of that which lies
beyond all earthly institutions. As the love of God which became man in Jesus Christ is the fulfilment of the law, it is also
the end of law. That is what remains when all institutions have
passed away. That is what we hope for in the midst of the just
and unjust institutions of this world. And as long as we live in
them, it is that which does not let us rest in the struggle for
earthly justice.

NOTES

(1) In the *Nicomachean Ethics*, the φύσει δίκαιον is shown only in its function as a criterion; in the *Rhetoric*, 1, 13, its theological character is emphasized. Aristotle quotes with approval Sophocles' saying: "The unwritten, irrefragable law of the gods."

(2) This pure formalism reaches its culmination in Kelsen's *Jurisprudence*. But even Stammler's purely formal conception of law contributed to this formalism, in spite of its contrary intention.

(3) Jellinek: *Die Erklärung der Bürger- und Menschenrechte.* Salander: *Vom Werden der Menschenrechte.* F. Ernst: *Die Sendung des Kleinstaates.* Cf. also my inaugural lecture as rector of the university: *Die Menschen rechte nach reformierter Lehre.* (Jarhesbericht der Zürcher Universität, 1942).

(4) Aristotle, *Nic. Ethics*, p. 54: "that there is, beside the general, another, particular" (ἄλλη ἐν μέρει).

(5) Neither Protestant theology nor the New Testament acknowledges the dual structure of Catholic morals, the distinction between "natural" and "supernatural" or theological virtues. There is only *one* ultimately legitimate motive of moral action—love. But there is a prescript of material action which, however, is justice, not love. The connection between justice and love was not made clear by the Reformers. See inf. Note 19.

(6) According to Plato, *Republic*, 1, 331, the *suum cuique*, though not in this clear and definite form, goes back to Simonides. It is explicitly formulated by Aristotle, *Rhet.* 1, 9. That it was, however, *the* principle of justice, not only in the Catholic law of nature, but also for the Reformers, is proved by hundreds of texts in Luther, Zwingli and Calvin (Cf. Arnold, *Zur Frage des Naturrechts bei Luther.* Dreske, *Zwingli und das Naturrecht.* Bohatec, *Calvin und das Recht*).

(7) From the philosophical point of view the relation to time here becomes important. The man in the institution is always the man already understood as the past, while man as the person in the face of God is understood as pure present. Cf. Heim, *Glauben und Denken*, p. 153 f.

(8) It was more especially Luther who contrasted the *jus naturale* as that which is "right and proper" with the letter of the law or bookish law, which he calls "diseased law." "For what happens by the force of nature goes boldly on its way even without law, and even

wends its way through all laws. But where nature is not, and laws must do the work, there is but beggarly patchwork." In this connection "nature" is equivalent to pure reason, the reason which is so rarely found. (*Auslegung des 101 Psalms, Werke*, pp. 51, 204 f.)

(9) *Ethics*. Cf. Luther; the *aequalitas arithmetica* belongs *ad emptionem aut venditionem, ad forum*, to the market: the *geometrica*, on the other hand, *ad personas*. (*Werke*, pp. 43, 641.)

(10) This idea of a mistaken belief appears arrogant to a relativistic age because it naturally involves an assertion of a faith which is not in error. On the other hand, the "relativity" or "subjectivity" of all propositions of faith is inferred from the fact that all human beings do not share the same faith. That is exactly as if the examiner of a school class were to infer the relativity of all propositions in mathematics from the fact that the pupils arrived at different results in their arithmetic papers. The objection that the mathematical proposition can be proved, the proposition of faith cannot, loses all its force as soon as we see that even mathematical propositions are based on axioms which cannot be proved, and that the validity of the proof, of the conclusive process of reason, itself cannot be proved. Even *absolute* truth may not be susceptible of proof.

(11) Cf. the important work by the brothers Carlyle, *Medieval Political Theory in the West*. Dilthey, *Weltanschauung und Analyse des Menschen seit Renaissance und Reformation*, pp. 90 ff. and 153 ff. Further Troeltsch, *Die Soziallehren der christlichen Kirchen und Gruppen*, and the two essays: *Das christliche Naturrecht* and *Das stoisch-christliche Naturrecht. Gesammelte Schriften*, IV, p. 156 ff.

(12) Gierke, *Natural Law in the Middle Ages*. "A mere glance at medieval political and legal theory suffices to show that, in contrast to its classical prototype, the thought of the absolute and imperishable values of the individual, revealed by Christianity and felt in all its depths by the Germanic peoples, was already bearing fruit everywhere in it. That every individual, in virtue of his predestination to eternity, is, in his inmost soul, sacred and inviolable even for the state, that the smallest part is valuable, not only for the whole but also in itself, that the individual must never be regarded by the community only as a means, but also as an end, is not merely suspected, but expressed more or less explicitly." That is weighty testimony from a weighty witness.

(13) Zwingli's doctrine of justice rests on two recurrent, fundamental propositions. *Omnes leges in lege naturae fundatae nisi sunt, bonae esse haudquaquam possunt. Werke*, pp. 6, 244. All true law is based on the law of nature. Further: *Imaginem hanc similitudinem esse puto quod nos naturae jus dicimus* (pp. 5, 7). The law of nature is identical with the *imago Dei*. But it is precisely Zwingli who lays

particular stress on the fact that this *imago* and this law of nature can only be recognized through Scripture. That is the simple substance of his *Christian* doctrine of the law of nature.

Calvin's is similar. For the unprejudiced reader, there can be no doubt of the absolutely fundamental significance of the *lex naturae* for Calvin. Calvin too sees a close connection between the *lex naturae* and the *imago Dei*. The text from Gen. 9: 6 quoted above plays an important part in his thought. "For if we have in mind that man is made in the image of God, we must hold him sacred in such a way that he cannot be injured without the image of God being injured at the same time" (pp. 22, 42). Calvin explicitly bases on this text his important proposition: *legis suae (Dei) finem unicum esse, ut communem illis inter se humanitatem commendet.* The entire *humanitas* rests on the *imago*, and the whole ethic of the law on the *humanitas* (pp. 23, 146). To the objection that the image of God was destroyed by the evil in man, Calvin has two answers: firstly, *manere adhuc aliquid residuum ut praestet non parva dignitate homo*—the whole of Calvin's social ethic rests on the idea of the vestige of the imago; secondly, *utcunque corruptus sit homo . . . finem tamen primae creationis habere ante oculos . . . quorsum homines condiderit et qua excellentia eos dignitatus prae animantibus reliquis* (pp. 23, 147)—as a commentary to the whole passage of Genesis. Not only justice but all intercession for all men is founded on the fact "that they are created in the *image* of God and (hence) share the same nature with us" (pp. 47, 280). "Therefore we must ever come to this point, that we are united together as by one flesh and all shaped in the image of God (pp. 26, 304). Luther attributes the same importance to the idea of the *imago*, though it stands less in the foreground of his thought. However, in the passage of Luther mentioned, we also find a fundamental pronouncement: *haec est insignis ratio, cur nolit (Deus) hominem occidi privato arbitrio quia sit nobilissima creatura, non condita sicut coetera animantia sed ad Dei imaginem . . . Hanc imaginem vult ut alii in aliis revereamum . . . Ad hunc modum constituit hic locus politiam in mundo quar ante deluvium non fuit* (pp. 42, 361).

(14) In Nietsche's "Will to power," the theory of inequality oscillates between graduation of value on a basis of life force and on a basis of culture and intellect, between the Darwinistic theory of selection and a romantic worship of genius.

(15) *Est igitur, quoniam nihil est ratione melius eaque et in homine et in Deo, prima hominum cum deo rationis societas* Cicero (*De. Leg.* pp. 1, 7, 23). *Sacer inter nos spiritus sedet—habitat Deus* Seneca (*Ep.* pp. 41, 2). *Ratio nihil aliud est quam in corpus humanum pars divini spiritus mersa* (*Ep.* 66, 12). The *animus rectus . . .* is a *deus in corpore humano hospitans* (*Ep.* pp. 31, 11). "Every spirit is God and

has flowed from God" Marcus Aurelius (pp. xii, 26). A God permeates all, one substance, one law, one common reason of all reasonable beings, one truth (pp. vii, 9).

(16) In the same way, the souls transported to the air remain there awhile, are then transformed, strewn, purified, absorbed into the substance of the all . . . Marcus Aurelius (pp. iv, 21). The soul desires *reverti ad illa quorum fuit* (Ad. Marc, pp. xcii, 30).

(17) Cf. in connection with the whole problem of institutions in Luther the excellent and inadequately appreciated work by Lau, *Aeusserliche Ordnung und weltlich Ding in Luthers Theologie*. Anyone who is conscious of an obligation to historical truth must see the depreciation of Luther's social ethics by certain Protestant theologians in its true light, as a product of political bias.

(18) For the history of the law of nature in Christian Europe, cf. Gierke, *Natural Law in the Middle Ages*, and particularly the standard work by the brothers Carlyle already referred to.

(19) One of the most disastrous obscurities in the doctrine of the law of nature is that concerning the relationship between justice and love, *jus naturale* and *lex naturae*. Cf. on this subject, Bohatec, *Calvin und das Recht*, p. 3 ff. In Calvin especially the principle of *equitas, équité naturelle*, perpetually merges into the principle of love. *Op. cit.* p. 41 ff. The correct idea that on the one hand the order of justice *serves* love, and that the *motive* of love includes or gives birth to the just intention, is confused with the other, that justice and love are the same thing. The Biblical humanist Budé sees the point much more accurately; he distinguishes between the rational principles of the justice of the *jus naturae* and Christian love. *Christianismi praecipua dictata sensui communi sunt paradoxa*—even *antidoxa*. They are *sapientia coelestis*. Quoted by Bohatec, *op. cit.* p. 48. The same lack of clarity which we find in Calvin is also to be found in Zwingli, who, still more freely than Calvin, makes the Christian commandment of love equivalent to the *jus naturae*.

(20) Benjamin Constant's idea certainly stands in need of correction. *Chez les anciens, l'individu, souverain presque habituellement dans les affaires publiques, est esclave dans tous ses mouvements.* (*De la liberté des anciens, comparé à celle des modernes*, p. 842). This realization, however, is more difficult to refute in its more cautious formulation by R. von Mohl. "Among the ancients the individual served the state, and found in its welfare the indirect satisfaction of his aims." (*Enzyklopädie der Staatswissenschaften*, p. 319). All such generalized pictures are to be taken *cum grano salis*. Post-Periclean Athens experienced an exaggeration of democracy which casts some doubt on the above judgment. But as an average, as a

comprehension of the essential, it has its truth. Bluntschli and Gierke were of the same opinion.

(21) In his well-known work on the origin of the rights of man, Jellinek proves that the French declaration of the rights of man goes back to the first constitutional guarantee of religious tolerance given at Rhode Lsland. Cf. also F. Ernst, *op. cit.*, and my inaugural lecture, 1942.

(22) The church set an example to the totalitarian state by using the state to intervene in the inner life—inquisition, moral police, monopoly of propaganda, persecution of dissidents and compulsory uniformity must largely be laid to its charge.

(23) Of the Reformers, it was more especially Calvin who repeatedly emphasized the primal right to freedom as part of the order of creation and a "law of nature"—much more so than Zwingli, not to speak of Luther. He distinguishes, it is true, between spiritual and temporal freedom; *spiritualis libertas cum politica servitute optime stare potest.* (pp. 2, 1093). But the thought constantly recurs that laws exist *pour maintenir le droit de chacun, pour no point souffrir que nul ne soit outragé en sa personne ou en ses biens.* (pp. 28, 214), that *cuiusdam jus (sit) stabile* (pp. 41, 8). "Freedom means more than half of life," he says in speaking of the bondage of the Israelites in Egypt (pp. 24, 268). But his doctrine of freedom is contained as a rule in his conception of law, which always keeps the personal, subjective rights of each individual as much in view as the duties of that individual towards the community.

(24) Strange to say, even Grotius based slavery on the right of the victor over the vanquished. *De jure bello*, II, pp. 5, 27. For the history of the Christian attitude towards slavery, see Carlyle, *op. cit.*, p. 111 ff. A criticism, unfortunately only too well-founded, of empirical Christianity towards slavery is to be found in Westermarck's *Christianity and Morals*. Chap. 14.

(25) The view held by many Church Fathers that, by the order of creation, property is not private but communal, is derived from their monkish asceticism (Cf. Carlyle, Vol. I., Chap. 12). Among the Reformers private property, though not in the unlimited, absolute sense, is taken for granted. Calvin interprets the eighth commandment as *ut suum cuique jus salvum maneat* (pp. 24, 709). The subjective rights to freedom of the individual which the state has to protect are always summarized by Calvin as *droit de chacun en sa personne et en ses biens* (e.g. pp. 28, 214). The communism of primitive Christianity is expressly rejected as an economic standard (pp. 47, 60). The state certainly has the right to limit private property, but not to expropriate it. Every violation of the limits of property is a violation of the divine order of nature (pp. 27, 567 f.).

(26) It is the New Testament order of *agape* which presents in exemplary form the order of inequality founded on creation as the pre-condition of mutual give and take. It is there conceived as the basic law of the community. But in this charismatic order of the community, what is fulfilled is simply the sense of natural institutions, e.g. marriage and the family. Both are dominated, though at a different stage, by the law of exchange for the sake of completion.

(27) There are countless passages in all the Reformers which declare marriage to be *dei ordinatio in creatione* (Luther, pp. 44, 218), a creation of God (pp. 12, 112). The idea of the *ordo Dei* embraces what we today call orders of nature, laws of nature and the fundamental institutions of human life in community. The *order* of creation *debere esse instar legis ut vir conjugalem fidem tota vita colat* (Calvin, pp. 45, 528). Marriage is ordained from the beginning of time—it is a law of nature—inviolable (pp. 23, 29), *ordo naturae* (pp. 8, 366).

(28) The Reformers too, on occasion, call the state an order of creation; at other times they emphasize *politia ante peccatum nulla fuit* (Luther, pp. 42, 79) in contrast to marriage and the economic system, the œconomia (pp. 15, 293). Calvin includes both in the thought of the divinely created order of preservation. See Bohatec, *op. cit.*, p. 53. We can agree with Troeltsch that with Luther it is more the thought of an order rendered necessary by sin which stands in the foreground, with Calvin rather the order of creation. This comes out still more clearly in Thomist theology, and most likely in its spiritual descendant, Anglican theology.

(29) For the consequences for constitutional law entailed by these various conceptions of the state, see Gierke, *Natural Law in the Middle Ages*, p. 57 ff. Gierke's realization that religious ideas have at all times determined the fundamental trends of political theory is infinitely deeper than Jellinek's view that "no political inference of any kind can be drawn from ecclesiastical doctrines since every religious-minded party has deduced the principles favourable to it with infallible certainty from theological premises" (*Allgemeine Staatslehre*, p. 189).

(30) The difference of emphasis in the very similar theories of the state held by Calvin and Luther might be analysed thus: Luther lays stress on the *establishment* of the state by God, Calvin on its *limitation* by God. But Calvin repeatedly emphasizes that there is an obligation of obedience even to the unjust, tyrannical prince, and most cautiously limits the right to resistance. Luther, in his turn, teaches that there is a right of resistance against tyrannical princes, and even a right to armed resistance. "Therefore shall no man let himself and his be forced into idolatry and a false worship, but shall defend him-

self against it with *force* as long as he can. For obedience is to God and not to men." (pp. 52, 757). There is no trace of the blind obedience which has always been attributed to Luther.

(31) While these actual words may not be found in Rousseau, their substance may. For every proper assembly of the people is to be opened with the two questions: *"S'il plaît au Souverain de conserver la présente forme du gouvernement?* and: *S'il plaît au Peuple d'en laisser l'administration à ceux qui en sont actuellement chargés?"* *Contrat Social,* p. 189.

(32) This confusion, or the uncritical application of the notion "the Stoic-Christian law of nature" is above all to be laid to the charge of Troeltsch, and has, through him, spread widely. This casts no reflection on his great contribution to a proper understanding of the relationship between Christianity and the law of nature.

(33) The contract theory has been nowhere more thoroughly expounded than by Locke in his *Treatise on Civil Government.* Gierke, *op. cit.* pp. 70-122 gives an excellent account of the idea of the social contract. "The theoretical deduction of the community from the individual was manifested with increasing definiteness as the inevitable basis of the theory of the social contract" (p. 105). The determining element is "The idea of the freedom and equality of men and of an original sovereignty of the individual resulting from it" (p. 107). Gierke also draws attention to the fact that the most logical form of individualism, by virtue of the principle of *aliénation totale* leads to the boundless despotism of the sovereign manifested in the will of the majority (p. 117), i.e. totalitarian democracy.

In Fichte, the development is similar; the purely contractual state generates something like the totalitarian state, which even lays its hands on the family.

(34) Among theologians, the dispute about the law of nature first became acute in the sphere of Reformation history. As early as 1901, E. Ehrhardt, in *La notion du droit naturel chez Luther,* propounded and attempted to prove that "in Luther the law of nature is the source of all positive law, indeed, of all temporal standards, hence even of morality" and further that "the notion of the law of nature has its roots in the fundamental principles of Luther's theology." This view was then taken up by Troeltsch and transformed in the light of the researches of Dilthey and the brothers Carlyle. In opposition, Holl entered the lists for Luther, Lang for Calvin. In doing so, Holl and Lang set out from what was obviously the form of the law of nature familiar to them—the modern one, which is to be found neither in Luther nor in Calvin. Further, it was always misinterpreted by Holl in a naturalistic sense. In their polemic against Troeltsch, however, one point was right, namely that the *Stoic* conception of the law of

nature is to be found neither in Luther nor in Calvin. Further, it must be said against Troeltsch that his notion of the "relative law of nature" was of his own devising and there is documentary evidence for it nowhere (Cf. also Note 40). Lau, *Aeusserliche Ordnung und weltlich Ding bei Luther*, and Bohatec, *Calvin und das Recht*, and *Calvins Lehre von Staat und Kirche*, have proved conclusively the enormous importance for Luther and Calvin of the conception of the *lex naturae* and *jus naturale*, though they show at the same time that both conceptions, for both Reformers, are genuinely Christian in character and, as Ehrhardt had rightly seen, are actually an integral part of their theology and drawn from its fundamental sources. It is a *genuinely* Christian doctrine of the law of nature, that is, a knowledge of the order of creation rooted in the divine revelation of Scripture, and of the law of justice founded on it. For both, the proposition which they repeatedly put forward holds good—that even Scriptural law, insofar as it relates to the conduct of men in temporal institutions and to those institutions themselves, is founded on God's *ordo naturae*. The subjective conception of the law of nature, according to which this knowledge is accessible even to unbelievers, plays a subordinate part in both, and this is the main difference from the Catholic theory of the law of nature, which laid the main stress on the rational obviousness of the law of nature. The Reformers too establish the closest connection between *ordo naturae* and *ratio*, but they emphasize at the same time that this *ratio* is exhibited only in a poor and uncertain fashion in human reason, and hence is not "rational" in the sense of being familiar to and obvious to everyone. Even these important distinctions, however, leave a large number of problems unsolved, as Lau, in particular, shows. But two points nevertheless are clearly established for anyone who is ready to learn from the sources themselves: one the absolutely decisive importance of the law of nature for Luther and Calvin, the other the genuinely Christian conception of the law of nature in both.

The objection of the jurists to the law of nature (cf. in particular Bergbohm, *Jurisprudenz und Rechtsphilosophie*) may be summarized as follows:

1. The law of nature is individualistic.
2. It is abstract, and lacks the sense of historical reality.
3. It is dangerous as a rival to positive law.

These objections are sound as far as they represent the modern, subjectivist conception of natural law, especially in its systematic form. The third too is also correct as regards the mediaeval Catholic view. But all these statements overlook the Christian law of nature of the Reformers, which is neither individualistic nor unhistorical, and which does not set itself up as a legally valid system side by side with positive law. On the contrary, it combines the rights of man with the conception of community as a corporation or federation, is understood as a criterion which must be accommodated to historical reality and hence has its main significance as the element of justice in positive law, in which it serves both as a source and standard for the framing of laws.

The newly awakened interest among jurists for the law of nature is simply a reaction from positivism and from historical relativism to the realization that the law of nature, being the knowledge of a higher order is "eternal and inevitable" (Triepel, *Veröffentlichungen der Vereinigung der deutschen Staatsrechtslehrer*, H. 3, 1927, quoted by Arnold, *loc. cit.*). "The general insecurity and uncertainty of both the cultural and economic life of the individual lent an increasing urgency to the question of what is right law and of established standards of jurisdiction. In jurisprudence the entire legal dogma of the younger generation is united against historical relativism and positivism, and finds its weapons in the arguments of the law of nature. We unquestionably stand on the threshold of a new epoch of the embodiment of natural law."

"As a method of general theory of the nature of law, unless all appearances are deceptive, the law of nature will see in the future a glorious resurrection," says the jurist Erik Wolf (Article, *Naturrecht* in *Theologisches Handwörterbuch*, RGG, IV, p. 450 f.). This *volte-face* was inevitable. The jurist, if he does not want to lose all solid ground under his feet, cannot dispense with valid standards of justice transcending the law of the state. The question is merely *which* law of nature. Are we to understand by it, as naturalist pantheism does, "the essential coincidence of the legislator with the substance of the people," or a Fichtean idealism of freedom? Or will jurisprudence at last consent to accept the realization that only the Christian law of nature, the doctrine of justice founded on the divine order of creation, offers a way out between rationalistic individualism on the left and authoritarian naturalism on the right?

A group of modern theologians who, on the one hand, recognize the necessity of a divine law of justice, but on the other reject the idea of a Christian law of nature and the foundation of justice on the divine order of creation, have made an attempt to create a "Christological foundation" for law and the state. If nothing were meant by this Christological foundation but this, that the doctrine of the orders of creation and of the divine law of justice must be sought in the Scriptural revelation of Christ, it would simply amount to the view that is to be found in the Reformers and is upheld in the present work. The Reformers' theory of reason has a Christological basis, the divine logos, Christ, being recognized as the principle of all rational knowledge, and their doctrine of the orders of creation and the *jus naturae* is part of the faith in Christ. But the new tendency stands in overt opposition to this reformed doctrine, and attempts quite another thing, namely to deduce the order of law and the state from the historical event Christ, the cross of Christ. How fantastic this deduction is must be plain to any unprejudiced mind. Even jurists consciously standing on the ground of Christian faith reject it. But apart from this impossibility, (cf. my essay on the subject in the *Kirchenblatt der reformierten Schweiz*, 1943), the theory is very dangerous, since it must lead to an emotional fusion of church and state, of the gospel of love and the doctrine of justice.

(35) Rümelin, *Die Idee der Gerechtigkeit*, and Stammler, *Der Gedanke der Gerechtigkeit*, who both refrain from dealing with the substance of justice, have this in common, that they both make far-reaching but tacit assumptions, especially of the moral conception of personality. This latter, which is effective, indeed fundamental even in such a positivist as Jellinek, subsumes the occidental tradition of the law of nature. We can see today what these great jurists were still unable to see—that this idea is not self-evident and that without it, law becomes the plaything of power.

(36) The Reformers' identification and confusion of the objective ontological, with the subjective epistemological conception of the law of nature has contributed largely to confuse the issues, as also the combination of a critical with an uncritical and empirical conception of reason.

(37) Gierke's last words at the end of his *Natural Law in the Middle Ages* must sound a little melancholy to those who realize that it is precisely the Reformers' conception of the law of nature which satisfies the postulate he sets up: "The idea of right born with man," "not to deny it entrance into the body of natural law." Nothing is more characteristic of the eager endeavours of the Reformers to prevent any conflict between positive law and the law of nature than that they, especially Calvin, sought a formula for the right to resist in positive law. Cf. Wolzendorf, *Staatsrecht und Naturrecht in der Lehre vom Widerstand des Volkes*, 1916.

(38) The danger to positive law from the law of nature is the greater, the more it is combined with the view that a law of the state which does not coincide with the moral law or the law of nature is thereby invalidated. This is the point at which the Protestant doctrine of the law of nature most definitely deviates from the doctrine of mediaeval Catholicism. According to the Protestant view, the law of nature can only *reveal* the injustice of a decree of the state; it cannot release the citizen from his duty of obeying that unjust decree.

The mediaeval theory took the opposite standpoint. "The original and permanent doctrine (of the Middle Ages) declared every act of the sovereign which violated the limits appointed by the law of nature to be formally null and void . . . also the unlawful *law*, whether promulgated by Pope or Emperor" (Gierke, *op. cit.* p. 275). From this point of view we can understand Luther's insistence on obedience to the government as a recognition of the necessity of a solidly founded system of law.

(39) Cf. Wolzendorf, *Staatsrecht und Naturrecht in der Lehre vom Widerstand des Volkes*, where the importance of the Calvinistic theory of resistance in the formation of the constitutional state is very finely demonstrated. On the other hand, we can also see here the beginnings of the later theory of the rights of man which led to the rationalistic individualism of the social contract.

(40) It was Troeltsch who introduced the notion "relative law of nature," thereby causing great confusion. Thus it misled even so distinguished a thinker as Bohatec to denote the specifically Christian law of nature of the Reformers as a "relative law of nature" because it is actually different from the "absolute law of nature" of individualistic rationalism—both Stoic and modern—and includes within itself the idea of corporation or of membership. The element of truth in the "relative law of nature" is simply and solely the necessary accommodation of the "just in itself" to historical and sinful reality. Insofar as this sinful reality contains certain constants, it is true that something like general adjustments come about, modifications, that is, of the "absolutely just" which can be embodied in laws. But we must be clear that there are different and widely divergent systems of the absolute law of nature, especially the Christian and the Stoic individualistic. The difference between the Christian and the Stoic-individualistic law of nature has nothing to do with the difference between absolute and relative except in one point, namely that the difference between absolute and relative is much greater in Christian than in Stoic thought because the opposition between creation and sin is much sharper than that between original and depraved nature in the Stoic or in modern rationalistic thought. It would be a good thing if the conception "relative law of nature" were abandoned altogether.

(41) This demand for the accommodation of the "absolutely just" to historical reality is the reason why the Reformers related "the law of nature" much more closely to positive law than mediaeval Catholicism and refused to admit that the claims of natural law—with the rare exception of the right to resist—could invalidate the force of positive law. Here we approach a type of legal thought—in the limitation and in the assertion of the Christian law of nature—such as is

represented by Stammler in his work: *Ueber die Methode der ge-schichtlichen Rechtstheorie*, with the great difference, already pointed out, that we regard the Christian conception of justice as fully sub-stantial, and not formal, while Stammler's Kantianism prevented him from doing so, however much his Christianity actually impelled him.

(42) Luther's view, which he never abandoned, that the Old Testament is not binding on us in all its legal provisions, that it is the "Code of the Hebrews" (pp. 18, 81) is well known. It is not so well known that Calvin thought, in principle, exactly in the same way. That can be seen in his candid estimate of Roman law as superior to Jewish law (v. Bohatec, *op. cit.*, p. 114 ff), and in the fact that he only accepts Jewish law insofar as it is in accordance with the com-mandment of *aequitas* and love. The political laws of the Old Testa-ment "are of the kind that can be abolished according to the circum-stances of time and place" (pp. 10, 236). "The law of Moses is political, and is only binding upon us within the limits of lawfulness and *la raison d'humanité*." (pp. 10, 246). On the special question of the prohibition of interest: "But this must be regarded as an element of the *political* order. It follows that interest is not prohibited in our day" (pp. 24, 682). "Political laws are guided by the customs of mankind" (pp. 45, 180). On a Mosaic civil law: "It is true that this is part of the political order which God gave to the ancient people: it must at the same time be borne in mind that that which is prescribed is drawn from the source of right itself, of the divine feeling innate in us" (pp. 24, 661). In the same way, the authoritative pronounce-ments in the final chapter of the *Institutio*, IV, Chap. pp. 20, 15 and 16. The ceremonial and legal law of the Old Testament are not bind-ing upon us. They have been abolished; they were given by God to His chosen people of Israel, not to the other nations. Moses was the legislator of *his* people. "It is folly to think that where the law of Moses is abolished and other laws preferred, the law of God is con-temned." That part of the political law of Israel which still stands is to be traced back to *naturalis aequitas*. But even the Ten Command-ments or the moral law are nothing but a testimony to natural law and the law which God has written in men's conscience. The fact that Calvin regarded the legal system of the Old Testament as a model, and always drew upon it, does not separate him from Luther.

(43) Luther was franker in his judgment of the Decalogue than Calvin, who, as a Biblicist, is more bound to the letter of the law. Whoever imposes a law as the law of Moses must impose all the laws of Moses (pp. 18, 77). The laws of Moses are binding insofar as they coincide with the *lex naturae* (EA, pp. 33, 12). "We heathens" i.e. non-Jews, "are not bound by the Ten Commandments, but the

Jews alone" (EA, pp. 36, 32). This is, of course, in principle, Calvin's view also.

(44) A detailed summary from Oldendorp's interesting Lutheran jurisprudence is to be found in Kaltenborn, *Vorläufer des Hugo Grotius*. Even Oldendorp's use of the Decalogue shows that he did not regard it as a source of knowledge, but only as an instrument of method. What he "reads into" the Decalogue he actually takes either from the New Testament or the law of nature, and explicitly assumes the identity of the Decalogue with the law of nature. Cf. Erik Wolf's fine work, *Grosse Rechtsdenker*, pp. 101-139.

(45) For Kant, the respect for the persons of others is identical with the brotherly love of the New Testament. Even in Zwingli and Calvin there is often little distinction between the two, the cause of confusion being the "golden rule" of Matt. 7: 12.

(46) The idea of the reality of the collective personality has run in the blood of German jurisprudence, in especial, since the Romantic period and, although it was upheld by distinguished thinkers such as Gierke, doubtless paved the way for national socialist totalitarianism.

(47) Strangely enough, even this formulation is Aristotelian, κοινωνικὸν ἄνδρωπος ζῷον as we read in the Eudem. Ethics, pp. 10, 1242a. But in this form the idea never became effective. It certainly plays a prominent part in the *Politics* of the Calvinistic jurist Althusius, but never became popular.

(48) It is impossible to pronounce the word "organic" without conjuring up the misunderstanding of the Romantic theory of organism. Cf. my ethics: *The Divine Imperative*, p.

(49) "Federalism" can mean many things, but *one* element is always essential—that the independence of those who unite is never forfeited, that the whole which is formed never absorbs all the rights of the parts. Federalism is always the negation of the "*aliénation totale de chaque associé de tous ses droits à toute la communauté*," (Rousseau, *Contrat Social, loc. cit.* p. 78). In federalism the individual element retains as much of his freedom as is just compatible with the common aim. The idea is that this union of parts which are and remain independent makes the supreme welfare of the whole and an otherwise unattainable wealth of community possible. We Swiss can best define federalism by our national existence, which is unparalleled in the European world of states, not by reason of its democracy, but by reason of its federalism.

(50) For the early Christian rejection of private property as the result of an ascetic conception of Christian life, Cf. Wünsch, *Evangelische Wirtschaftsethik*, p. 665. That the Old Testament always regards private property—though in a very restricted sense—as right

can be seen in the laws relating to the inviolability of landmarks, Deut., 19: 14.

(51) With the *moral* problem of wealth, of wealth as a danger for the soul, as a temptation to pride or godlessness, which stands in the foreground of the Bible, a theory of justice is not directly concerned. We are dealing, not with the conduct of the individual in institutions, but with the justice or injustice of the institutions themselves.

(52) As is well known, the problem of the partition of land and of the right of ownership to land plays a great part in the Old Testament, where it is dominated by two principles: the supreme owner is Jehovah, ownership is a fief. The moral principle is deduced from this religious principle: ownership of land is a concern of the community. It is not unconditionally, but very largely taken out of the power of disposition of the individual. Cf. Lev. 25: 4; Num. 36. The very peculiar institution of the Sabbatical and jubilee year, whether it was merely a priestly requirement or a legal reality, was designed to put a check upon land speculators. Cf. the reference to unrestrained acquisition of land in Isa. 5: 8. "Woe unto them that join house to house, that lay field to field, till there be no place, that they may be placed alone in the midst of the earth!"

(53) An instructive general view of the changes in the legal view of landed property is given by K. Fehr, *Grundfragen eines bäuerlichen Boden rechtes.* Zürich, 1943.

(54) While wealth only appears in the New Testament as a spiritual problem, as a danger to the relationship with God and a powerful temptation to lovelessness, pride, false security, etc., we can recognize in the Old Testament, especially in the Prophets, a distinct bias against great wealth and the abuse of power it so easily entails, though more from the standpoint of the doctrine of justice and of the institutions of law. Cf. especially the equal partition of land, Num. 26: 53, and elsewhere.

(55) With the rise of a money economy, the mediaeval church abandoned, or at any rate largely modified, the prohibition of interest, both in theory and practice. The Papal Curia itself "became a centre of the capitalism of the late middle ages more than any royal court." Sommerlad, *Kirchliche Wirtschaftsgeschichte*, in RGB, Col. 1980.

(56) As is well known, it is upon this theory of saving as a manifestation of spiritual asceticism that Max Weber founded his famous theory of the connection between Calvinism and capitalism (*Geschichtliche Aufsätze zur Religionssoziologie*, I, p. 17-206), which, in its turn acquired through Troeltsch an importance it hardly deserves (Cf. Tawney, *Religion and the Rise of Capitalism*).

(57) The element of risk in the estimation of interest is, of course

exhibited in the graduation of interest upon savings, debentures, shares.

(58) As regards the taking of interest, Luther is certainly far more guarded than Calvin. Yet his rejection of the *purchase* of interest must not be confused with a rejection of interest itself. After all, he approved tithes because they gave the capitalists a share in the risk. "Therefore the tithe is the most refined form of interest, and has been practised since the beginning of the world, and was praised and confirmed in the ancient law as that *most justified by divine and natural law.* (after WA, 15, 321). But where there is no question of tithes, i.e. of interest calculated on yield, he proposes an interest of 5 per cent as a rough standard (*loc. cit.*).

(59) The mediaeval theory of *justum pretium*, which is also upheld by Luther (*op. cit.* p. 296) is based on the principle of the expenditure of labour. The theory of *justum pretium* sketched by St. Thomas Aquinas in his theological system is highly elaborate. (*Summa Theol.* 2, 2, q. 77). It takes careful account of all the factors which enter into the determination of an objectively just price. His doctrine is no longer condemned as "pure scholasticism" in our day, which has become accustomed to the state regulation of prices. It is even taken seriously by economists, however inadequate it is to our own economic circumstances. It would be worth while for Protestant economists to attack this problem from a fresh angle. My own remarks are intended rather to exhibit than to solve the problem.

(60) Of course, not every *entrepreneur* is a capitalist—business can be conducted with "outside" money. But it is more important that not every capitalist is an *entrepreneur*. All shareholders, indeed everyone with a savings bank book, are capitalists, but practically none of them have a share in the business direction of the enterprise which they finance along with many others. As a rule, however, the *entrepreneur* is the chief financier of his concern, while on the other hand, the limited company is the ultimate direction by a board of directors. In the more recent developments of the large-scale enterprise, the *entrepreneur* is being ousted by the capitalist, the trust magnate.

(61) A number of writers would prefer to obliterate the word capitalism from modern terminology because it is far too ambiguous (Röpke). On the other hand, I hold, with Sombart, that this term, properly defined, is extremely valuable as a means of knowledge and can be replaced by no other. Cf. Sombart's great work: *Der moderne Kapitalismus*, and, as a briefer summary and final formulation of his theory, the article "Capitalism" in the *Handwörterbuch der Soziologie*, pp. 258-277. For his definition, cf. also p. 93.

(62) Both "socialism" and "Communism" are notions which can be interpreted in widely different ways, and are at the same time

ideal aims to which very different meanings can be given. Many idealistic socialists and Communists will rebel against my assertion that Communism inevitably leads to totalitarian dictatorship. To justify my view, I can refer to the fact that the only communistic economic system the world has yet known, namely the Russian experiment, *is* actually a dictatorship. What idealistic socialism has in mind is a free corporation on a basis of "socialistic" ideas and independent of the state. There are doubtless corporations of the kind, and I cannot say what objections could be raised to them from the standpoint of justice. On the contrary, morally speaking, they represent a very valuable solution of the economic problem. They have only one flaw, namely that, being bound to that highly moral conception, they can only be experimental and exceptional. This type of socialism on an ethical or Christian basis is as impossible in this sinful world as a stateless society. As soon as such corporations expand, they become collective and egoistic aggressive organizations which may certainly have, as such, their justification, but whose justice becomes the more dubious, the greater the power they acquire. Corporations recruit their adherents either on the basis of advantage or on that of ideal aims of activity. Insofar as they abide by the latter, it is notorious that they remain small. When they grow, as a matter of experience, they revert to the former method. In neither case, however, do they lead to a total reformation of the economic system in the sense of social justice. For only a small minority will be moved by the ethical ideal, but the interests of the group provide no guarantee of justice. Only socialism united with state coercion can hope for a thorough reformation of the economic system and for a leading voice in the total system. But since this state coercion cannot for the present be brought to support the idea of collective economy by democratic methods, it was, and still is, necessary to proclaim the dictatorship of the proletariat. The minority pledged to collectivism gets the machinery of state into its hands and introduces by force the communistic totalitarian state. That is, unfortunately, the only form of socialism which has to be seriously reckoned with. Honest democratic socialism is that which certainly has the same aims as this form of communism, but desires to attain them by democratic methods. It will, however, only attain them when the majority of the citizens has become so blinded as to see the future salvation of humanity in the communistic totalitarian state. For the moment there is good reason to hope that the desire for freedom felt by the majority of men is too great for them to make voluntary sacrifice of their freedom to this illusory ideal of welfare with its fiction of freedom. Hence such socialism as does not secretly foster the idea of the dictatorship of the proletariat will always have to remain in the position of the bourgeois democratic opposition and be useful in that sense.

(63) The problem of capitalism versus Communism has certainly undergone an essential change of late, in that capitalism has taken on collectivistic form in the way of trusts, syndicates, etc. The free *entrepreneur* has largely become a fiction. From the standpoint of the right to freedom, it would not make much immediate difference if these limited companies were nationalized. Indirectly, however, by the state economy it would promote, and by its effects on the really free economy, it would have a total effect in the sense of state social-ism which must be judged unfavourably on account of this appalling aim. The true interest of the community, however, is the reduction of this mammoth capitalism with its monopolistic character to a manageable system of small and medium-sized concerns. This pro-gram has, it is true, only restricted prospects of success at present, since technology, on the whole, favours the large-scale concern. But there were, even in the last generation, signs of a reverse development, i.e. of a decentralization, which is moving abreast of the growth of capitalistic centralization. The community must in any case realize that it has every reason to promote the first and to check the second of these movements. Seen from the standpoint of freedom, state Com-munism simply means a maximum of subjection to trusts. Of all trusts, the total trust of Communism is the worst because it possesses not only economic power, but also the coercive power of the state.

(64) This is the point at which I become aware of my opposition to Röpke's theory of the middle way, in spite of the fact that his work appeals to me very deeply and that I regard his book: *Die Gesell-schaftskrisis der Gegenwart* as a notable achievement. But Röpke's antipathy to state planning is largely mitigated by his own principle of "adequate intervention," and hence he arrives at a combination of free and state-supervised—not state-controlled—industry which is not very far removed from that proposed here.

(65) The phenomenon of the mass can be regarded and explained from very various standpoints—e.g. by the "psychology of the crowd" as a kind of psychic infection; sociologically by the realization "there are many of us," or by certain *gleichschaltende*, anonymous factors of mental influence, such as wireless propaganda etc. All these explana-tions are justified, but none is exhaustive. The decisive question is: Why are some groups susceptible to these mass factors and others not? Why do some seek these mass stimuli and others not? The factors named are not the real producers of the phenomenon of the mass but only its immediate cause. F. Toennies' distinction between "society" and "community" goes far deeper. But even it requires a spiritual interpretation. Community exists only where there is a real awareness

of personality and a real and spontaneous sense of the union of personalities; both point to the religious sphere. The mass is the extreme pole of mere "society," of lack of community, through which men become susceptible to mass suggestion, etc, which reduces them to a structureless bulk, a "unit," a collective factor without personality.

(66) When that great preacher of social justice, Hermann Kutter, made the assertion in his famous book: *Sie Müssen*, "The socialist working man's movement comes from God, for all its atheism," he meant just this deep emotion of justice which springs from religious sources, and which cannot be denied even to the first great Marxists. It has been declared, perhaps not without justification, that something of the spirit of the Old Testament prophecy inspired those Jewish social revolutionaries. But that is no reason for taking Marxist ideas and the Marxist program as Christian. Socialism in its purely ethical form and spiritual communism have very little to do with it. But it is disastrous when adherents of this ethical or religious socialism imagine they can see the political next of kin of their own socialism in Marxism.

(67) Locke's repugnance to all patriarchalism can be understood not only by his rationalistic individualism, but also by his opposition to the politically absolute patriarchalism of his exact opposite, Sir Robert Filmer who, in his *Patriarcha*, deduced absolute monarchy from Scriptural patriarchalism (Adam). In opposition to him, Locke proclaimed with intransigeant logic and superb moral feeling man's right to freedom, but in the course of his defense of that right arrived at an individualistic notion of freedom which left community no alternative but the contract.

(68) Thought is dangerously coloured by resentment if the idea of leadership is altogether abhorred because it has been compromised by National Socialism. The notion of leadership is indispensable. It is one of those that must not be surrendered whatever the discredit into which it may have fallen. The general is the leader of the army. The director of a big industrial concern is a leader and must be a leader, just as the soundly democratic scout patrol has its patrol leader. It is just the democratic citizen who must know that leaders are necessary even in democracy, and not merely an "executive."

(69) We hear little today of syndicalism as an alternative to state Communism. It has been realized that this solution is either a purely voluntary one or, where it is a question of big unions, creates a dangerous state within the state which no state can tolerate. The alliance of unions, such as, for instance, the "big four" in England, gives them a position of monopoly which must be felt as intolerable not only by the other economic groups but also by the state. Syndicalism on this

scale is either the beginning of anarchy or it leads to the dictatorship of the proletariat, to state communism.

(70) The importance of the idea of honour is underrated nearly everywhere in modern Protestant theology because it is confused with that "vainglory before God" which the Bible condemns most sharply, or with moral self-righteousness. How little the depreciation of the notion of honour can appeal to the Scriptural doctrine of grace we can see by the fact that the Apostle of grace, who was most severe in his condemnation of this "glory before God" quite unequivocally commands "honour to whom honour is due."

(71) The estimation of peace—inward and outward—as the most precious factor in political life is quite unambiguous with the Reformers. Luther even rates it higher than justice. "If one (of either) must yield, then right shall yield to peace and not peace to right" (WA 30, III, p. 223). Calvin: the *coacta justitia necessaria est publicae hominum communitati, cujus hic tranquillitati consulitur, dum cavetur, ne omnia permisceantur tumultu* (pp. 2, 260).

(72) As regards this fourth stage of justice, namely the question of the form of the state, Scripture is almost indifferent. In a general way, monarchy is acknowledged, and even in relatively unlimited form. Even the theocratic dictatorship of the epoch of the Judges, which is regarded as the really right form of state, is by no means a democratic constitutional form. Its contrast to the monarchy (Saul) is not constitutional but religious. The leader of the people should not be a monarch, but a charismatic, whom God has charged directly with the power of leadership, and whom He leaves in office as long as he does His will. It is true that not only this charismatic dictatorship, but also the hereditary monarchy, included in Israel very far-reaching rights on the part of the communities and the tribes. Federalism was always preserved, whatever the form of the state.

(73) Thus, for instance, before America's entry into the war, it was obvious that the syndicalism of the workers on the one hand and trust capitalism on the other meant a grave threat to the democratic power of the state, in spite of the fact that the Constitution of the United States has introduced a strong element of authoritarianism into its democracy by the institution of the Presidency. The precarious situation of the democratic political power in France for several generations past is familiar to everybody.

(74) While the Old Testament is not greatly interested in the question of the constitution, it lays all the more stress on the justice of the government. That justice consists in the king giving validity to the law of God. The idea of the just king, which was based on the image of the absolute, but just King David, becomes the very heart of the Messianic hope (Isa. 9: 6).

(75) *On doit concevoir par là, que ce qui généralise la volonté est moins le nombre des voix que l'intérêt commun qui les unit; car, dans cette institution (contrat social) chacun se soumet nécessairement aux conditions qu'il impose aux autres: accord admirable de l'intérêt et de la justice.* (Rousseau, *Contrat Social, loc. cit.* p. 98).

(76) This assertion of the novelty of the totalitarian state may be countered by the example of Sparta, of Calvinistic Geneva, or of the absolute monarchy in France (Louis XIV). It must be admitted that small states of a military and centralized type represent a kind of totalitarian state because the exiguity of their circumstances permits complete control over the individual and his private life. The mediaeval and post-mediaeval city, however, possessed so large an area intentionally left free of state control, and had in the divine law so powerful a safeguard against the unlimited sovereignty of the state that, in spite of all suggestions to the contrary, they cannot in any way be regarded as examples of the totalitarian state. A great power like seventeenth century France, on the other hand, had neither the desire nor the necessary technique of organization to *gleichschalten* its citizens, although it attempted to do so in the religious sphere with considerable success. But this highly centralized organization was only a forerunner of the totalitarian state. The scope of the state-free space was enormous in comparison with actual totalitarianism.

(77) It is painful to reflect that the struggle of the church against the totalitarian state was for so long not directed against the principle of totalitarianism, but only set in when the state attacked the church. The violation of the freedom of preaching is a grave wrong against which the church must protest. But the church only has the full moral right to do so when it has already protested against the totalitarian principle as such. It must be said to the credit of the practising Protestant church that it subsequently made good its neglect with energy.

(78) There is perhaps this difference between the continental European and the Englishman that the former sees rather the horrors of totalitarianism, the latter the anarchy of liberalism.

(79) Rousseau upholds the view, which had a vogue in the age of positivism, that conscience replaced instinct only by means of the state and its law, *donnant à ses actions la moralité qui leur manquait auparavant* (*op. cit.* p. 83). The great jurist Ehering says: "The state is the sole source of law" (*Der Zweck im Recht*, pp. 1, 318). Jellinek arrives at a similar conclusion because he regards the "guarantee"— not necessarily coercion—as an essential characteristic of the idea of law (*Allg. Staatslehre*, p. 307).

(80) If Roman Catholic jurisprudence opposes the theory of the uniqueness of the law of the state, it is right insofar as it takes its stand on current terminology, but not right insofar as it does not admit

that the law which is prior to or beyond the state, where it diverges from the law of the state, has no such binding force that it could invalidate the binding force of the law of the state.

(81) This idea was put forward with particular emphasis by W. Burckhardt, *Einführung in die Rechtswissenschaft.* Cf. also Egger's fine work: *Ueber die Rechtsethik des Schweizerschen Zivilgesetzbuches,* which interprets the leading ideas of freedom, humanity, the common welfare, as they have here been summarized under the idea of justice, and as they have always been summarized by the Christian doctrine of the law of nature.

(82) This positivistic notion gained enormous importance by Marx's historical materialism. His variation of the theme ran: The present state of the law is the product of bourgeois-capitalist power. Hence the contempt of law in Marxism. Cf. also Gumplowitz, *Allg. Staatsrecht,* who even declares that the idea of morality altogether is "nothing but the intellectual deposit of historical and political conditions," p. 343.

(83) Cf. Bundesrichter Strebel's *Geschiedene Ehen.* It is a well-known fact that the criminal law of the Old Testament is highly developed and, to our mind, incredibly severe. The number of transgressions which were punishable by death, e.g. by stoning, was very large. This might be borne in mind by those who imagine that they can base their opposition to capital punishment on the commandment: "Thou shalt not kill." They should read on into the next chapter to see how this commandment is *not* to be interpreted.

(84) The *jus talionis* is the primitive form of the principle of all criminal law; equal guilt, equal punishment. Criminal law is not, as the doctrine of the *justitia vindicativa* maintains, a special kind of justice. Like all justice, it declares what is due to each, in this case to the disturber of order, and proceeds by the rule of equality, namely equality of transgression and punishment.

(85) The modern view that the idea of expiation is sub-moral has unfortunately infected a large number of Christians. Expiation means restoration of the disturbed order by a suffering corresponding to the transgression. But the opinion that because Christ alone made atonement, no atoning character must be introduced into human atonement, is untenable. Human atonement is no more abolished by the divine atonement than human punishment by forgiveness. Besides, without atonement, all improvement is an illusion. Only he who feels the just punishment to be necessary, i.e. who regards it as atonement, has admitted his wrong and can improve.

(86) The appeal to the fact that Christ has been made Lord of all nations and states (Matt. 28: 18; Col. 2: 15 and elsewhere) makes no difference to *this* dualism, that in the temporal political world, the

community of those who follow Christ is separated from the world of unbelievers, and will remain separated from it until the end of earthly time.

(87) When Carr, in his important work *Conditions of Peace*, criticizes the policy of security of the statesmen of 1918, he is right insofar as the mere will to stablize any *status quo* is the very policy which cannot guarantee a lasting peace. But the title and substance of his book show clearly enough that he too recognizes the primacy of the order of peace.

(88) Cf. Max Huber, *Die allgemeinen politischen Grundlagen des völkerbundsvertrages, Zeitschrift für Völkerrecht,* 1920. Also, *Einige Betrachtungen zum christlichen Verständnis der internationalen Rechtsordnung* in *Die Kirche Christi und die Welt der Nationen.*

(89) This rather confusing notion does not mean the church, the *Corpus Christi,* but the social order and cultural community, more or less ruled, or at any rate determined, by Christian principles, as it existed before the Age of Reason, and has since yielded to a purely secular order which is only very indirectly influenced by Christianity.

(90) This does not imply that the great power bears the main political blame or should be judged as an absolute evil. Historically speaking, the great power is a necessary stage of transition between the multitude of small national states and a universal order of the nations. It has, as such, of course great merits. But when statesmen who belong to great powers again begin to regard the great power as the actually normal form of the state, as though the small states should really apologize for their existence, they are guilty of pure topsy-turvyism. That is precisely the totalitarian manner of thought which was to be combated in the struggle against National Socialism. We might also recall that the imperialism of the great powers is the main cause of world wars, and not the disputes of the small states. It is because the great powers always regard the latter from the standpoint of their "spheres of interest" that the interstate conflicts of today necessarily expand into world war.

(91) That comes out very forcibly in the peace encyclica of the Pope (Pope Pius XII, *The Peace of the Nations*). On the other hand, those proclamations are characterized by a notable vagueness with respect to the more precise interpretation of the main principles, which is probably to be explained by the fact that the Pope was embarrassed by political conditions.

(92) This is the aspect of Carr's very valuable book which gives rise to the gravest misgivings. As he regards the problem mainly from the economic angle, and reckons with the policy of the great power as a self-evident fact, the small state appears to him obsolete and the neutral state a parasite on the order established by the great powers.

From the standpoint of justice, it is, of course, the other way round. The small states have to efface themselves as if they were inferior merely because they do not command the military apparatus of the great powers. The neutrals, however, who are reproached with their non-participation in the war, can justifiably complain that the policy of the great powers repeatedly plunges the world into fresh wars, whereby they, the neutrals, have to suffer.

(93) The following authoritative pronouncements on the whole question of international order have been issued by the churches:

1. The encyclica of the Pope (Pope Pius XII, *The Peace of the Nations*).
2. A proclamation by the Federation of American Churches.
3. A statement relative to that proclamation by prominent English churchmen.

1. The Papal encyclica are restricted to the pronouncement of very general principles, such as: security of the right to live and independence for all nations, disarmament, establishment of international courts of justice, satisfaction of the just claims of nations and minorities, the safeguarding of the principles of national and international order, the abolition of economic injustice (of extreme inequalities), the protection of the rights more especially of small states and minorities, the unhampered activity of the church. Substantially, these postulates entirely coincide with our own. What is almost entirely lacking is any reference to the difficulties arising from the opposition of right and might, and their solution. 2. The proclamation of the Federation of American Churches is far more concrete. It lays down six propositions and adds to each a commentary. What is demanded is (1) a political framework for the collaboration of the Allied nations (as the victorious powers), the others to be called in later, (2) endeavours to reach an agreement in international questions of economics and finance, (3) creation of an organization which will adjust the economic structure to varying conditions, (4) an organization for the gradual restoration of the autonomy of countries now under foreign occupation, (5) control of all national armies, which are to be reduced and placed at the disposal of international organizations which will serve the common welfare, (6) guarantee of the intellectual and religious freedom of the individual.

These postulates unquestionably issue from an attitude which is essentially similar to that of the present work, and are a move in the right direction. What is striking is that the main problem, the subjection of imperialistic power politics to law is left untouched. This unintentional concealment of the real heart of the problem stands revealed in the terminology: organization and co-operation. The creation of international corporations does not mean *real* collaboration, but only, in the first instance, that people "get together." The question then arises, who sets the tone, who leads and what triumphs? The existence of this apparatus does not, in itself, mean much for justice and still less for peace. It is assumed, with remarkable optimism, that the powers negotiating in such committees will naturally desire the good. What appears as the main cause of war is not the imperialism of the great powers but the fact that there are twenty-five states in Europe. It is not the will of power and egoism that are regarded as the cardinal evil, but inadequate co-ordination and the lack of international organization. Hence organization is taken to mean in itself co-operation, and the fact that there is also an international organization at the service of exploitation and oppression is hardly touched on. Resistance to the resolutions of the council taken in the sense of justice is made light of as the reaction of an asocial minority, against which the national militias can be mobilized by the council. The document takes too little account of the ruthlessness and egoism inherent in the power state.

3. The English statement on the American proclamation sets out by expressing its entire agreement, but proceeds to add a number of very curious new standpoints. It places in the foreground the principle that might must be subordinated to right, explicitly stresses the necessity of the safeguarding of peace, and admits openly that the latter, for the time being, lies in the hands of the victorious powers, but that the neutrals and enemy powers can be called in later to form a "co-operative system of world order." It regards as unfeasible the third point—the possibility of an organization for the continuous adaptation of international law to perpetually changing real circumstances, but desires that the demand for autonomy should also cover the problems to be dealt with by a colonial committee, whose business it would be to introduce and direct the development towards self-administration of the colonies. The question of military power is to be settled less by disarmament than by using armed forces in the service of the whole.

Thus the English statement is decidedly more realistic in tone. It sees more clearly the source of the real danger to peace and justice. Yet even here the essential problems are not touched. How is a difference of opinion between the individual members of a coalition of great powers to be solved, or a conflict between the coalition of great powers and the rest? Thus even here we can feel that the statement was issued at a moment when the future peace alliance of the great powers was unanimously fighting against the common enemy, hence when the central problem of the future, the further unanimity of the great powers, had not quite become a reality. To assume the will to justice of all main participants is the $\pi\rho\hat{\omega}\tau o\nu\ \psi\epsilon\hat{\upsilon}\delta o\varsigma$ of all programs of peace. There are only two things that can be assumed with certainty, (a) the continuance of the bias to power of all the states whose size gives them prospects of success in power politics, (b) on the other hand the readiness to pay a high price for the peace which has cost such toil.

The real task of statesmanship confronting a Christian statesman is to make use of this second factor, as long as it remains as forcible as it is immediately after the end of the war, in order to raise a barrier against the first factor which will stand when the second has weakened.

INDEX

Adam, Karl, 280

Advertising, artificial stimulus of, 181, 182

Agape (defined), 126

Age of Reason, beginning of, 47
classical concept of justice in, 6
English and French philosophers of, 86, 284

Althusius, 275

Anarchy, and human nature, 197
no justice in, 198

Anglican theology, 268

Apostles, ethical teaching of, 113, 114, 115

Aristotle, acceptance of institution of slavery, 54
agreement with Plato, 33
between individualism and collectivism, 76
did not know Scriptural love, 126
on democracy and mob rule, 201
doctrine of law of nature, 90
on double meaning of word "just," 13
use of word since, 14
early Christian acceptance of teachings, 81
first to inquire into nature of justice, 27, 28
classical master of theory of, 29
formal theory of, 45
on question of just price, 165, 166
regarding nature of justice, 6
regarding a truly just justice, 47
limitations of achievement, 30
on love as friendship between noble minds, 125
Politics, 38n, 91
on punishment, 222n, 263
teachings of inequality, 37
term, "political animal," 137
questions left unsolved by, 92
on right of state against individual, 80
theory of unfruitfulness of money, 158
what would appear madness to, 127

Armament, restriction of, 246

Army, idea of honour in, 195
not constituted on basis of democracy, 190, 191

Arnold, Carl Franklin, 263, 271

Balkans, example of, 243

Barth, Karl, 129

Berne, lobbying in, 217

Bible, conception of equality of sexes, 41
differs from Epictetus, Rosseau and Kant, 84
on dignity of difference of sex, 40
divine commandments of, 51
not exclusive source of all truth, 91
on man created by and for love, 41
on meaning of justice, 13, 14
contrast between justice and love, 21
peasant inheritance mentioned in, 152n
presupposes private property as normal, 60
proclaims Kingdom of God, not earthly justice, 112
revelation concerning marriage, 52
righteousness of God central theme, 110
view of prohibition of interest, 163

Bluntschli, Johann Kasper, 267

Bohatec, Josef, 44n, 266, 268, 270, 273, 274

Brotherly love, Biblical contrast to justice, 21
commandment of, 50
higher good than justice, 16
required of men, 20

Brunner, Emil, *Divine Imperative*, 43n, 145n
Man in Revolt, 39n
Offenbarung und Vernunft, 98n

Burckhardt, Jakob, 212 220n

Burckhardt, W. 283

Caesar, and parable of talents, 112

Calvin, John, admiration for Roman law, 91

Punishment—*Continued*
and justice, 222
retribution *vs* vengeance, 223

Rationalism, doctrine of law of
nature, 87
equalitarian theory of, 192
modern view derived from Stoic
philosophy, 38, 39, 40, 41
idea of freedom and equality, 185
since Locke, 189
Rousseau's ideology, 186
Reconstruction, postwar, Christian
theology share of work of,
10
concept of justice necessary in, 9
of institutions of Western World,
15
Reformation, concept of justice in, 6
guild system after, degeneration of,
187
Lutheran jurisprudence, 120
Reformers, acceptance of teachings of
classical scholars, 91
Calvin and Luther on equality, 44
divergence from mediaeval Cath-
olics, 93
doctrine of law of nature, 87
estimate of man's capacity for
rational knowledge, 92
new understanding of "divine
justice," 88
respect for positive law, 94
view of interest, 162
Relativism, or scepticism, of present
era, 258
Rembrandt, 166
Renaissance, concept of justice in, 6
Machiavellianism product of, 234
Renan, Ernest, definition of the
nation, 242
Rights of man, Christians and Stoics
originators of, 55
to education, 62
to error, given by Creator, 57
expression of in Christian ideas,
10
given at birth, 89
of press, trade, commerce, not
primal, 63
to physical freedom, 61
religious toleration fundamental
to, 57
to resist tyranny, 94

Rights of Man—*Continued*
to sexual freedom, 61
to work, 61
Roman Empire, Apostle's teachings
concerning, 114
breakdown of, 35
Christian community in, 118
comfortable life, 233
of Nero, 104
religious uniformity enforced in,
57
Roman law, development of, 35
good and evil in, 115
jurists' teachings accepted by early
Christians, 91
patria potestas, 62
and private property, 79
property and, 153
spirit of, 97
Romantic period, and concept of
justice, 6
theory of organism, 43
Röpke, Wilhelm, theory of the
middle way, 277, 279
Rousseau, Jean Jacques, belief in
goodness of human nature,
202
Contrat Social, 42n, 141
differences from Bible, 84
ideology of revolution, 186
influence on theory of justice, 39
logic of fired by Christian feeling,
77
non-Rousseauesque democracy, 217
and sovereignty of the people, 74,
201
view of human dependence, 42
of human interdependence, 70
views, references to, 269, 282
Rumelin, Gustave, 272
Russia, experiment in communism,
141, 177, 179
theory of proletariat, 37

Savings, compulsory, 163
lending of, 161
ridicule of unjustified, 159
small, 160
in Switzerland, 160n
Scandinavian, Christian law of
nature, 93
Schoolmen, doctrine of law of nature,
87, 88